# THREE PLAYS

2

# THREE PLAYS

## ABSURD PERSON SINGULAR
## ABSENT FRIENDS
## BEDROOM FARCE

## ALAN AYCKBOURN

*New York*

*Printed in the United States of America*

Library of Congress Cataloging-in-Publication Data

Ayckbourn, Alan, 1939–
    Three plays.

    Reprint of the ed. published by Chatto & Windus,
    London.
    CONTENTS: Absurd person singular.—Absent
    friends.—Bedroom farce.
        1. Title.
PR6051.Y35A19    1979      822'.9'14      78-20339
ISBN 0-8021-3157-3

Grove Press
841 Broadway
New York, NY 10003

00 01 02 03   10 9 8 7 6 5 4 3

# CONTENTS

# PREFACE

*Absurd Person Singular* – the title was originally intended for a play I didn't write and subsequently, because I rather cared for it, given to the play I did write – was first produced in Scarborough in 1972.

At that time, I remember, I was becoming increasingly fascinated by the dramatic possibilities of offstage action. Not a new device, granted, but one with plenty of comic potential still waiting to be tapped. Very early on in my career as a dramatist I discovered that, given the chance, an audience's imagination can do far better work than any number of playwright's words. The offstage character hinted at but never seen can be dramatically as significant and telling as his onstage counterparts. Offstage action is more difficult. Unless care is taken, if the dramatist chooses to describe rather than show his action, the audience can rapidly come to the conclusion that they're sitting in the wrong auditorium.

Thus, when I came to write *Absurd Person* and started by setting the action in Jane and Sidney Hopcroft's sitting room, I was halfway through the act before I realised that I was viewing the evening from totally the wrong perspective. Dick and Lottie were indeed monstrously overwhelming, hearty and ultimately very boring, and far better heard occasionally but not seen. By a simple switch of setting to the kitchen, the problem was all but solved, adding incidentally far greater comic possibilities than the sitting room ever held. For in this particular case, the obvious offstage action was far more relevant than its onstage counterpart.

As a footnote: since I was writing about parties and guests arriving, it also relieved me of the tedium of all that hallo-how-are-you-goodbye-nice-to-see-you business.

*Absurd Person*, then, could be described as my first offstage action play. It is also, some critics have observed, a rather weighty comedy. Its last scene darkens considerably. I make no apologies for this. As I've grown in confidence as a dramatist (confidence, that is, that I can get most of the techniques right most of the time), I have also grown in the conviction that I owe it to the characters I've created to develop and therefore to a certain extent to dictate how a play should run.

I've always had an aversion to comedies that rely upon natty, superimposed denouements in order to round off the evening. Why comedies should have to do this whereas dramas are allowed to finish as they like is beyond me. As a nation, we show a marked preference for comedy when it comes to playgoing, as any theatre manager will tell you. At the same time, over a large area of the stalls one can detect a faint sense of guilt that there is something called enjoyment going on. Should we, people seem to be asking, be sitting here laughing like this? It's to do with the mistaken belief that because it's funny, it can't be serious — which of course isn't true at all. Heavy, no; serious, yes. It would therefore seem unwise to compound this guilt feeling by artificially resolving the play. In other words, it can be funny, but let's make it truthful.

*Absent Friends,* first produced in Scarborough in 1974, followed *The Norman Conquests,* which to all intents and purposes was the end of my exploration of offstage action. Three plays, two of which were happening offstage simultaneously with the one onstage, were quite enough. *Absent Friends* was almost a drawing-in of forces. It was significant for me in several ways. Its use of time, for one. The stage action matches real time almost second for second. Most plays have their own time span where hours or months can pass quite happily in the space of minutes. *Absent Friends'* time span, being what it is, had the intended consequence of making the play far more claustrophobic, almost oppressive.

Its single set, its small detailed action, helped. It is a play for a small intimate theatre where one can hear the actors breathing and the silences ticking away. It was a terrifying risk when it was first produced. I'd never pitched anything in quite such a low key before.

Following this (with only the five short plays entitled *Confusions* between them) came the far more robust *Bedroom Farce.* This play has, I think, elements of both *Absurd Person* and *Absent Friends* in it. It has its moments of near farce and yet still contains elements of the claustrophobic — maybe because it's all in bedrooms. It is also the first time I've made use, to quite such an extent, of the cross-cut device. Jumping the action from bedroom to bedroom gives the play an added rhythm over and above what the dialogue normally provides. Again, I've allowed the characters to progress, develop and resolve very much in their own way. Perhaps, as in my other plays, none of them finds instant happiness or sudden great self-insight. But at least they retain the dignity of resolving their own destinies.

Alan Ayckbourn
Scarborough 1976

# ABSURD PERSON SINGULAR

First produced at the Library Theatre, Scarborough, in June 1972 and subsequently by Michael Codron at the Criterion Theatre, London, on the 4th July 1973, with the following cast:

| | |
|---|---|
| Sidney | Richard Briers |
| Jane | Bridget Turner |
| Ronald | Michael Aldridge |
| Marion | Sheila Hancock |
| Geoffrey | David Burke |
| Eva | Anna Calder-Marshall |

The play directed by Eric Thompson
Settings by Alan Tagg

Act I Sidney and Jane's Kitchen. Last Christmas
Act II Geoffrey and Eva's Kitchen. This Christmas
Act III Ronald and Marion's Kitchen. Next Christmas

# ACT ONE

SIDNEY *and* JANE HOPCROFT'*s kitchen of their small suburban house. Last Christmas*
*Although on a modest scale, it is a model kitchen. Whilst not containing all the gadgetry, it does have an automatic washing machine, a fridge, an electric cooker and a gleaming sink unit. All these are contained or surrounded by smart formica-topped working surfaces with the usual drawers and cupboards. The room also contains a small table, also formica-topped, and matching chairs.*
*When the* CURTAIN *rises,* JANE, *a woman in her thirties, is discovered bustling round wiping the floor, cupboard doors, working surfaces—in fact, anything in sight—with a cloth. She sings happily as she works. She wears a pinafore and bedroom slippers, but, under this, a smart new party dress. She is unimaginatively made up and her hair is tightly permed. She wears rubber gloves to protect her hands.*
*As* JANE *works,* SIDNEY *enters, a small dapper man of about the same age. He has a small trimmed moustache and a cheery, unflappable manner. He wears his best, rather old-fashioned, sober suit. A dark tie, polished hair and shoes complete the picture.*

SIDNEY: Hallo, hallo. What are we up to out here, eh?
JANE: [*without pausing in her work*] Just giving it a wipe.
SIDNEY: Dear oh dear. Good gracious me. Does it need it? Like a battleship. Just like a battleship. They need you in the Royal Navy.
JANE: [*giggling*] Silly . . .
SIDNEY: No—the Royal Navy.
JANE: Silly . . .
   [SIDNEY *goes to the back door, turns the yale knob, opens it and sticks his hand out*]
SIDNEY: Still raining, I see.
JANE: Shut the door, it's coming in.
SIDNEY: Cats and dogs. Dogs and cats. [*He shuts the door, wiping his wet hand on his handkerchief. Striding to the centre of the room and staring up at his digital clock*]

Eighteen-twenty-three. [*Consulting his watch*] Eighteen-twenty-three. Getting on. Seven minutes — they'll be here.

JANE: Oh. [*She straightens up and looks round the kitchen for somewhere she's missed*]

SIDNEY: I've got a few games lined up.

JANE: Games?

SIDNEY: Just in case.

JANE: Oh good.

SIDNEY: I've made a parcel for "Pass the Parcel", sorted out a bit of music for musical bumps and thought out a few forfeits.

JANE: Good.

SIDNEY: I've thought up some real devils. [*He puts his leg on the table*]

JANE: I bet. [*She knocks his leg off, and wipes*]

SIDNEY: Just in case. Just in case things need jollying up. [*Seeing* JANE *still wiping*] I don't want to disappoint you but we're not going to be out here for our drinks, you know.

JANE: Yes, I know.

SIDNEY: The way you're going . . .

JANE: They might want to look . . .

SIDNEY: I doubt it.

JANE: The ladies might.

SIDNEY: [*chuckling knowingly*] I don't imagine the wife of a banker will particularly choose to spend her evening in our kitchen. Smart as it is.

JANE: No?

SIDNEY: I doubt if she spends very much time in her own kitchen. Let alone ours.

JANE: Still . . .

SIDNEY: Very much the lady of leisure, Mrs Brewster-Wright. Or so I would imagine.

JANE: What about Mrs Jackson?

SIDNEY: [*doubtfully*] Well—again, not a woman you think of in the same breath as you would a kitchen.

JANE: All women are interested in kitchens. [*She turns to the sink*]

SIDNEY: [*ironically*] Oh, if you're looking for a little job . . .

JANE: What's that?

SIDNEY: A small spillage. My fault.

JANE: [*very alarmed*] Where?

SIDNEY: In there. On the sideboard.

JANE: Oh, Sidney. [*She snatches up an assortment of cloths, wet and dry*]

SIDNEY: Nothing serious.

JANE: Honestly.

[*Sidney goes to the back door, opens it, sticks a hand out*]

SIDNEY: Dear oh dear. [*He closes the door and dries his hand on his handkerchief*]

JANE: [*returning*] Honestly.

SIDNEY: Could you see it?

JANE: You spoil that surface if you leave it. You leave a ring. [*She returns her dish cloth to the sink, her dry cloths to the drawer and now takes out a duster and a tin of polish*] Now that room's going to smell of polish. I had the windows open all day so it wouldn't.

SIDNEY: Well then, don't polish.

JANE: I have to polish. There's a mark. [*She goes to the door and then pauses*] I know, bring the air freshener.

SIDNEY: Air freshener?

JANE: Under the sink.

[*JANE exits*]

SIDNEY: Ay, ay, Admiral. [*He whistles a sailor's horn-pipe, amused*] Dear oh dear. [*He opens the cupboard under the sink, rummages and brings out an aerosol tin. He is one of those men who like to read all small print. This he does, holding the tin at arm's length to do so. Reading*] "Shake can before use." [*He does so. Reading*] "Remove cap." [*He does so. Reading*] "Hold away from body and spray into air by depressing button." [*He holds the can away from his body, points it in the air and depresses the button. The spray hisses out over his shirt front*] Dear oh dear [*He puts down the tin, wipes his shirt-front with a dishcloth*]

[*JANE enters*]

JANE: What are you doing?

SIDNEY: Just getting this to rights. Just coming to terms with your air freshener.

JANE: That's the fly spray.

SIDNEY: Ah.

JANE: Honestly. [*She takes the canister from him and puts it on top of the washing machine*]

SIDNEY: My mistake.

JANE: For someone who's good at some things you're hopeless.

SIDNEY: Beg your pardon, Admiral, beg your pardon.

[JANE *puts away the duster and polish*]

[*Checking his watch with the clock*] Four and a half minutes to go.

JANE: And you've been at those nuts, haven't you?

SIDNEY: Nuts?

JANE: In there. In the bowl. On the table. Those nuts. You know the ones I mean.

SIDNEY: I may have had a little dip. Anyway, how did you know I'd been at those nuts? Eh? How did you know, old eagle-eye?

JANE: Because I know how I left them. Now come on, out of my way. Don't start that. I've got things to do.

SIDNEY: [*closing with her*] What about a kiss then?

JANE: [*trying to struggle free*] Sidney . . .

SIDNEY: Come on. Christmas kiss.

JANE: Sidney. No, not now. What's the matter with you? Sidney . . . [*She pauses, sniffing*]

SIDNEY: What's the matter now?

JANE: What's that smell?

SIDNEY: Eh?

JANE: It's on your tie. What's this smell on your tie?

[*They both sniff his tie*]

There. Can you smell?

SIDNEY: Oh, that'll be the fly spray.

JANE: Fly spray?

SIDNEY: Had a bit of a backfire.

JANE: It's killed off your after-shave.

SIDNEY: [*jovially*] As long as it hasn't killed off my flies, eh.

[*He laughs*]

[JANE *laughs*]

[*Suddenly cutting through this*] Eighteen-twenty-eight. Two minutes.

JANE: [*nervous again*] I hope everything's all right.

SIDNEY: When?

JANE: For them. I want it to be right.

SIDNEY: Of course it's right.

JANE: I mean. I don't want you to be let down. Not by me. I

want it to look good for you. I don't want to let you down . . .

SIDNEY: You never have yet . . .

JANE: No, but it's special tonight, isn't it? I mean, with Mr and Mrs Brewster-Wright and Mr and Mrs Jackson. It's important.

SIDNEY: Don't forget Dick and Lottie Potter. They're coming, too.

JANE: Oh, well, I don't count Dick and Lottie. They're friends.

SIDNEY: I trust by the end of this evening, we shall all be friends. Just don't get nervous. That's all. Don't get nervous. [*He consults the clock and checks it with his watch*] One minute to go.

[*A slight pause. The front door chimes sound*]

What was that?

JANE: The front door.

SIDNEY: They're early. Lucky we're ready for them.

JANE: Yes. [*In a sudden panic*] I haven't sprayed the room.

SIDNEY: All right, all right. You can do it whilst I'm letting them in. Plenty of time.

JANE: It doesn't take a second.

[*JANE snatches up the air freshener and follows SIDNEY out into the sitting-room. A silence. JANE comes hurrying back into the kitchen*]

[*JANE puts away the air freshener, removes her pinny, straightens her clothing and hair in the mirror, creeps back to the kitchen door and opens it a chink. Voices are heard— SIDNEY's and two others. One is a jolly hearty male voice and one a jolly hearty female voice. They are DICK and LOTTIE POTTER, whom we have the good fortune never to meet in person, but quite frequently hear whenever the door to the kitchen is open. Both have loud, braying distinctive laughs. JANE closes the door, cutting off the voices, straightens her hair and dress for the last time, looks at a mirror on the wall, grips the door handle, takes a deep breath, is about to make her entrance into the room when she sees she is still wearing her bedroom slippers*]

Oh.

[*She takes off her slippers, puts them on the table and scuttles round the kitchen looking for her shoes. She cannot find them. She picks up the slippers and wipes the table with their fluffy side, where they have made a mark*]

Oh.

[*She hurries back to the door, opens it a fraction. Jolly chatter and laughter is heard.* JANE *stands for a long time, peeping through the crack in the door, trying to catch sight of her shoes. She sees them. She closes the door again. She stands lost*]

Oh. Oh. Oh.

[*The door opens. Loud laughter from off.* SIDNEY *comes in laughing. He closes the door. The laughter cuts off abruptly*]

SIDNEY: [*fiercely, in a low voice*] Come on. What are you doing?

JANE: I can't.

SIDNEY: What?

JANE: I've got no shoes.

SIDNEY: What do you mean, no shoes?

JANE: They're in there.

SIDNEY: Where?

JANE: By the fireplace. I left them so I could slip them on.

SIDNEY: Well, then, why didn't you?

JANE: I didn't have time. I forgot.

SIDNEY: Well, come and get them.

JANE: No . . .

SIDNEY: It's only Dick and Lottie Potter.

JANE: You fetch them.

SIDNEY: I can't fetch them.

JANE: Yes, you can. Pick them up and bring them in here.

SIDNEY: But I . . .

JANE: Sidney, please.

SIDNEY: Dear oh dear. What a start. I say, what a start. [*He opens the door cautiously and listens. Silence*] They've stopped talking.

JANE: Have they?

SIDNEY: Wondering where we are, no doubt.

JANE: Well, go in. Here.

SIDNEY: What?

JANE: [*handing him her slippers*] Take these.

SIDNEY: What do I do with these?

JANE: The hall cupboard.

SIDNEY: You're really expecting rather a lot tonight, aren't you?

JANE: I'm sorry.

SIDNEY: Yes, well it's got to stop. It's got to stop. I have to entertain out there, you know. [*He opens the door and starts laughing heartily as he does so*]

[SIDNEY *goes out, closing the door*]

[JANE *hurries about nervously, making still more adjustments to her person and checking her appearance in the mirror*]

[*At length the door opens, letting in a bellow of laughter.* SIDNEY *returns, carrying* JANE's *shoes*]

[*Behind him*] Yes, I will. I will. I'll tell her that, Dick . . . [*He laughs until he's shut the door. His laugh cuts off abruptly. Thrusting* JANE's *shoes at her, ungraciously*] Here.

JANE: Oh, thank goodness.

SIDNEY: Now for heaven's sake, come in.

JANE: [*struggling into her shoes*] Yes, I'm sorry. What did Dick say?

SIDNEY: When?

JANE: Just now? That you told him you'd tell me.

SIDNEY: I really can't remember. Now then, are you ready?

JANE: Yes, yes.

SIDNEY: It's a good job it's only Dick and Lottie out there. It might have been the Brewster-Wrights. I'd have had a job explaining this to them. Walking in and out like a shoe salesman. All right?

JANE: Yes.

SIDNEY: Right. [*He throws open the door, jovially*] Here she is. [*Pushing* JANE *ahead of him*] Here she is at last.

[*Hearty cries of "Ah ha" from* DICK *and* LOTTIE]

JANE: [*going in*] Here I am.

[JANE *and* SIDNEY *exit*]

SIDNEY: [*closing the door behind him*] At last.

[*A silence. A long one.*]

[SIDNEY *returns to the kitchen. Conversation is heard as he opens and closes the door. He starts hunting round the kitchen opening drawers and not bothering to shut them. After a second, the door opens again, and* JANE *comes in*]

JANE: [*as she enters*] Yes, well you say that to Lottie, not to me. I don't want to know that . . . [*She closes the door*] What are you doing? Oh, Sidney, what are you doing? [*She hurries round after him, closing the drawers*]

SIDNEY: Bottle-opener. I'm trying to find the bottle-opener. I can't get the top off Lottie's bitter lemon.

JANE: It's in there.

SIDNEY: In there?

JANE: Why didn't you ask me?

SIDNEY: Where in there?

JANE: On the mantelpiece.

SIDNEY: The mantelpiece?

JANE: It looks nice on the mantelpiece.

SIDNEY: It's no use having a bottle-opener on a mantelpiece, is it? I mean, how am I . . . ?

[*The door chimes sound*]

JANE: Somebody else.

SIDNEY: All right, I'll go. You open the bitter lemon. With gin.

JANE: Gin and bitter lemon.

SIDNEY: And shake the bottle first.

[SIDNEY *opens the door. Silence from the room. He goes out, closing it*]

JANE: [*to herself*] Gin and bitter lemon — shake the bottle first — gin and bitter lemon — shake the bottle first . . . [*She returns to the door and opens it very slightly. There can now be heard the chatter of five voices. She closes the door and feverishly straightens herself*]

[*The door opens a crack and* SIDNEY's *nose appears. Voices are heard behind him*]

SIDNEY: [*hissing*] It's them.

JANE: Mr and Mrs Brewster-Wright?

SIDNEY: Yes, Ronald and Marion. Come in.

JANE: Ronald and Marion.

SIDNEY: Come in.

[SIDNEY *opens the door wider, grabs her arm, jerks her through the door and closes it*]

JANE: [*as she is dragged in*] Gin and bitter lemon — shake the bottle first . . .

[*Silence. Another fairly long one. The door bursts open and* JANE *comes rushing out*]

[*Murmur of voices*]

[*Over her shoulder*] Wait there! Just wait there! [*She dashes to the sink and finds a tea towel and two dish cloths*]

[RONALD, *a man in his mid-forties, enters. Impressive with-*

*out being distinguished. He is followed by an anxious* SIDNEY.
RONALD *is holding one leg of his trousers away from his*
*body. He has evidently got drenched*]

SIDNEY: Oh dear oh dear. I'm terribly sorry.

RONALD: That's all right. Can't be helped.

JANE: Here's a cloth.

RONALD: Oh, thank you—yes, yes. [*He takes the tea towel*]
I'll just use this one, if you don't mind.

SIDNEY: Well, what a start, eh? What a grand start to the
evening. [*With a laugh*] Really, Jane.

JANE: I'm terribly sorry. I didn't realize it was going to splash
like that.

RONALD: Well, tricky things, soda siphons. You either get a
splash or a dry gurgle. Never a happy medium.

JANE: Your nice suit.

RONALD: Good God, it's only soda water. Probably do it
good, eh?

JANE: I don't know about that.

RONALD: [*returning the tea towel*] Thanks very much. Well,
it's wet enough outside there. I didn't expect to get wet inside
as well.

SIDNEY: No, no . . .

JANE: Terribly sorry.

RONALD: Accidents happen. Soon dry out. I'll run around for
a bit.

SIDNEY: I'll tell you what. I could let you have a pair of my
trousers from upstairs just while yours dry.

JANE: Oh, yes.

RONALD: No, no. That's all right. I'll stick with these. Hate to
break up the suit, eh? [*He laughs*]
[*So do* SIDNEY *and* JANE]
[MARION, *a well-groomed woman, a little younger than*
RONALD *and decidedly better preserved, comes in*]

MARION: All right, darling?

RONALD: Yes, yes.

MARION: Oh! [*She stops short in the doorway*] Isn't this
gorgeous? Isn't this enchanting.

JANE: Oh.

MARION: What a simply dishy kitchen. [*To* JANE] Aren't you
lucky.

JANE: Well . . .

MARION: It's so beautifully arranged. Ronnie, don't you agree? Isn't this splendid.

RONALD: Ah.

MARION: Just look at these working surfaces and you must have a gorgeous view from that window, I imagine.

SIDNEY: Well . . .

MARION: It must be stunning. You must look right over the fields at the back.

SIDNEY: No—no.

JANE: No, we just look into next door's fence.

MARION: Well, which way are the fields?

JANE: I've no idea.

MARION: How extraordinary. I must be thinking of somewhere else.

SIDNEY: Mind you, we've got a good ten yards to the fence . . .

RONALD: On a clear day, eh?

SIDNEY: Beg pardon?

MARION: Oh look, Ronnie, do come and look at these cupboards.

RONALD: Eh?

MARION: Look at these, Ronnie. [*Opening and shutting the cupboard doors*] They're so easy to open and shut.

JANE: Drawers—here, you see . . .

MARION: Drawers! [*Opening them*] Oh, lovely deep drawers. Put all sorts of things in these, can't you? And then just shut it up and forget them.

SIDNEY: Yes, yes, they're handy for that . . .

MARION: No, it's these cupboards. I'm afraid I really do envy you these. Don't you envy them, Ronnie?

RONALD: I thought we had cupboards.

MARION: Yes, darling, but they're nothing like these. Just open and shut that door. It's heaven.

RONALD: [*picking up a booklet from the counter*] Cupboard's a cupboard. [*He sits and reads*]

JANE: [*proudly*] Look. [*Going to the washing machine*] Sidney's Christmas present to me . . .

MARION: [*picking up the air freshener from the top of the washing machine*] Oh lovely. What is it? Hair spray?

SIDNEY: No, no. That's the fly spray, no. My wife meant the

machine. [*He takes the spray from her and puts it down*]

MARION: Machine?

JANE: Washing machine. Here . . .

MARION: Oh, that's a washing machine. Tucked under there. How thrilling. What a marvellous Christmas present.

JANE: Well, yes.

MARION: Do tell me, how did you manage to keep it a surprise from her?

SIDNEY: Well . . .

MARION: I mean, don't tell me he hid it or wrapped it up. I don't believe it.

SIDNEY: No, I just arranged for the men to deliver it and plumb it in.

JANE: They flooded the kitchen.

MARION: Super.

JANE: You see, it's the automatic. It's got—all the programmes and then spin-drying and soak.

MARION: Oh, good heavens. Ronnie, come here at once and see this.

RONALD: [*reading avidly*] Just coming . . .

MARION: [*bending to read the dial*] What's this? Whites—coloureds—my God, it's apartheid.

JANE: Beg pardon?

MARION: What's this? Minimum icon? What on earth is that?

JANE: No, minimum iron.

MARION: Don't tell me it does the ironing too.

JANE: Oh, no, it . . .

MARION: Ronnie, have you seen this extraordinary machine?

RONALD: Yes. Yes . . .

MARION: It not only does your washing and your whites and your blacks and your coloureds and so on, it does your ironing.

SIDNEY: No, no . . .

JANE: No . . .

MARION: [*to* JANE] We shall soon be totally redundant. [*She picks up the spray and fires it into the air and inhales*] What a poignant smell. It's almost too good to waste on flies, isn't it. Now where . . .? It's a little like your husband's gorgeous cologne, surely?

JANE: Oh, well . . .

[*The doorbell chimes*]

MARION: Oh, good gracious. What was that? Does that mean your shirts are cooked or something.

SIDNEY: No, front doorbell.

MARION: Oh, I see. How pretty.

SIDNEY: Somebody else arrived.

JANE: Yes, I'd better . . .

SIDNEY: Won't be a minute.

JANE: No, I'll go.

SIDNEY: No . . .

JANE: No, I'll go.

[JANE *hurries out, closing the door*]

MARION: I do hope your Mr and Mrs Potter don't feel terribly abandoned in there. They're spendidly jolly, blooming people, aren't they?

SIDNEY: Yes, Dick's a bit of a laugh.

MARION: Enormous. Now, you must tell me one thing, Mr Hopcraft. How on earth did you squeeze that machine so perfectly under the shelf? Did you try them for size or were you terribly lucky?

SIDNEY: No, I went out and measured the machine in the shop.

MARION: Oh, I see.

SIDNEY: And then I made the shelf, you see. So it was the right height.

MARION: No, I mean how on earth did you know it was going to be right?

SIDNEY: Well, that's the way I built it.

MARION: No. You don't mean this is you?

SIDNEY: Yes, yes. Well, the shelf is.

MARION: Ronnie!

RONALD: Um?

MARION: Ronnie, darling, what are you reading?

RONALD: [*vaguely consulting the cover of his book*] Er . . .

SIDNEY: Ah, that'll be the instruction book for the stove.

RONALD: Oh, is that what it is. I was just trying to work out what I was reading. Couldn't make head or tail.

MARION: Darling, did you hear what Mr Hop—er . . .

SIDNEY: Hopcroft.

MARION: Sidney, isn't it? Sidney was saying . . . ?

RONALD: What?

MARION: Darling, Sidney built this shelf on his own. He went out and measured the machine, got all his screws and nails and heaven knows what and built this shelf himself.

RONALD: Good Lord.

SIDNEY: I've got some more shelves upstairs. For the bedside. And also, I've partitioned off part of the spare bedroom as a walk-in cupboard for the wife. And I'm just about to panel the landing with those knotty pine units, have you seen them?

MARION: Those curtains are really the most insistent colour I've ever seen. They must just simply cry out to be drawn in the morning.

[JANE *sticks her head round the door*]

JANE: Dear—it's Mr and Mrs Jackson.

SIDNEY: Oh. Geoff and Eva, is it? Right, I'll be in to say hallo.

MARION: Geoff and Eva Jackson?

SIDNEY: Yes. Do you know them?

MARION: Oh yes. Rather. Darling, it's Geoff and Eva Jackson.

RONALD: Geoff and Eva who?

MARION: The Jacksons.

RONALD: Oh, Geoff and Eva Jackson. [*He goes and studies the washing machine*]

MARION: That's nice, isn't it?

RONALD: Yes?

JANE: Are you coming in?

SIDNEY: Yes, yes.

MARION: Haven't seen them for ages.

JANE: They've left the dog in the car.

SIDNEY: Oh, good.

MARION: Have they a dog?

JANE: Yes.

MARION: Oh, how lovely. We must see him.

JANE: He's—very big . . .

SIDNEY: Yes, well, lead on, dear.

[JANE *opens the door. A burst of conversation from the sitting room.* JANE *goes out.* SIDNEY *holds the door open for* MARION, *sees she is not following him and torn between his duties as a host, follows* JANE *off*]

We'll be in here. [*He closes the door*]

MARION: Ronnie . . .

RONALD: [*studying the washing machine*] Mm?

MARION: Come along, darling.

RONALD: I was just trying to work out how this thing does the ironing. Don't see it at all. Just rolls it into a ball.

MARION: Darling, do come on.

RONALD: I think that woman's got it wrong.

MARION: Darling . . .

RONALD: Um?

MARION: Make our excuses quite shortly, please.

RONALD: Had enough, have you?

MARION: We've left the boys . . .

RONALD: They'll be all right.

MARION: What's that man's name?

RONALD: Hopcraft, do you mean?

MARION: No, the other one.

RONALD: Oh, Potter, isn't it?

MARION: Well, I honestly don't think I can sit through many more of his jokes.

RONALD: I thought they were quite funny.

MARION: And I've never had quite such a small gin in my life. Completely drowned.

RONALD: Really? My scotch was pretty strong.

MARION: That's only because she missed the glass with the soda water. Consider yourself lucky.

RONALD: I don't know about lucky. I shall probably have bloody rheumatism in the morning.

[SIDNEY *sticks his head round the door. Laughter and chatter behind him*]

SIDNEY: Er—Mrs Brewster-Wright, I wonder if you'd both . . .

MARION: Oh, yes, we're just coming. We can't tear ourselves away from your divine kitchen, can we, Ronnie? [*Turning to* RONALD, *holding up the fingers of one hand and mouthing*] Five minutes.

RONALD: Righto.

[*They all go out, closing the door*]

[*Silence*]

[JANE *enters with an empty bowl. She hurries to the cupboard and takes out a jumbo bag of crisps and pours them into the bowl. She is turning to leave when the door opens again and* SIDNEY *hurries in, looking a little fraught*]

SIDNEY: Tonic water. We've run out.

JANE: Tonic water. Down there in the cupboard.

SIDNEY: Right.

JANE: Do you think it's going all right?

SIDNEY: Fine, fine. Now get back, get back there.

JANE: [*as she goes*] Will you ask Lottie to stop eating all these crisps? Nobody else has had any.

[JANE *goes out closing the door behind her*]

[SIDNEY *searches first one cupboard, then another, but cannot find any tonic*]

SIDNEY: Oh dear, oh dear.

[SIDNEY *hurries back to the party closing the door behind him. After a second* JANE *enters looking worried, closing the door behind her*]

[*She searches where* SIDNEY *has already searched. She finds nothing*]

JANE: Oh. [*She wanders in rather aimless circles round the kitchen*]

[SIDNEY *enters with a glass with gin and a slice of lemon in it. He closes the door*]

SIDNEY: Is it there?

JANE: Yes, yes. Somewhere . . .

SIDNEY: Well, come along. She's waiting.

JANE: I've just—got to find it.. . .

SIDNEY: Oh dear, oh dear.

JANE: I tidied them away somewhere.

SIDNEY: Well, there was no point in tidying them away, was there? We're having a party.

JANE: Well—it just looked—tidier. You go back in, I'll bring them.

SIDNEY: Now that was your responsibility. We agreed buying the beverages was your department. I hope you haven't let us down.

JANE: No. I'm sure I haven't.

SIDNEY: Well, it's very embarrassing for me in the meanwhile, isn't it? Mrs Brewster-Wright is beginning to give me anxious looks.

JANE: Oh.

SIDNEY: Well then.

[SIDNEY *goes back in*]

[JANE *stands helplessly. She gives a little whimper of dismay. She is on the verge of tears. Then a sudden decision. She goes to a drawer. reaches to the back and brings out her house-keeping purse. She opens it and takes out some coins. She runs to the centre of the room and looks at the clock*]

JANE: Nineteen-twenty-one. [*Hurried calculation*] Thirteen—fourteen—fifteen—sixteen—seventeen—eighteen—nineteen . . . seven-twenty-two. [*She hurries to the back door and opens it. She holds out her hand, takes a tentative step out and then a hasty step back again. She is again in a dilemma. She closes the back door. She goes to the cupboard just inside the door and, after rummaging about, she emerges holding a pair of men's large wellington boots in one hand and a pair of plim-solls in the other. Mentally tossing up between them, she returns the plimsolls to the cupboard. She slips off her own shoes and steps easily into the wellingtons. She puts her own shoes neatly in the cupboard and rummages again. She pulls out a large man's gardening raincoat. She holds it up, realizes it's better than nothing and puts it on. She hurries back to the centre of the room buttoning it as she does so*] Nineteen-twenty-four. [*She returns to the back door, opens it and steps out. It is evidently pelting down. She stands in the doorway holding up the collar of the coat and ineffectually trying to protect her hairdo from the rain with the other hand. Frantical-ly*] Oh . . . [*She dives back into the cupboard and re-emerges with an old trilby hat. She looks at it in dismay. After a moment's struggle she puts it on and hurries back to the centre of the room*] Twenty-five.

[JANE *returns to the back door, hesitates for a second and then plunges out into the night, leaving the door only very slightly ajar. After a moment, SIDNEY returns still clutching the glass*]

SIDNEY: Jane? Jane! [*He looks round, puzzled*] Good gracious me. [*He peers around for her*]

[EVA *comes in. In her thirties, she makes no concessions in either manner or appearance*]

EVA: May I have a glass of water?

SIDNEY: Beg your pardon?

EVA: I have to take these. [*She holds out a couple of tablets enclosed in a sheet of tinfoil. She crosses to the back door and stands taking deep breaths of fresh air*]

SIDNEY: Oh, yes. There's a glass here somewhere, I think.

EVA: Thanks.

SIDNEY: [*finding a tumbler*] Here we are. [*He puts it down on the washing machine*]
[*EVA stands abstractedly staring ahead of her, tearing at the paper round the pills without any effort to open them. A pause. SIDNEY looks at her*]
Er . . .

EVA: What? Oh, thanks. [*She closes the back door and picks up the glass*]

SIDNEY: Not ill, I hope?

EVA: What?

SIDNEY: The pills. Not ill?

EVA: It depends what you mean by ill, doesn't it?

SIDNEY: Ah.

EVA: If you mean do they prevent me from turning into a raving lunatic, the answer's probably yes. [*She laughs somewhat bitterly*]

SIDNEY: [*laughing, too*] Raving lunatic, yes—[*he is none too certain of this lady*] —but then I always say, it helps to be a bit mad, doesn't it? I mean, we're all a bit mad. I'm a bit mad. [*Pause*] Yes. [*Pause*] It's a mad world, as they say.

EVA: [*surveying the pills in her hand which she has now opened*] Extraordinary to think that one's sanity can depend on these. Frightening, isn't it? [*She puts them both in her mouth and swallows the glass of water in one gulp*] Yuck. Alarming. Do you know I've been taking pills of one sort or another since I was eight years old. What chance does your body have? My husband tells me that even if I didn't need them, I'd still have to take them. My whole mentality is geared round swallowing tablets every three hours, twenty-four hours a day. I even have to set the alarm at night. You're looking at a mess. A wreck. [*She still holds the glass and is searching round absently as she speaks, for somewhere to put it*] Don't you sometimes long to be out of your body and free? Free just to float? I know I do. [*She opens the pedal bin with her foot and tosses the empty glass into it*] Thanks.
[*She puts the screwed up tinfoil into* SIDNEY's *hand and starts for the door.* SIDNEY *gawps at her.* EVA *pauses*]

My God, was that our car horn?

SIDNEY: When?

EVA: Just now.

SIDNEY: No, I don't think so.

EVA: If you do hear it, it's George.

SIDNEY: George?

EVA: Our dog.

SIDNEY: Oh, yes, of course.

EVA: We left him in the car, you see. We have to leave him in the car these days, he's just impossible. He's all right there, usually, but lately he's been getting bored and he's learnt to push the horn button with his nose. He just rests his nose on the steering-wheel, you see.

SIDNEY: That's clever.

EVA: Not all that clever. We've had the police out twice.

SIDNEY: A bit like children, dogs.

EVA: What makes you say that?

SIDNEY: Need a bit of a firm hand now and again. Smack if they're naughty.

EVA: You don't smack George, you negotiate terms.

SIDNEY: Ah. [*He retrieves the glass from the waste-bin*]

EVA: He was only this big when we bought him, now he's grown into a sort of yak. When we took him in, he—my God was that me?

SIDNEY: What?

EVA: Did I put that glass in there?

SIDNEY: Er—yes.

EVA: My God, I knew it, I'm going mad. I am finally going mad.
[*She goes to the door and opens it*]
[*Chatter is heard*]
Will you please tell my husband, if he drinks any more, I'm walking home.

SIDNEY: Well, I think that might be better coming from you as his wife.

EVA: [*laughing*] You really think he'd listen to me? He doesn't even know I'm here. As far as he's concerned, my existence ended the day he married me. I'm just an embarrassing smudge on a marriage licence.
[EVA *goes out, closing the door*]

SIDNEY: Ah. [*He puts the glass on the washing machine and*

*finds* JANE's *discarded shoes on the floor. He picks them up, stares at them and places them on the draining-board. Puzzled, he crosses to the back door and calls out into the night*] Jane!
[*He listens. No reply*]
[MARION *comes in*]
Jane!

MARION: I say . . .

SIDNEY: Rain . . . [*He holds out his hand by way of demonstration, then closes the back door*]

MARION: Oh, yes, dreadful. I say, I think you dashed away with my glass.

SIDNEY: Oh, I'm so sorry. [*Handing it to her*] Here.

MARION: Thank you. I was getting terribly apprehensive in case it had gone into your washing machine. [*She sips the drink*] Oh, that's lovely. Just that teeny bit stronger. You know what I mean. Not too much tonic . . .

SIDNEY: No, well . . .

MARION: Perfect.

SIDNEY: Actually, that's neat gin, that is.

MARION: Oh, good heavens! So it is. What are you trying to do to me? I can see we're going to have to keep an eye on you, Mr – er . . .

SIDNEY: No, no. You're safe enough with me.

MARION: Yes, I'm sure . . .

SIDNEY: The mistletoe's in there.

MARION: Well, what are we waiting for? Lead on, Mr–er . . .
     [*She ushers him in front of her*]

SIDNEY: Follow me.
     [SIDNEY *goes through the door*]

MARION: [*as she turns to close it, looking at her watch*] My God.
     [MARION *goes out and closes the door*]
     [*A pause*]
     [JANE *arrives at the back door still in her hat, coat and boots. She is soaking wet. She carries a carton of tonic waters. She rattles the back door knob but she has locked herself out. She knocks gently then louder, but no-one hears her. She rattles the knob again, pressing her face up against the glass. We see her mouth opening and shouting but no sound. Eventually, she gives up and hurries away. After a second,* SIDNEY

*returns. He has the crisp bowl which is again empty. He is about to refill it when he pauses and looks round the kitchen, puzzled and slightly annoyed. He goes to the back door and opens it*]

SIDNEY: Jane! Jane!

[SIDNEY *turns up his jacket collar and runs out, leaving the door ajar*]

[*As soon as* SIDNEY *has gone, the doorbell chimes. There is a pause, then it chimes again, several times*]

[RONALD *enters from the sitting-room*]

RONALD: I say, old boy, I think someone's at your front—oh.
[*He sees the empty room and the open back door*]
[RONALD *turns and goes back into the room*]
No, he seems to have gone out. I suppose we'd better ... [*His voice cuts off as he closes the door*]
[*The doorbell chimes once more*]
[SIDNEY *returns, closing the back door. He finds a towel and dabs his face and hair*]

SIDNEY: Dear oh dear. [*He shakes his head and returns to his crisps. Suddenly, the living-room door bursts open and* JANE *enters hurriedly in her strange garb, her boots squelching. She shuts the door behind her and stands against it, shaking and exhausted*]
[SIDNEY *turns and throws the bag of crisps into the air in his astonishment*]

JANE: Oh, my goodness.

SIDNEY: What are you doing?

JANE: Oh.

SIDNEY: [*utterly incredulous*] What do you think you're doing?

JANE: [*still breathless*] I went—I went out—to get the tonic.
[*She puts a carton of tonic waters on the table*]

SIDNEY: Like that?

JANE: I couldn't find—I didn't want ...

SIDNEY: You went out—and came in again, like that?

JANE: I thought I'd just slip out the back to the off-licence and slip in again. But I locked myself out. I had to come in the front.

SIDNEY: But who let you in?

JANE: [*in a whisper*] Mr Brewster-Wright.

SIDNEY: Mr Brewster-Wright? Mr Brewster-Wright let you in like that?

[JANE *nods*]
What did he say?

JANE: I don't think he recognized me.

SIDNEY: I'm not surprised.

JANE: I couldn't look at him. I just ran straight past him and right through all of them and into here.

SIDNEY: Like that?

JANE: Yes.

SIDNEY: But what did they say?

JANE: They didn't say anything. They just stopped talking and stared and I ran through them. I couldn't very well . . .

SIDNEY: You'll have to go back in there and explain.

JANE: No, I couldn't.

SIDNEY: Of course you must.

JANE: Sidney, I don't think I can face them.

SIDNEY: You can't walk through a respectable cocktail party, the hostess, dressed like that without an apology.

JANE: [*on the verge of tears again*] I couldn't.

SIDNEY: [*furious*] You take off all that—and you go back in there and explain.

JANE: [*with a wail*] I just want to go to bed.

SIDNEY: Well, you cannot go to bed. Not at nineteen-forty-seven. Now, take off that coat.

[JANE *squelches to the cupboard*]

[RONALD *opens the kitchen door. He is talking over his shoulder as he comes in, carrying a glass of scotch*]

RONALD: Well I think I'd better, I mean . . .

JANE: Oh, no.

[JANE *has had no time to unbutton her coat. Rather than face* RONALD, *she rushes out of the back door hatless, abandoning her headgear in the middle of the kitchen table*]

[SIDNEY, *trying to stop* JANE, *lunges after her vainly. The door slams behind her.* SIDNEY *stands with his back to it*]

RONALD: [*in the doorway, having caught a glimpse of violent activity, but unsure what*] Ah, there you are, old chap.

SIDNEY: Oh, hallo. Hallo.

RONALD: Just popped out, did you?

SIDNEY: Yes, just popped out.

RONALD: Well—something rather odd. Someone at the door just now. Little short chap. Hat, coat, boots and bottles. Just stamped straight through. You catch a glimpse of him?

SIDNEY: Oh, him.

RONALD: Belong here, does he? I mean . . .

SIDNEY: Oh, yes;

RONALD: Ah. Well, as long as you know about him. Might have been after your silver. I mean, you never know. Not these days.

SIDNEY: No, indeed. No, he — he was from the off-licence. [*He shows* RONALD *the carton*]

RONALD: Really?

SIDNEY: Brought round our order of tonic, you see.

[RONALD *stares at the hat on the table.* SIDNEY *notices and picks it up*]

Silly fellow. Left his hat. [*He picks up the hat, walks to the back door, opens it and throws out the hat. He closes the door*]

RONALD: Not the night to forget your hat.

SIDNEY: No, indeed.

RONALD: [*Sitting at the table*] Mind you, frankly, he didn't look all there to me. Wild eyed. That's what made me think. . .

SIDNEY: Quite right.

RONALD: Ought to get him to come round the back, you know. Take a tip from me. Once you let tradesmen into the habit of using your front door, you might as well move out, there and then.

SIDNEY: Well, quite. In my own particular business, I always insist that my staff . . .

RONALD: Oh, yes, of course. I was forgetting you're a — you're in business yourself, aren't you?

SIDNEY: Well, in a small way at the moment. My wife and I. I think I explained . . .

RONALD: Yes, of course. And doing very well.

SIDNEY: Well, for a little general stores, you know. Mustn't grumble.

RONALD: Good to hear someone's making the grade.

SIDNEY: These days.

RONALD: Quite. [*He picks up the booklet and looks at it*]

[*A pause*]

SIDNEY: I know this isn't perhaps the moment, I mean it probably isn't the right moment, but none the less, I hope you've

been giving a little bit of thought to our chat. The other day.
If you've had a moment.

RONALD: Chat? Oh, yes—chat. At the bank? Well, yes, it's—
probably not, as you say, the moment but, as I said then—and
this is still off the cuff you understand—I think the bank could
probably see their way to helping you out.

SIDNEY: Ah well, that's wonderful news. You see, as I envisage
it, once I can get the necessary loan, that means I can put in a
definite bid for the adjoining site — which hasn't incidentally
come on to the market. I mean, as I said, this is all purely
through personal contacts.

RONALD: Quite so, yes.

SIDNEY: I mean the site value alone—just taking it as a site—you
follow me?

RONALD: Oh, yes.

SIDNEY: But it is a matter of striking while the iron's hot—
before it goes off the boil . . .

RONALD: Mmm . . .

SIDNEY: I mean, in this world it's dog eat dog, isn't it? No
place for sentiment. Not in business. I mean, all right, so on
occasions you can scratch mine. I'll scratch yours . . .

RONALD: Beg your pardon?

SIDNEY: Tit for tat. But when the chips are down it's every
man for himself and blow you Jack, I regret to say . . .

RONALD: Exactly.

[*The sitting-room door opens.* GEOFFREY *enters. Mid-
thirties. Good-looking, confident, easy-going. He carries a glass
of scotch*]

GEOFFREY: Ah. Is there a chance of sanctuary here?

RONALD: Hallo.

GEOFFREY: Like Dick Potter's harem in there.

SIDNEY: Dick still at it?

GEOFFREY: Yes. Keeping the ladies amused with jokes . . .

RONALD: Is he? Oh, dear. I'd better—in a minute . . .

GEOFFREY: You'll never stop him. Is he always like that? Or
does he just break out at Christmas?

SIDNEY: Oh, no. Dick's a great laugh all the year round . . .

GEOFFREY: Is he?

RONALD: You don't say.

SIDNEY: He's very fascinating character, is Dick. I thought

you'd be interested to meet him. I mean, so's she. In her way.
Very colourful. They're both teachers, you know. But he's
very involved with youth work of all types. He takes these
expeditions off to the mountains. A party of lads. Walks in
Scotland. That sort of thing. Wonderful man with youngsters . . .

RONALD: Really?

SIDNEY: Got a lot of facets.

RONALD: Got a good-looking wife . . .

SIDNEY: Lottie? Yes, she's a fine-looking woman. Always very
well turned out. . .

GEOFFREY: Yes, she seems to have turned out quite well.

SIDNEY: She does the same as him with girls . . .

RONALD: I beg your pardon?

SIDNEY: Hiking and so on. With the brownies, mainly.

RONALD: Oh, I see.

GEOFFREY: Oh.

[*Pause*]

RONALD: Better join the brownies, then, hadn't we? [*He
laughs*]

SIDNEY: [*at length; laughing*] Yes, I like that. Better join the
brownies. [*He laughs*] You must tell that to Dick. That would
tickle Dick no end.

GEOFFREY: [*after a pause*] Nice pair of legs.

RONALD: Yes.

SIDNEY: Dick?

GEOFFREY: His wife.

SIDNEY: Lottie? Oh, yes. Mind you, I don't think I've really
noticed them . . .

GEOFFREY: Usually, when they get to about that age, they
tend to go a bit flabby round here. [*He pats his thigh*] But she's
very trim . . .

RONALD: Trim, oh yes.

GEOFFREY: Nice neat little bum . . .

SIDNEY: Ah.

RONALD: Has she? Hadn't seen that.

GEOFFREY: I was watching her, getting up and stretching out
for the crisps. Very nice indeed.

RONALD: Oh, well, I'll keep an eye out.

[*Pause*]

SIDNEY: That'll be the hiking . . .

GEOFFREY: What?

SIDNEY: [*tapping his thighs; somewhat self-consciously*] This—
you know. That'll be the hiking . . .

RONALD: Yes. [*After a pause*] How did you happen to see
those?

GEOFFREY: What?

RONALD: Her . . . [*He slaps his thighs*] I mean when I saw her
just now she had a great big woolly—thing on. Down to here.

GEOFFREY: Oh, you can get around that.

RONALD: Really?

GEOFFREY: I've been picking imaginary peanuts off the floor
round her feet all evening.

[RONALD *laughs uproariously.* SIDNEY *joins in, a little out
of his depth*]

RONALD: You'll have to watch this fellow, you know.

SIDNEY: Oh, yes?

RONALD: Don't leave your wife unattended if he's around.

SIDNEY: Oh, no?

RONALD: Lock her away . . .

SIDNEY: [*getting the joke at last and laughing*] Ah-ha! Yes . . .
[JANE *suddenly appears outside the back door, peering in*]
[SIDNEY *waves her away with urgent gestures*]

GEOFFREY: Still raining, is it?

SIDNEY: [*holding out his hand*] Yes. Yes.

RONALD: I'll tell you what I've been meaning to ask you . . .

GEOFFREY: What's that?

RONALD: Remember that party we were both at—during the
summer—Malcolm Freebody's . . . ?

GEOFFREY: When was this?

RONALD: Eva—your wife was off sick . . .

GEOFFREY: That's nothing unusual.

RONALD: I remember it because you were making tremendous
headway with some woman that Freebody was using on his
public relations thing. . .

GEOFFREY: Was I?

RONALD: Blonde. Sort of blonde.

GEOFFREY: [*a short thought*] Binnie.

RONALD: Binnie, was it?

GEOFFREY: Binnie something. I think . . .

RONALD: Make out all right, did you?

GEOFFREY: Well—you know . . .

RONALD: Really?

GEOFFREY: You have no idea. Absolute little cracker. Married to a steward on P. and O. Hadn't seen him for eight months . . .

RONALD: [chuckling] Good Lord . . .

SIDNEY: Ah – ha – oh – ha – ha-ha. [And other noises of sexual approval]

[The others look at him]

GEOFFREY: What have you done with yours? Buried her in the garden?

SIDNEY: [guiltily] What? No, no. She's about. Somewhere.

GEOFFREY: Wish I could lose mine, sometimes. Her and that dog. There's hardly room for me in the flat—I mean between the two of them, they have completely reduced that flat to rubble. I mean I'm very fond of her, bless her, she's a lovely girl—but she just doesn't know what it's all about. She really doesn't.

RONALD: Maybe. I still think you're pretty lucky with Eva . . .

GEOFFREY: Why's that?

RONALD: Well, she must have a jolly good idea by now about your—er . . .

GEOFFREY: Yes. I should imagine she probably has . . .

RONALD: Well, there you are . . .

GEOFFREY: Oh now, come off it. Nonsense. She chooses to live with me, she lives by my rules. I mean we've always made that perfectly clear. She lives her life to a certain extent; I live mine, do what I like within reason. It's the only way to do it . . .

SIDNEY: Good gracious.

RONALD: I wish you'd have a chat with Marion. Convince her.

GEOFFREY: Any time. Pleasure.

RONALD: Yes, well, perhaps not—on second thoughts.

GEOFFREY: No, seriously. Any man, it doesn't matter who he is—you, me, anyone— [pointing at SIDNEY] —him. They've just got to get it organized. I mean face it, there's just too much good stuff wandering around simply crying out for it for you not . . .

[The living-room door opens. EVA appears. Behind, DICK POTTER still in full flow, laughing]

[To SIDNEY, altering his tone immediately] Anyway, I think

that would be a good idea. Don't you?

EVA: [*coolly*] Are you all proposing to stay out here all night?

SIDNEY: Oh, dear. We seem to have neglected the ladies.

EVA: Neglected? We thought we'd been bloody well abandoned.

GEOFFREY: Can't manage without us, you see.

EVA: We can manage perfectly well, thank you. It just seemed to us terribly rude, that's all.

GEOFFREY: Oh, good God . . .

EVA: Anyway. Your jolly friends are leaving.

SIDNEY: Oh, really. Dick and Lottie? I'd better pop out and see them off, then. Excuse me . . .

[SIDNEY *goes off to the sitting-room*]

EVA: And, darling, unless you want to see our car towed away again, horn blazing—we'd better get our coats.

GEOFFREY: He's not at it again . . .

EVA: Past his supper time . . .

GEOFFREY: Oh, honestly, Eva . . .

EVA: Don't honestly Eva me, darling. He's your dog.

GEOFFREY: What do you mean, he's my dog?

EVA: [*sweetly*] Your house, your dog, your car, your wife—we all belong to you, darling—we all expect to be provided for. Now are you coming, please?

[RONALD *smiles*]

And your wife is looking slightly less than pleased, I might tell you.

[RONALD's *smile fades*]

[EVA *goes out*]

RONALD: Oh. [*He looks at his watch*] I suppose I'd better, er. . .

GEOFFREY: Oh. Ronnie. By the way . . .

RONALD: Mmmm?

GEOFFREY: I wondered if you heard anything on the grapevine about the new building Harrison's having put up . . .

RONALD: Oh, this new shopping complex of his.

GEOFFREY: Has he got anyone yet?

RONALD: What, you mean in your line?

GEOFFREY: Yes. Has he settled on an architect? Or is it still open?

RONALD: Well, as far as I know, it's still wide open. I mean, it's still a gleam in his eye as far as I know.

GEOFFREY: Well. If you get a chance to put in a word. I know you're fairly thick with him.

RONALD: Yes, of course, I'll mention it, if the topic comes up. I mean, I'm sure you could do as a good a job as anyone.

GEOFFREY: Look, I can design, standing on my head, any building that Harrison's likely to want.

RONALD: Yes, well, as I say, I'll mention it.

GEOFFREY: I'd be grateful . . .

[MARION *comes in*]

RONALD: Ah.

MARION: All right, darling, we're off . . .

RONALD: Right.

MARION: Had a nice time out there?

RONALD: Oh, yes, grand.

MARION: Good. As long as you have . . .

[RONALD *goes off into the living-room*]
This really is a simply loathsome little house. I mean how can people live in them. I mean, Geoff, you're an architect, you must be able to tell me. How do people come to design these sort of monstrosities in the first place, let alone persuade people to live in them?

GEOFFREY: Well . . .

MARION: Oh, God. Now he's going to tell me he designed it.

GEOFFREY: No. I didn't do it. They're designed like this mainly because of cost and people who are desperate for somewhere to live aren't particularly choosey.

MARION: Oh, come. Nobody can be this desperate.

GEOFFREY: You'd be surprised.

MARION: Anyway, it's been lovely to see you. It's been ages. You must come up and see us . . .

[SIDNEY *and* RONALD, *now in his overcoat and carrying* MARION's *coat, return*]

RONALD: Darling . . .

MARION: Sidney, we've had a simply lovely time. Now some time you must come up and see us—and your wife, that's if you ever find her . . .

SIDNEY: Yes, yes, indeed . . .

[*They all go out, chattering, closing the door*]
[*Silence*]
[*After a pause*, SIDNEY *returns. He closes the door*]
[*Rubbing his hands together*] Hah! [*He smiles. Quite pleased.*

*He takes up his drink and sips it. He munches a crisp]*
*[There is a knock at the back door–rather tentative. It is JANE]*
*[SIDNEY frowns. His concentration is disturbed]*
Just a minute. *[He opens the back door]*
*[JANE falls in–a sodden mass]*
*[Recoiling]* My word.

JANE: I saw them leaving.

SIDNEY: Yes. All gone now. They said for me to say good-bye to you.

JANE: Oh.

SIDNEY: Where have you been?

JANE: In the garden. Where else? Where do you think?

SIDNEY: Oh–I don't know. You might have been for a stroll.

JANE: In this?

SIDNEY: Oh. Still raining, is it?

JANE: Yes. *[Pause]* Sidney, if you'd only explained to them – I could've – I mean I've been out there for ages. I'm soaking. . .

SIDNEY: Yes, well, your behaviour made things very difficult. Explanations, that is. What could I say?

JANE: You could have explained.

SIDNEY: So could you. It was really up to you, wasn't it?

JANE: Yes, I know but–I just thought that you might have–that you would've been . . . *[She gives up]*
*[JANE starts to peel off her things]*

SIDNEY: All went off rather satisfactorily, anyway . . .

JANE: *[emptying a wellington boot into the sink]* Good–I'm glad . . .

SIDNEY: So am I. I mean these people just weren't anybody. They are people in the future who can be very, very useful to us. . .

JANE: *[emptying the other boot]* Yes. . .

SIDNEY: Now, you mustn't do that, Jane. You really mustn't. You see, you get yourself all worked up. And then what happens?

JANE: Yes.

SIDNEY: Right. Enough said. All forgotten, eh? *[Pause]* Oh dear . . .

JANE: What?

SIDNEY: We never got round to playing any of our games, did we?

JANE: No.

SIDNEY: In all the excitement. Never mind. Another year. Well, I think I'll have a look at television. Should be something. Christmas Eve. Usually is. Coming in, are you?

JANE: In a minute.

SIDNEY: Right then.

[SIDNEY *goes out closing the door*]

[JANE *stands. She sniffs. She has finished putting away her things. Her eye lights on the dirty things scattered about. She picks up a glass or so and puts them in the sink. She picks up the damp cloth and wipes first where the glasses were standing and then slowly, in wider and wider circles, till she has turned it, once more, into a full-scale cleaning operation. As she cleans she seems to relax. Softly at first, then louder, she is heard to sing happily to herself, and—*

*the* CURTAIN *falls*

# ACT TWO

GEOFFREY *and* EVA JACKSON's *kitchen in their fourth-floor flat. This Christmas.*
*One door leads to the sitting-room, another into a walk-in cup-board. The room gives an immediate impression of untidiness. It is a room continually lived in, unlike the* HOPCROFT's *immaculate ship's bridge. While it gives signs that the owners have a certain taste for the trendy homespun in both equipment and furnishings, some of the equipment, particularly the gas stove, has seen better days. Besides the stove, the room contains a table* [natural scrubbed wood], *kitchen chairs* [natural scrubbed wood], *a chest of drawers* [natural scrubbed wood] *and a fridge and sink.*
*When the* CURTAIN *rises* EVA, *unmade, unkempt and baggy-eyed, sits at the table in her dressing-gown. She is writing with a stub of pencil in a notepad. Whatever it is, it is difficult to word. She and the floor around her are ringed with screwed-up pieces of paper. In front of her is an open scotch bottle. After a minute she tears out the page she has been working on, screws that up as well, and tosses it on the floor to join the others. She starts again.*
*A door slams. From the sitting-room comes the sound of a large dog barking.* EVA *looks up alarmed, consults her watch, gives a moan, and quickly closes the notepad to cover up what she has been writing.* GEOFFREY's *voice is heard off.*

GEOFFREY: [off] Darling? Eva—Eva! Quiet, George!
[GEOFFREY *backs in from the sitting-room*]
[GEORGE *is still barking with wild glee*]
George! That's enough, George! Don't be silly, boy. Sit, George. Sit, boy. At once. That's a good boy. Sit. Good George. Good . . .
[GEORGE *has quietened.* GEOFFREY *goes to close the door.* GEORGE *barks with fresh vigour*]
George. . .! [*Giving up*] Oh, all right, suit yourself. [*He closes the door, turning to face* EVA *for the first time*] Hallo, darling. [*He gives her a kiss as he passes*]
[EVA *hardly seems to notice. Instead, she sits fiddling with one of her pieces of screwed-up paper. Her face is a tense blank*]

God, I need a drink. You want a drink? [*Without waiting for a reply, he takes the scotch, finds a glass and pours himself a drink*] You want one? No? [*He puts the bottle back on the table and drinks*] Cheers. I think we're running into some sort of trouble with the Harrison job. Helluva day. Would you believe I could spend two months explaining to them exactly how to assemble that central-dome. I go along this morning, they're trying to put a bloody great pillar up the middle, straight through the fountain. I said to them, "Listen, you promise to put it up as you're told to—I promise it'll stay up, all right?" I now have to tell Harrison that his super Shopperdrome that he thought was only going to cost so much is going to finish up at twice that. He is not going to be pleased. No, I think I'm in trouble unless I can . . . Oh well, what the hell, it's Christmas. [*Going to the window*] You know, I think it's going to snow. By Boxing Day, that site'll be under six foot of slush, mark my words. That'll put us another six months behind. [*Returning from the window*] Why didn't I pick something simple? [*Seeing the screwed-up paper*] What've you been up to? [*He tries to take* EVA'*s writing pad*]

[EVA *clings to the pad.* GEOFFREY *shrugs, moves away, then turns and looks at her*]

You all right? You're still in your dressing-gown, did you know? Eva? Are you still thinking about this morning? I phoned you at lunch, you know. Were you out? Eva? Oh, come on, darling, we talked it over, didn't we? We were up till four o'clock this morning talking it over. You agreed. You did more than agree. I mean, it was your idea. And you're right. Believe me, darling, you were right. We can't go on. Sooner or later one of us has got to do something really positive for once in our lives—for both our sakes. And it's absolutely true that the best thing that could happen to you and me, at this point in our lives, is for me to go and live with Sally. You were absolutely right. You know, I was thinking on the way home—I nipped in for a quick one, that's why I'm a bit late—I was thinking, this could actually work out terribly well. If we're adult about it, I mean. Don't behave like lovesick kids or something. Sally and I will probably get somewhere together—and by that time you'll probably have got yourself fixed up—we could still see each other, you know. What I'm really saying is, let's not go through all that nonsense

— all that good-bye, I never want to see you again bit. Because I do want to see you again. I always will. I mean, five years. We're not going to throw away five years, are we? Eva? Eva, if you're sitting there blaming yourself for this in any way, don't. It's me, love, it's all me. It's just I'm—okay, I'm weak, as you put it. I'm unstable. It's something lacking in me, I know. I mean, other men don't have this trouble. Other men can settle down and be perfectly happy with one woman for the rest of their lives. And that's a wonderful thing. Do you think I don't envy that? [*Banging the table*] God, how I envy them that. I mean, do you really think I enjoy living out my life like some sexual Flying Dutchman? Eva, please—please try and see my side just a little, will you? Look, it's Christmas Eve. The day after Boxing Day, I promise—I'll just clear everything of mine that you don't need out of the flat. That way, you can forget I even existed, if that's what you want. But can't we try, between us to make the next couple of days ... [*He breaks off*] Did I say it's Christmas Eve? Haven't we got some people coming round? Yes, surely we . . . What time did we ask them for? [*He looks at his watch*] Oh, my God. You didn't remember to put them off by any chance, did you? No. Well then . . . Have we got anything to drink in the house? Apart from this? [*He holds up the bottle of scotch*] Oh well, we'll have that for a start. Now then. . . [*He finds a tray, puts it on the table and puts the scotch bottle on the table*] What else have we got? [*He rummages in the cupboards*] Brandy. That'll do. Bottle of coke. Aha, what's this? Tonic wine? Who's been drinking tonic wine? Is that you? Eva? Oh, for heaven's sake, Eva—you've made your point, now snap out of it, will you? We have lots of people coming round who were due five minutes ago. Now come on . . . [*He looks at her and sighs*] O.K. I get the message. O.K. There is no help or co-operation to be expected from you to-night, is that it? All systems shut down again, have they? All right. All right. It won't be the first time—don't worry. [*He returns to his hunt for bottles*] I mean it's not as if you're particularly famous as a gracious hostess, is it? It hasn't been unheard of for you to disappear to bed in the middle of a party and be found later reading a book. [*Producing a couple more bottles—gin and sherry*] I should think our friends will be a little disappointed if you do put in an appearance. [*Finding an assortment of glasses*] When, I say our friends, perhaps I should say yours. I will remind you that, so far as I can remember, all the people coming tonight come under the heading of your friends and not mine. And if I'm left to entertain them tonight because you choose to opt out, I shall probably finish up being very, very rude to them. Is that clear? Right. You have been warned. Yes, I know. You're very anxious, aren't you, that I should go and work for the up and coming Mr. Hopcroft? So is up and coming Mr. Hopcroft. But I can tell you both, here and now, I have no intention of helping to perpetrate his squalid little developments. What I lack in morals – I make up in ethics.

[GEOFFREY *stamps out into the sitting-room with the tray*]

[*Off, as* GEORGE *starts barking again*] George – no, this is not for you. Get down, I said get down. [*There is a crash as of a bottle coming off the tray*] Oh, really – this damn dog – get out of it . . .

[GEOFFREY *returns with a couple of old coffee-cups which he puts in the sink*]

That room is like a very untidy cesspit. [*He finds a dish cloth*] One quick drink, that's all they're getting. Then it's happy Christmas and out they bloody well go.

[GEOFFREY *goes out again. He takes with him the dish cloth*]

[EVA *opens her notepad and continues with her note*]

[GEOFFREY *returns. He still has the cloth. In the other hand he has a pile of bits of broken dog biscuit*]

Half-chewed biscuit. Why does he only chew half of them, can you tell me that? [*He deposits the bits in the waste bin. He is about to exit again, then pauses*] Eva? Eva – I'm being very patient. Very patient indeed. But in a minute I really do believe I'm going to lose my temper. And we know what happens then, don't we? I will take a swing at you and then you will feel hard done by, and by way of reprisal, will systematically go round and smash everything in the flat. And come tomorrow breakfast time, there will be the familiar sight of the three of us, you, me and George, trying to eat our meals off our one surviving plate. Now, Eva, *please* . . .

[*The doorbell rings.* GEORGE *starts barking*]

Oh, my God. Here's the first of them. [*Calling*] George. Now, Eva, go to bed now, please. Don't make things any more embarrassing. [*As he goes out*] George, will you be quiet.

[GEOFFREY *goes out. The door closes. Silence*]

[EVA *opens her notepad, finishes her note and tears it out. She pushes the clutter on the table to one side slightly. She goes to a drawer and produces a kitchen knife. She returns to the table and pins the note forcibly to it with the knife. She goes to the window*]

[GEOFFREY *returns*]

[*Barking and chattering are heard in the background – two voices.* EVA *stands motionless, looking out*]

[*Calling back*] He's all right. He's quite harmless. Bark's worse than his bite. [*He closes the door*] It would be the bloody Hopcrofts, wouldn't it. Didn't think they'd miss out. And that lift's broken down, would you believe it. [*Finding a bottle-opener in a drawer*] Every Christmas. Every Christmas, isn't it? Eva, come on, love, for heaven's sake.

[GEOFFREY *goes out, closing the door*]

[EVA *opens the window. She inhales the cold fresh air. After a second, she climbs uncertainly on to the window ledge. She stands giddily, staring down and clutching on to the frame*]

[*The door opens, chatter,* GEOFFREY *returns, carrying a glass*]

[*Calling behind him*] I'll get you a clean one, I'm terribly sorry. I'm afraid the cook's on holiday. [*He laughs*]

[*The Hopcrofts' laughter is heard.* GEOFFREY *closes the door*]

Don't think we can have washed these glasses since the last party. This one certainly didn't pass the Jane Hopcroft Good Housekeeping Test, anyway. [*He takes a dish cloth from the sink and wipes the glass rather casually*] I sometimes think that woman must spend . . . Eva! What are you doing?

[EVA, *who is now feeling sick with vertigo, moans*]

Eva! Eva – that's a good girl. Down. Come down – come down – that's a good girl – down. Come on . . . [*He reaches Eva*] That's it. Easy. Come on, I've got you. Down you come. That's it.

[*He eases* EVA *gently back into the room. She stands limply. He guides her inert body to a chair*]

Come on, sit down here. That's it. Darling, darling, what were you trying to do? What on earth made you want to . . . ? What was the point of that, what were you trying to prove? I mean . . . [*He sees the note and the knife for the first time*] What on earth's this? [*He reads it*] Oh, no. Eva, you mustn't think of . . . I mean, what do you mean, a burden to everyone? Who said you were a burden? I never said you were a burden . . . [*During the above,* EVA *picks up the bread-knife, looks at it, then at one of the kitchen drawers. She rises, unseen by* GEOFFREY, *crosses to the drawer and, half opening it, wedges the knife inside so the point sticks out. She measures out a run and turns to face the knife.* GEOFFREY, *still talking, is now watching her absently.* EVA *works up speed and then takes a desperate run at the point of the knife.* GEOFFREY, *belatedly realizing what she's up to, rushes forward, intercepts her and re-seats her*]

Eva, now, for heaven's sake! Come on . . . [*He studies her nervously*] Look, I'm going to phone the doctor. I'll tell him you're very upset and overwrought. [*He backs away and nearly impales himself on the knife. He grabs it*] He can probably give you something to calm you down a bit.

[*The doorbell rings*]

Oh God, somebody else. Now, I'm going to phone the doctor. I'll just be two minutes, all right? Now, you sit there. Don't move, just sit there like a good girl. [*Opening the door and calling off*] Would you mind helping yourselves? I just have to make one phone call . . .

[GEOFFREY *goes out*]

[*Silence.* EVA *finishes another note. A brief one. She tears it out and weights it down, this time with a tin of dog food which happens to be on the table. She gazes round, surveying the kitchen. She stares at the oven. She goes to it and opens it, looking inside thoughtfully. She reaches inside and removes a casserole dish, opens the lid, wrinkles her nose and carries the dish to the draining-board. Returning to the oven, she removes three shelves and various other odds and ends that seem to have accumulated in there. It is a very dirty oven. She looks at her hands, now grimy, goes to the kitchen drawer and fetches a nearly clean tea towel. Folding it carefully, she lays it on the floor of the oven. She lies down and sticks her head inside, as if trying it for size. She is apparently dreadfully uncomfortable. She wriggles about to find a satisfactory position*]

[*The door opens quietly and* JANE *enters*]

[*The hubbub outside has now died down to a gentle murmur so not much noise filters through.* JANE *carries rather carefully two more glasses she considers dirty. She closes the door. She looks round the kitchen but sees no-one. She crosses, rather furtively, to the sink and rinses the glasses.* EVA *throws an oven tray on to the floor with a clatter.* JANE, *startled, takes a step back and gives a little squeak.* EVA, *equally startled, tries to sit up in the oven and hits her head with a clang on the remaining top shelf*]

JANE: Mrs Jackson, are you all right? You shouldn't be on the cold floor in your condition, you know. You should be in bed. Surely? Here . . .

[*She helps* EVA *to her feet and steers her back to the table*] Now, you sit down here. Don't you worry about that oven now. That oven can wait. You clean it later. No point in damaging your health for an oven, is there? Mind you, I know just what you feel like, though. You suddenly get that urge, don't you? You say, I must clean that oven if it kills me. I shan't sleep, I shan't eat till I've cleaned that oven. It haunts you. I know just that feeling. I'll tell you what I'll do. Never say I'm not a good neighbour – shall I have a go at it for you? How would that be? Would you mind? I mean, it's no trouble for me. I quite enjoy it, actually – and you'd do the same for me, wouldn't you? Right. That's settled. No point in wasting time, let's get down to it. Now then, what are we going to need? Bowl of water, got any oven cleaner, have you? Never mind, we'll find it – I hope you're not getting cold, you look very peaky. [*Hunting under the sink* ] Now then, oven cleaner? Have we got any? Well, if we haven't, we'll just have to use our old friend Mr. Vim, won't we? [*She rummages*]

[*The door opens.* GEOFFREY *enters and goes to* EVA. *Conversation is heard in the background*]

GEOFFREY: Darling, listen, it looks as if I've got . . . [*Seeing* JANE] Oh.

JANE: Hallo, there.

GEOFFREY: Oh, hallo – anything you – want?

JANE: I'm just being a good neighbour, that's all. Have you by any chance got an apron I could borrow?

GEOFFREY: [*rather bewildered, pointing to the chair*] Er – yes

—there.

JANE: Oh, yes. [*Putting it on*] Couldn't see it for looking.

GEOFFREY: Er—what are you doing?

JANE: Getting your oven ready for tomorrow, that's what I'm doing.

GEOFFREY: For what?

JANE: For your Christmas dinner. What else do you think for what?

GEOFFREY: Yes, well, are you sure . . .?

JANE: Don't you worry about me. [*She bustles around singing loudly, collecting cleaning things and a bowl of water*]

GEOFFREY: [*over this, irritated*] Oh. Darling — Eva, look I've phoned the doctor but he's not there. He's apparently out on a call somewhere and the fool of a woman I spoke to has got the address and no number. It'll be quicker for me to try and catch him there than sitting here waiting for him to come back. Now, I'll be about ten minutes, that's all. You'll be all right, will you?

JANE: Don't you fret. I'll keep an eye on her. [*She puts on a rubber glove*]

GEOFFREY: Thank you. [*He studies the immobile* EVA. *On a sudden inspiration, crosses to the kitchen drawer and starts taking out the knives. He scours the kitchen, gathering up the sharp implements*]

[JANE *watches him, puzzled*]

[*By way of explanation*] People downstairs are having a big dinner party. Promised to lend them some stuff.

JANE: Won't they need forks?

GEOFFREY: No. No forks. They're Muslims. [*As he goes to the door*] Ten minutes.

[*The doorbell rings*]

JANE: There's somebody.

GEOFFREY: The Brewster-Wrights, probably.

JANE: Oh . . .

[GEOFFREY *goes out, the dog barking as he does so, until the door is closed*]

Hark at that dog of yours. Huge, isn't he? Like a donkey—huge. Do you know what Dick's bought him? Dick Potter? He's bought George a Christmas present. One of those rubber rings. You know the ones you throw in the air. One of those. He loves

it. He's been running up and down your hallway out there —
Dick throwing it, him trying to catch it. But he's really
wonderful with dogs, Dick. He really understands them. Do
you know he nearly became a dog handler only he didn't have
his proper eyesight. But he knows how to treat them. Doesn't
matter what sort of dog it is . . . He knows all their ways. [*Turning to the oven*] Now then — oh, this is going to be a big one,
isn't it? Dear oh dear. Never mind. Where there's a will. [*Removing the tea towel from the oven*] You haven't been trying
to clean it with this, have you? You'll never clean it with this.
Good old elbow grease — that's the way. [*She sets to work, her
head almost inside the oven*] Shall I tell you something —
Sidney would get so angry if he heard me saying this — but I'd
far sooner be down here on the floor, on my knees in the oven
— than out there, talking. Isn't that terrible. But I'm never at
ease, really, at parties. I don't enjoy drinking, you see. I'd just
as soon be out here, having a natter with you. [*She starts to sing
cheerily as she works, her voice booming round the oven*]
[*During this, EVA rises, opens the cupboard, pulls out a tin
box filled with first-aid things and searches through the con-
tents. Eventually, she finds a white cylindrical cardboard pill
box which is what she's looking for. She goes to the sink with
it and runs herself a glass of water. She opens the box, takes
out a couple of small tablets and puts the box back on the
draining-board. She swallows one tablet with a great deal of
difficulty and water. The same with the second. She leaves the
tap running, pulls the cotton-wool out of the box — and the
rest of the pills rattle down the drain. EVA tries desperately to
save some with her finger before they can disappear, turning
off the tap. This proving ineffective, she tries with a fork*]
[*The door opens. Barking and chatter are heard. SIDNEY
enters*]
SIDNEY: Hallo, hallo. Where's everyone gone then . . . [*Seeing
JANE*] Dear oh dear. I just can't believe it. I just can't believe
my eyes. You can't be at it again. What are you doing?
JANE: She's under the weather. She needs a hand.
SIDNEY: Do you realize that's your best dress?
JANE: Oh, bother my best dress.
SIDNEY: Mr and Mrs Brewster-Wright have arrived, you know.
Ron and Marion. I hope they don't chance to see you down

there. [*Turning to* EVA *who is still fishing rather half-heartedly with the fork*] And what's the trouble over here, eh? Can I help – since it seems to be in fashion this evening?

[SIDNEY *takes the fork from* EVA *and seats her in her chair*] Now. I'll give you a little tip, if you like. You'll never get a sink unblocked that way. Not by wiggling a fork about in it, like that. That's not the way to unblock a sink, now, is it? All you'll do that way, is to eventually take the chrome off your fork and possibly scratch the plug hole. Not the way. Let's see now . . . [*He runs the tap for a second and watches the water running away*] Yes. It's a little on the sluggish side. Just a little. But it'll get worse. Probably a few tea-leaves, nothing more. Let's have a look, shall we? [*He opens the cupboard under the sink*] Ten to one, this is where your troubles lie. Ah-ha. It's a good old-fashioned one, isn't it? Need the wrench for that one.

JANE: He'll soon fix that for you, won't you, Sidney?

SIDNEY: Brace of shakes. Shake of braces as we used to say in the Navy. I've got the tools. Down in the car. No trouble at all. [*He turns to* EVA] Nothing serious. All it is, you see – where the pipe bends under the sink there – they call that the trap. Now then. [*He takes out a pencil*] I'll show you. Always useful to know. Paper? [*He picks up* EVA'S *latest suicide note*] This is nothing vital, is it . . . ? Now then [*He glances curiously at it, then turns it over and starts to draw his diagram on the back*] Now – here's your plug hole, do you see, here – if I can draw it – and this is your pipe coming straight down and then almost doubling back on itself like that, for a second, you see? Then it runs away here, to the drain . . .

JANE: You want to know anything, you ask Sidney . . .

SIDNEY: And this little bit here's the actual drain trap. And all you have to do is get it open and out it all comes. Easy when you know. Now I suppose I'll have to walk down four flights for my tools. [*He screws up the paper and throws it away. At the door*] Now, don't worry. Lottie's keeping them entertained at the moment and Dick's busy with George, so everybody's happy, aren't they?

[SIDNEY *opens the door and goes out. We hear* LOTTIE'S *laughter and the dog barking distantly for a moment before the door closes*]

JANE: It's at times like this you're glad of your friends, aren't

you? [*She goes at the oven with fresh vigour, singing cheerily*]
[*During the above* EVA *writes another brief note and places it in a prominent position on the table. She now rises and goes to a chair where there is a plastic washing basket filled with clean but unironed clothes. Coiled on top is a washing line. She returns to the table.* JANE, *emerging for fresh water, catches sight of her*]
Sorting out your laundry? You're a terror, aren't you? You're worse than me. [*She returns to her oven and resumes her song*]
[EVA *begins to pull the washing line from the basket. She finds one end and ties it in a crude noose. She tests the effectiveness of this on one wrist and, satisfied, pulls the rest of the rope from the basket. Every foot or so is a plastic clothes peg which she removes*]
I think I'm beginning to win through. I think I'm down to the metal, anyway, that's something. There's about eight layers on here.
[EVA *comes across a pair of knickers and two pairs of socks still pegged to the line. She removes these and replaces them in the basket*]
There's something stuck on the bottom here like cement. You haven't had cement for dinner lately, have you? [*She laughs*]
[EVA *now stands with her clothes line gazing at the ceiling. There are two light fittings and her eyes rest on the one immediately above the table. She crosses to the door, clicks a switch and just this one goes out*]
Whooo! Where was Moses . . . ? What's happened? Bulb gone, has it? We'll get Sidney to fix that when he comes back. Keep him on the go. [*She returns to the oven again, changing her tune to something suitable like "Dancing in the Dark"*]
[EVA *climbs first on to a chair then on to the table holding her rope. She removes the bulb and shade in one from the socket and places them on the table at her feet. She is beginning to yawn more and more frequently and is obviously beginning to feel the effect of the sleeping pills. Swaying slightly, she starts to tie the rope round the flex above the holder. This proves a difficult operation since she has far too much rope for the job. She finally manages a knot which loosely encircles the flex. She gives the rope a gentle tug – it holds. She tries again. It still remains in position. She gives it a*

*third tug for luck. The rope slides down the flex as far as the
bulb-holder and promptly pulls this away from the wires. The
holder clatters on to the table and she is left clutching the rope.
She stands swaying more pronouncedly now, a faint look of
desperation on her face*]

[RONALD *enters. Behind him we hear* LOTTIE POTTER'S
*laughter and, more distant, a dog barking*]

RONALD: Now then, how's our little invalid getting . . . [*Seeing*
EVA] Oh, good God. [*He dashes forward and steadies* EVA]
My dear girl, what on earth are you doing up there?

JANE: [*emerging from her oven*] Oh, no. She's a real terror, you
know. [*She goes to assist* RONALD *in helping* EVA *off the
table and back on to a chair*] She can't keep still for a minute.
[*Reprovingly to* EVA] You could have hurt yourself up there,
you silly thing.

[RONALD *folds up the rope, which is looped round* EVA'S
*wrist, and leaves it in her hand*]

RONALD: Lucky I . . .

JANE: Yes, it was.

RONALD: I mean. What was she trying to do?

JANE: Bulb's gone.

RONALD: [*looking up*] Yes, so it has. Well, you could have
asked me to do that, you know. I'm no handyman but even I
can change a bulb.

[SIDNEY *enters with a large bag of tools. Behind him we hear*
LOTTIE'S *laughter and a dog barking*]

SIDNEY: Here we are, back again. I've brought everything, just in
case. Everything except the kitchen sink and that's already
here, eh? [*He laughs*]

RONALD: What? Oh, yes. Very good.

JANE: [*amused*] Except the kitchen sink. Honestly.

SIDNEY: [*noticing the light*] Hallo, hallo. More trouble? [*He
puts the tool bag by the sink*]

RONALD: Nothing much. Just a bulb gone.

SIDNEY: You've lost more than a bulb, by the look of it. You've
lost the whole fitting.

RONALD: Good gracious me. So we have. Look at that.

SIDNEY: Just the bare wires, you see.

RONALD: Yes. There's no thingummyjig.

JANE: Just the wires, aren't there?

SIDNEY: Don't like the look of that.

RONALD: No.

JANE: No.

SIDNEY: I mean, if that was to short across like it is . . .

RONALD: Yes.

JANE: Yes.

SIDNEY: You could finish up with a fuse, or a fire . . .

RONALD: Or worse.

JANE: Worse.

SIDNEY: I mean, you've only got to be carrying, say, for instance, a pair of aluminium steps across the room and you happen accidentally to knock against the wires, electricity would be conducted down the steps and straight into you. Natural earth, you see. Finish.

RONALD: I suppose that would go for a very tall man in, say, a tin hat, eh? [*He laughs*]

SIDNEY: True, true. Not so probable. But true.

JANE: Lucky it's not the war time.

SIDNEY: Oh, yes. In certain cases, one touch could be fatal.

RONALD: Better fix it, I suppose.

SIDNEY: I'd advise it. Going to have a go, are you?

RONALD: Well — I don't know. Looks a bit technical for me.

SIDNEY: Oh, no. Very simple. Nothing to it. Look, you've got your two wires coming down . . . Look, I'll draw it for you. [*He whips out his pencil again and, searching for a piece of paper, picks up* EVA's *suicide note. With a casual glance at it*] Nothing important this, is it? [*Without waiting for a reply, he turns it over and starts to sketch*]
[EVA *stares – fascinated*]
You've got your two wires coming down here, you see – like that. They go through the top of the plug, here — excuse the drawing, and then they just screw in to the little holes on the prongs, you see? Tighten your grubs. Screw your top to your bottom and away you go.

RONALD: Let there be light.

SIDNEY: Exactly.
[EVA *scrawls another note*]

RONALD: Oh, well, that looks – simple enough. [*He still seems doubtful*]

SIDNEY: Right. I'll get you a screwdriver and I'll get going on

the sink. [*Opening his tool bag*] Now then, let's get you fixed
up. What've we got here? [*He rummages through his tools,
taking out a screwdriver and a spare fitting*]

RONALD: Good gracious. What a collection.

SIDNEY: This is just the set I keep in the car.

RONALD: Really? Get a lot of trouble with it, do you?

[*During the above* EVA *climbs slowly on to her chair, steps on
to the table and reaches out with both hands towards the bare
wires.* JANE, *who has returned to her oven, turns in time to
see her*]

JANE: Watch her!

SIDNEY: Hey-hey . . .

RONALD: Hoy . . .

[*All three of them run, grab* EVA *and pull her back in the chair*]

SIDNEY: They might have been live.

RONALD: Yes. [*A thought*] Might they?

SIDNEY: Yes.

RONALD: Well, how do we know they're not?

SIDNEY: Check the switches first.

RONALD: Yes, well, don't you think we'd better? I mean, I'm
going to be the one who . . .

SIDNEY: [*striding to the door*] Check the switches, by all means.
[SIDNEY *plays with both switches, plunging the room into
darkness a couple of times*]

JANE: [*During this, still with* EVA] She's got a charmed life,
honestly. The sooner that doctor gets here . . .

RONALD: He'll fix her up.

JANE: He'd better.

SIDNEY: [*completing his check*] Yes, all safe. [*He takes off his
jacket and puts it over the back of a chair*]

RONALD: Ah.

SIDNEY: Should be, anyway. Unless they've put this switch on
upside down, of course.

RONALD: How do we know they haven't?

SIDNEY: Well, you'll be the first to find out, won't you? [*He
roars with mirth*]

JANE: [*equally tickled*] You'll be the first . . .
[RONALD *is less amused*]

SIDNEY: Well, let's get down to it, shall we?

RONALD: [*gazing at the light*] Yes.

SIDNEY: Each to his own. [*He starts work under the sink*]
JANE: Each to his own. [*She returns to the oven*]
 [*They prepare for their various tasks*]
 This is coming up a treat.
SIDNEY: Ought to get—er—Marion out here, eh? Find her something to do.
RONALD: [*clearing the things off the table*] No—no. I don't think she'd contribute very much. Probably better off with the Potters. Matter of fact, she's just a bit—on her pins. You know what I mean.
SIDNEY: Ah, well. Christmas.
JANE: If you can't do it at Christmas . . .
SIDNEY: Once a year, eh?
RONALD: Not in my wife's case. Festive season recurs rather more frequently. Every three or four days.
SIDNEY: [*under the sink*] Ah-ha! You're going to be a tricky little fellow, aren't you? Nobody's opened you since you were last painted.
 [SIDNEY *clatters under the sink.* JANE *scrubs cheerfully on.* RONALD *sets to work, standing on the table and on* EVA's *latest note. He tackles his own particular job extremely slowly and with many false starts. He is not particularly electrically-minded.* EVA *attempts, under the following, to rescue her note from under* RONALD's *feet. It rips. She scrawls another rapidly*]
RONALD: Must be pretty pleased with your year, I should imagine.
SIDNEY: Beg pardon?
RONALD: Had a good year. Must be pretty pleased.
SIDNEY: Oh, yes. Had a few lucky hunches. Seemed to pay off.
RONALD: I should say so.
SIDNEY: Mustn't complain, anyway.
JANE: No. Mustn't complain.
SIDNEY: As long as you're looking after our money. Eh?
 [*He laughs*]
RONALD: Oh, yes. Yes.
 [*They work.* SIDNEY *whistles.* RONALD *hums.* JANE *sings. Occasionally, the workers break off their respective melodies to make those sounds that people make when wrestling with inanimate objects. "Come on, you little. . . Just one more. . .*

*get in, get in, etc." During this* EVA, *having finished her note, sees* SIDNEY's *bag of tools. Unseen by the others, she goes to the bag and removes a lethal-looking tin of paint stripper. Also a hammer and a nail. She nails her latest note to the table with the hammer which she leaves on the table. Turning her attention to the paint stripper, she tries to get the top off. It is very stiff. She struggles vainly, then goes to the room door, intending to use it as a vice* ]

[*At this moment* MARION *enters*]

[EVA *is pushed behind the door, and, as it swings shut, she clings to the handle and falls across the floor. While the door is open the dog barks and raised voices are heard* ]

MARION: [*holding a gin bottle and glass*] I say – something rather ghastly's happened.

RONALD: [*concentrating hard*] Oh, yes?

MARION: Goodness! Don't you all look busy? Darling, what are you doing up there?

[EVA *tries to open the bottle with the walk-in cupboard door*]

RONALD: Oh, just a little light electrical work or should I say a little electrical light work? [*He laughs*]

SIDNEY: Electrical light work. [*He laughs*]

JANE: Electrical light work. [*She laughs*]

SIDNEY: I like that – yes . . .

MARION: Yes, very funny, darling. Now do come down, please, before you blow us all up. You know absolutely nothing about that sort of thing at all.

RONALD: I don't know . . .

MARION: Absolutely nothing.

RONALD: I fixed that bottle lamp with a cork in it, didn't I?

MARION: Yes, darling, and we all had to sit round admiring it while the lampshade burst into flames.

[EVA *goes to the toolbag for a screwdriver*]

RONALD: [*irritably*] That was entirely the fault of the bloody lampshade.

MARION: I was terrified. The whole thing was an absolute death trap. I had to give it to the Scouts for jumble.

SIDNEY: What was the trouble?

MARON:: It was like modern sculpture. Bare wires sticking out at extraordinary angles.

[EVA *goes and sits down in a corner*]

SIDNEY: No. I meant when you came in.

MARION: Oh, yes. What was it? Something awful. [*She remembers*] Oh, yes. I came for help, that's right. That dog . . .

JANE: George?

MARION: Is that his name – George – yes. Well, he's just bitten that Potter man in the leg.

JANE: Oh, dear.

MARION: Terribly nasty. Right through his trousers. Of course, it was entirely his fault. I mean, he was leaping about being desperately hearty with the poor animal till it had froth simply foaming from its jowls and didn't know where it was.

JANE: Oh, dear, are they . . .

SIDNEY: Yes, what are they . . . ?

MARION: Well, I think they were thinking of going. If they haven't gone. They seem to think he might need an anti-something.

SIDNEY: Rabies.

MARION: Probably. I'll see. [*She opens the door*]
[*Silence*]
[*Calling*] I say, hallo. Hallo there.
[*There is a low growl*]
Oh, dear.

RONALD: What's the matter?

MARION: It's sort of crouching in the doorway chewing a shoe and looking terribly threatening.

RONALD: Really?

MARION: I don't think it's going to let us through, you know.

RONALD: [*picking up the tin of dog meat and moving tentatively to the sitting-room*] He's probably all right, he just needs calming down. Here, boy, boy, good boy. Hallo, boy, good boy.
[*A growl. RONALD returns, closes the door, and goes back to his work*]
No, well, best to leave them when they're like that. Just a bit excited.

SIDNEY: Mind you, once they've drawn blood, you know . . .

JANE: Old Mr Allsop's Alsatian . . .

SIDNEY: Yes.

MARION: Yes. Well, it's lucky I brought the drink. Keep the workers going. And the invalid. How is she?

RONALD: Very groggy.

MARION: [*peering at her*] Golly, yes. She's a dreadful colour. How are you feeling?

JANE: I don't think she really knows we're here.

MARION: Hallo. Hallo, there . . . [*No response*] No, you're right. She's completely gone. Poor thing. Oh well, drink, everyone?

JANE: Not just at the moment. Nearly finished.

MARION: Jolly good. [*Nudging* SIDNEY *with her leg*] What about you?

SIDNEY: In a moment. In just a moment.

RONALD: Darling, I wouldn't drink too much more of that.

MARION: Oh, Ronnie, don't be such a misery. Honestly, he's such a misery. He's totally incapable of enjoying a party.

RONALD: No, all I'm saying is . . .

MARION: Well, Eva and I'll have one, won't we, Eva?

[MARION *pours out two glasses*]

SIDNEY: [*from under the sink*] Ah!

JANE: All right?

SIDNEY: Got it off.

JANE: Oh, well done.

MARION: What's he got off?

[EVA *finally gets the lid off the paint stripper and is about to drink it*]

SIDNEY: That was a wrestle and no mistake. But I got it off. The big question now is, can I get it on again.

MARION: Eva, dear, now you drink that. [*She puts the glass in* EVA'S *hand, removing the tin of stripper*] That'll do you far more good than all the pills and patent medicines put together. [*She puts the paint stripper on the draining-board*]

RONALD: Marion, seriously, I wouldn't advise . . .

MARION: [*hitting him on the foot with the gin bottle*] Oh, Ronnie, just shut up!

RONALD: Ah!

MARION: [*to* EVA; *confidentially*] You'd never think it but he was a really vital young man, Eva. You'd never think it to look at him, would you?

[MARION *fills* EVA'S *glass of gin so that she is forced in her inert state to drink some*]

SIDNEY: [*emerging from his sink*] Well, time for a break. Now then, did somebody promise a drink?

MARION: [*pushing the bottle towards him*] Help yourself.

SIDNEY: Thank you.

JANE: I think that's as much as I can do. It's a bit better.

MARION: [*going to the stove*] Oh, look, isn't that marvellous. Look at that splendid oven.

SIDNEY: Well done. Well done.

JANE: Bit of a difference. [*She picks up her bowl of water and carries it to the sink*]

RONALD: [*having difficulty*] Ah . . .

SIDNEY: How's the electrical department?

RONALD: [*muttering*] Damn fiddly thing.

SIDNEY: [*seeing* JANE] Hey! Don't pour that down now!

JANE: Oh. Nearly forgot.

SIDNEY: You'd have been popular. [*He puts the gin bottle on the table*]

JANE: I'd have been popular.

MARION: Well, I'm just going to sit here all night and admire that oven. I think she's honestly better than our Mrs Minns, isn't she, darling?

RONALD: Anyone's better than our Mrs Minns.

MARION: Oh, she means well. We have our Mrs Minns. She's a dear old soul. She can hardly see and she only comes in for two hours a day and when she's gone we spend the rest of the time cleaning up after her. But she's got an absolute heart of gold.

RONALD: Largely paid for by us.

SIDNEY: Good health. Happy Christmas to all.

MARION: Happy New Year.

JANE: Yes.

SIDNEY: Get this lot finished, maybe there'll be time for a game . . .

JANE: Oh, yes . . .

MARION: What sort of game do you mean?

SIDNEY: You know. Some good party game. Get everyone jumping about.

MARION: What an obscene idea.

SIDNEY: Oh, they're great fun. We've had some laughs, haven't we?

JANE: Talk about laughs . . .

RONALD: Blast.

SIDNEY: What's the matter?

RONALD: Dropped the little thing. Could you see if you can see it. I've got to keep holding on to this or it'll drop off. Little thing about so big.

MARION: What little thing?

RONALD: A whajamacallit.

JANE: Small was it?

RONALD: Lord, yes. Tiny little thingy.

SIDNEY: Oh dear oh dear.

[*They hunt,* SIDNEY *crawls on hands and knees*]

JANE: Might have rolled anywhere.

MARION: What are we looking for?

RONALD: Little whosit. Goes in here.

MARION: Darling, do be more precise. What's a whosit?

JANE: You know, one of those – one of those – isn't that silly, I can't think of the word.

MARION: Well, I refuse to look till I know what we're looking for. We could be here all night. I mean, from the look of this floor it's simply littered with little whosits.

SIDNEY: [*under the table*] Can't see it.

JANE: It's on the tip of my tongue . . . that's it, a nut. Little nut.

MARION: [*searching by the sink*] Oh, well then, a nut. Now we know. Everyone hunt for a little nut.

[EVA *goes and sits at the table*]

SIDNEY: I didn't know we were looking for a nut.

JANE: Aren't we?

RONALD: No. A screw. That's what I'm after, a screw.

SIDNEY: A screw, yes.

JANE: Oh, a screw.

MARION: All right, everybody, stop looking for nuts. Ronnie's now decided he wants a screw. I can't see a thing. And I think it would be terribly sensible if we put the light on, wouldn't it?

RONALD: Good idea.

[MARION *goes to the light switch*]

SIDNEY: [*realizing far too late*] No, I wouldn't turn that on . . .

[MARION *presses the switch*]

MARION: There.

[RONALD, *on the table, starts vibrating, emitting a low moan*]

SIDNEY: [*rising*] Turn it off.

JANE: Get him away.

MARION: Darling, what on earth are you doing?

JANE: [*reaching out to pull* RONALD *away*] Get him away.

SIDNEY: No, don't touch him, he's live. [*He goes to the switch*]
   [JANE *touches him and recoils, with a squeak*]

RONALD: [*through gritted teeth*] Somebody turn it off.
   [SIDNEY *turns it off*]

SIDNEY: All right. Panic over.
   [RONALD *continues to vibrate*]

JANE: Turn him off, Sidney.

SIDNEY: I have.

JANE: Turn him off!

SIDNEY: He is off. [*Calming* JANE] Now, pull yourself together. Help me get him down. Get him down.
   [SIDNEY *and* JANE *guide* RONALD *down from the table
   and to a chair.* MARION *watches them*]

MARION: Good lord. Wasn't that extraordinary?

SIDNEY: Easy now.

JANE: Take it slowly.
   [EVA *pours herself another drink*]

MARION: Whenever he fiddles about with anything electrical it
   always ends in disaster. This always happens. Is he all right?

SIDNEY: He's in a state of shock.

JANE: He would be.

SIDNEY: Sit him down and keep him warm — that's the way.
   Pass me my jacket. Jacket. Jacket.

MARION: He looks frightfully odd.

JANE: [*bringing* SIDNEY'S *jacket*] Here.

SIDNEY: He needs more. He really needs to be wrapped up,
   otherwise . . .

JANE: [*Looking round*] There's nothing much here.

SIDNEY: Well, find something. In the other room. We need
   blankets.

JANE: Right.
   [JANE *goes to the door whilst* MARION *looks vaguely round
   the kitchen*]

SIDNEY: Now easy, old chap. Just keep breathing . . .
   [JANE *opens the door. There is a fierce growling. She with-
   draws swiftly and closes it*]

JANE: He's still there.

SIDNEY: Who?

JANE: The dog.

SIDNEY: Well, step over him. This is an emergency.

JANE: I'm not stepping over him. You step over him.

SIDNEY: Oh dear oh dear.

MARION: [*who has found the washing basket*] What about these bits and bobs? [*She picks up an article of clothing*]

SIDNEY: What's that?

MARION: Last week's washing, I think. [*Sniffing it*] It seems fairly clean. Might be better than nothing.

SIDNEY: Yes, well, better than nothing.

MARION: It seems dry.

JANE: Better than nothing.

[*Between them, during the following, they cover* RONALD *in an assortment of laundry, both male and female. He finishes up more or less encased in it but still quivering*]

SIDNEY: Quick as you can. Come along, quick as you can.

JANE: [*examining a shirt*] She hasn't got this collar very clean.

SIDNEY: Jane, come along.

MARION: [*holding up a petticoat*] Oh, that's rather pretty. I wonder where she got this.

SIDNEY: Not the time for that now. That the lot?

MARION: Yes. Only socks left. And you-know-whats.

SIDNEY: Well, it'll keep his temperature up.

MARION: Oh, my God, what does he look like? Ronnie! You know I've got a terrible temptation to phone up his chief cashier. If he could see him now . . . [*She starts to laugh*]

JANE: I don't think he's very well, you know.

MARION: Yes, I'm sorry. It's just that I've never seen anything quite so ludicrous.

SIDNEY: [*moving a stool up beside* RONALD] Might I suggest that Marion sits down with her husband just until the doctor gets here for Mrs Jackson . . .

JANE: Then he can look at them both.

SIDNEY: Precisely.

JANE: Lucky he was coming.

SIDNEY: Yes, well, we'd better just finish off and clear up, hadn't we?

MARION: [*sitting beside* RONALD] Would you like a drink, darling? You look dreadful!

JANE: I'd better just go over the floor.

SIDNEY: [*preparing to go under the sink again*] No, dear, we don't want you to go over the floor. Not now . . .

JANE: Just where we've been tramping about. If Doctor's coming. It won't take a minute.

SIDNEY: All right. Carry on, Sister. Sorry I spoke.

JANE: [*going to the walk-in cupboard*] Now where does she keep her broom?

RONALD: [*strained tone*] You know, I feel very peculiar.

[*JANE finds the broom and starts clearing the immediate vicinity around the table*]

MARION: Well, I hope you won't be like this all over Christmas, darling. I mean we've got your mother over tomorrow for lunch and Edith and the twins on Boxing Day — I just couldn't face them alone. I just couldn't.

JANE: [*to* EVA] Excuse me, dear. I wonder if you could just . . . [*She winds up the rope, still looped to* EVA'S *wrist, and puts it in* EVA'S *hand*] Tell you what, why don't you sit up here? Just for a second. Then I won't get in the way of your feet. [*She assists* EVA *to sit on the edge of the table*] Upsidaisy.

SIDNEY: [*sliding under the sink*] She all right still?

JANE: I think so.

[EVA *yawns*]

Just a bit tired. Neglected you in all the excitement, haven't we? Never mind. Just sit there. Doctor'll be here soon. [*She sweeps under the table*]

MARION: You know, I believe I'm beginning to feel dizzy as well. I hope I haven't caught it from her.

JANE: I hope not. What a Christmas, eh?

SIDNEY: [*from under the sink*] We'll be laughing about this.

JANE: [*going to the sink and lifting* SIDNEY'S *feet*] Excuse me, dear. What's that?

SIDNEY: I say, in about two weeks' time, we'll —

[JANE *pours the water away in the sink*]

— all be sitting down and laughing about — aaaah!

JANE: Oh, no.

SIDNEY: Put the plug in.

JANE: [*feverishly following the plug chain*] I can't find the end.

SIDNEY: Put the plug in!

JANE: [*putting the plug in*] I'm sorry.

SIDNEY: [*emerging from under the sink, his top half drenched in dirty water*] Look what you've done.

JANE: I'm terribly sorry. [*She picks up a dish cloth*]

SIDNEY: Look what you have done! You silly woman!
[*She tries to mop him down with the dish cloth*]
[*Beating her away*] Don't do that! Don't do that! It's too late for that. Look at this shirt. This is a new shirt.

JANE: Well, it'll wash. It'll wash. I'll wash it. It's only oven grease.

SIDNEY: I told you, didn't I? I said, whatever you do — don't pour water down there, didn't I?

JANE: I didn't think . . .

SIDNEY: Obviously.

JANE: Well, take the shirt off now and I'll . . .

SIDNEY: And I'll go home in my singlet, I suppose?

JANE: Nobody'll notice.

SIDNEY: Of course they'll notice. Otherwise, there'd be no point in wearing a shirt in the first place, would there? If nobody noticed, we'd all be walking around in our singlets.

JANE: It's dark.

SIDNEY: Don't change the subject. It would really teach you a lesson if I caught pneumonia.

JANE: [*tearful*] Don't say that.

SIDNEY: Teach you, that would.
[JANE *sniffs.* SIDNEY *strides to the door*]
Dear oh dear.

JANE: [*following him*] Where are you going?

SIDNEY: To get my overcoat before I freeze. Where else do you think I'm going?

JANE: But, Sidney . . .
[SIDNEY *ignores her, flinging open the door and striding out, making a dignified exit. There is a burst of furious barking.* SIDNEY *reappears very swiftly and closes the door behind him*]

SIDNEY: [*to* EVA, *furiously*] That dog of yours is a liability. You ought to keep that animal under control. I can't even get to my overcoat. It's not good enough.
[EVA *slowly lies down on the kitchen table, oblivious*]

JANE: Come and sit down.

SIDNEY: Sit down? What's the point of sitting down?

JANE: Geoff should be back soon.

SIDNEY: I should hope so. This isn't what you expect at all. Not when you come round for a quiet drink and a chat. [*Almost screaming in* EVA'S *ear*] This is the last time I accept hospitality in this household.

JANE: Ssh.

SIDNEY: What?

JANE: She'll hear you.

SIDNEY: I don't care who hears me. [*He sits*]

JANE: Ssh. [*She sits*]

> [*A pause. The four of them are sitting.* EVA *lies.* RONALD *continues to look glassy, quivering slightly.* MARION'S *drinking has caught up with her.* JANE *looks abjectly miserable.* SIDNEY *shivers in his vest*]

SIDNEY: And we're missing the television.

JANE: Ssh.

> [*A silence. Then, from apparently nowhere, a sleepy voice begins to sing dreamily. It is* EVA]

EVA: [*singing*] "On the first day of Christmas my true love sent to me a partridge in a pear tree. On the second day of Christmas my true love sent to me, two turtle doves –

MARION: [*joining her*] – and a partridge in a pear tree. On the third day of Christmas my true love sent to me, three French hens –

JANE: [*joining her*] – two turtle doves and a partridge in a pear tree. On the fourth day of Christmas my true love sent to me, four calling birds –

RONALD: [*joining them*] – three French hens, two turtle doves and a partridge in a pear tree.

ALL: On the fifth day of Christmas my true love sent to me, five gold rings, etc.

> [*As the bedraggled quintet begin to open up, the singing gets bolder and more confident. Somewhere in the distance* GEORGE *begins to howl.* EVA, *still lying on her back, conducts them dreamily with both hands and then finally with the hammer*]

> [*The door bursts open.* GEOFFREY *enters hurriedly, calling behind him*]

GEOFFREY: Through here, Doctor. Please hurry, I . . .

> [GEOFFREY *is suddenly aware of the sound behind him.*

*He turns, still breathless from his run up four flights. His mouth drops further open as he surveys the scene. The singing continues unabated, as the Lights black-out and –*

*the* CURTAIN *falls*

# ACT THREE

*The Brewster-Wrights' kitchen. Next Christmas.*
*They live in a big old Victorian house, and the kitchen, though*
*modernized to some extent, still retains a lot of the flavour of the*
*original room. A sink, an electric stove [or even an Aga range], a*
*fridge, a dark wood sideboard, a round table and chairs form the*
*substantial furnishings for the room. On the table is an elderly*
*radio set. There is a door, half of opaque glass, to the hall, and a*
*garden door.*
*When the* CURTAIN *rises,* RONALD *is discovered sitting in an*
*armchair near the table. He wears a scarf and a green eye-shade.*
*Beside him is a lighted portable oil stove. At his elbow is an empty*
*teacup. The radio is on, playing very quietly a very jolly carol.*
RONALD *is reading a book. He is obviously enjoying it, for every*
*two or three seconds he chuckles to himself out loud. This con-*
*tinues for some seconds, until the door from the hall opens and*
EVA *enters. She wears a winter coat and carries an empty teacup*
*and a plate, which she puts down on the draining-board.*

RONALD: Oh. Hallo there.
EVA: All right?
RONALD: Oh, yes. [*He switches off the radio*]
EVA: Are you warm enough in here?
RONALD: Oh, yes. It's fine in here. Well, not too bad.
EVA: The rest of the house is freezing. I don't envy you going to
　　bed.
RONALD: Her room's all right though, is it?
EVA: Oh, she's got three electric fires blazing away.
RONALD: My God. That'll be the second power station I've paid
　　for this winter.
EVA: She seems to be rather dug in up there. Almost in a state of
　　hibernation. Doesn't she ever come out?
RONALD: Not if she can help it. Heating system went on the
　　blink, you see — usual thing and we had a few frosty words
　　over it and — the outcome was, she said she wasn't setting foot
　　outside her room until I got it fixed.
EVA: [*putting on a pair of gloves*] Well, how long's it been like

this?

RONALD: [*vaguely*] Oh, I don't know. Two or three weeks, I suppose.

EVA: Well, that's disgusting. Can't you get the men round to fix it?

RONALD: Yes, yes. I have phoned them several times. But I've been a bit unlucky up to now. They always seem to be at lunch . . .

EVA: [*taking off her coat and putting it on the back of a chair*] Well, I wouldn't put up with it. I'd scream the place down till Geoffrey got it fixed. [*She hunts in the cupboards*]

RONALD: Yes, we've had a packet of trouble with this central heating. Always goes on the blink. Either the day before Christmas, the day before Easter or the day before Whitsun. Always seems to manage it. Don't understand the principle it works on but whatever it is, seems to be very closely tied in with the Church calendar. [*He laughs*] Can I help you at all?

EVA: She said she'd like a sandwich. [*She puts a plate, knife, bread and a pot of peanut butter on a bread board*]

RONALD: [*looking at his watch*] Oh, yes. She's about due for a sandwich.

EVA: I'm looking for the butter.

RONALD: Oh, don't you bother to do that, I'll. . .

EVA: It's all right. Where do you keep your butter?

RONALD: Do you know, that's very interesting. I have absolutely no idea. A closely guarded secret kept by Mrs Minns. I suppose we could hazard a guess. Now then, butter. Try the fridge.

EVA: Fridge?

RONALD: Keeps it soft. It's warmer in there than it is outside.

EVA: [*looking in the fridge*] Right first time. [*She sets about making a sandwich, taking off one glove*]

RONALD: What's she want? Peanut butter?

EVA: Apparently.

RONALD: Good grief. She's got an absolute craving for that stuff lately. That and cheese footballs. All most alarming. She's not up there knitting little blue bootees, by any chance?

EVA: Not that I noticed.

RONALD: Thank God for that.

EVA: She looks a lot better than when I last saw her, anyway.

RONALD: Really? Yes, yes. Well, she got a bit overtired, I think.

Principally.

EVA: Geoff'll be here in a minute to pick me up. I'll get out of your way. I just heard Marion was — I hope you didn't mind . . .

RONALD: No, very good of you to look round. Sure she appreciated it. She doesn't get many visitors. Lottie Potter looked in briefly. That set her back a couple of weeks. No, the trouble with Marion you see, is she lives on her nerves. Far too much.

EVA: Marion does?

RONALD: Oh, yes. Very nervous, insecure sort of person basically, you know.

EVA: Really?

RONALD: That surprises you, does it? Well, I've got a pretty thorough working knowledge of her now, you know. I mean, she's calmer than she was. When I first met her she was really one of the jumpiest girls you could ever hope to meet. Still, as I say, she's much calmer since she's been with me. If I've done nothing else for her, I've acted as a sort of sedative.

EVA: You don't think that a lot of her trouble may be — drink?

RONALD: Drink? No, I don't honestly think so. She's always liked a — I mean, the doctor did say she should lay off. But that was only because it was acting as a stimulant. She hasn't touched it lately.

EVA: She has this evening.

RONALD: Really?

EVA: Yes.

RONALD: Well, you do surprise me.

EVA: She's got quite a collection up there.

RONALD: Oh, has she? Has she now?

EVA: Didn't you know?

RONALD: Well, I don't often have much cause to go into her room these days. She likes her privacy, you see. And I respect that. Not that it's not a mutual arrangement, you understand. I mean, she doesn't particularly choose to come into my room either. So it works out rather conveniently. On the whole.

EVA: Do you ever see each other at all?

RONALD: Good Lord, it's not as if we aren't in the same house. We bang into each other quite frequently. It's not always as quiet as this, believe me. In the holidays we've got the boys here. They thump about. No end of a racket. Boys, of course. Mind you, they're no trouble — they're usually out, too, most of the time – with their friends.

EVA: Pity they're not with you for Christmas.

RONALD: Oh well, it's greatly over-estimated, this Christmas business. That reminds me, would you like a drink? Seeing as it's Christmas.

EVA: No, I don't think so.

RONALD: Oh, go on. Just one. With me, for Christmas.

EVA: Well – all right, a little one.

RONALD: Right. [*He rises*] Good. I'll brave the elements then and try and make it as far as the sitting-room . . .

[*The doorbell rings*]

EVA: That's probably Geoff.

RONALD: [*opening the door*] I'll let him in, then. [*Stopping short*] Good Lord, is that dust on the hall table or frost? Won't be a minute.

[RONALD *goes out*]

[EVA, *alone, looks round the room rather sadly. She leaves the sandwich and plate on the table, puts the other things back on the sideboard, returns to the table, sits and starts to eat the sandwich*]

[GEOFFREY *enters in his overcoat*]

GEOFFREY: Blimey. Why aren't you sitting in the garden, it's warmer.

EVA: Hullo.

GEOFFREY: Ready then?

EVA: I'm just going to have a drink with Ronnie.

GEOFFREY: Oh. And how is *she*?

EVA: Drunk.

GEOFFREY: God.

[*Pause.* EVA *munches*]

EVA: How did you get on?

GEOFFREY: Well . . .

EVA: Did you ask him?

GEOFFREY: Well . . .

EVA: You didn't.

[GEOFFREY *does not reply*]

You didn't damn well ask him.

GEOFFREY: It's no good. I find it impossible to ask people for money.

[EVA *gives a short laugh*]

I'm sorry.

EVA: He owes it you. You're not asking him a favour, you know. He owes it you.

GEOFFREY: I know.

EVA: Well then.

GEOFFREY: It doesn't matter.

EVA: Oh, my . . . Oh well I'll have to get in touch with him then. After Christmas. I don't mind doing it.

GEOFFREY: You don't have to do that.

EVA: Well, somebody has to, darling. Don't they?

[*The door opens. A drinks trolley enters followed by* RONALD]

RONALD: Here we come. The Trans-Siberian Express. Thank you so much. We seem to be a bit depleted on the old alcohol stakes. Odd, thought I'd stocked up only recently. Probably old Mrs Minns been knocking them off, eh? The woman must have some vices. She hasn't got much else to recommend her. Now what are we having, Eva?

EVA: Could I have just a bitter lemon?

RONALD: Good gracious, nothing stronger?

EVA: Not just now.

RONALD: Well, if that's what you want . . . Geoff, what about you?

GEOFFREY: I think I'd like the same, actually.

RONALD: What? A bitter lemon?

GEOFFREY: Just what I feel like.

RONALD: You won't last through Christmas at that rate. [*Inspecting his trolley*] Well, that seems to be the only thing I haven't brought.

EVA: Oh well, it doesn't matter. Something else.

RONALD: No, no. I'll get it, I'll get it. We've got some somewhere.

[RONALD *goes out, closing the door*]

EVA: I mean, either you want me to help you or you don't.

GEOFFREY: Yes.

EVA: I mean, if you don't, just say so. I don't particularly enjoy working in that dark little office of yours. You're a terrible employer. You come in late even when I drive you to work. You take four-hour lunch breaks and then expect me to do all your damn typing at five o'clock in the evening.

GEOFFREY: That's the way I do business.

EVA: Not with me you don't.

GEOFFREY: That's what you're paid for.

EVA: That's what I'm what?

GEOFFREY: Look, if you don't like the job . . .

EVA: You asked me to help you. Now, if you didn't mean that, that's a different matter.

GEOFFREY: Well yes, I did, but . . .

EVA: All right, then. That's settled. You asked me to help you. I am bloody well going to help you.

GEOFFREY: O.K. O.K., thanks.

EVA: Not at all. [*A slight pause*] And you're not going to ask for that money?

GEOFFREY: No.

EVA: Even though we're owed it?

GEOFFREY: No.

EVA: And you won't let me ask?

GEOFFREY: No.

EVA: All right. Then we'll have to think of something else.

GEOFFREY: Exactly.

EVA: I'll phone Sidney Hopcroft after Christmas and talk to him.

GEOFFREY: Sidney Hopcroft.

EVA: He's always asking if you're interested.

GEOFFREY: If you think I'm going to get myself involved in his seedy little schemes . . .

EVA: Why not?

GEOFFREY: Have you seen the buildings he's putting up? Half his tenants are asking to be re-housed and they haven't even moved in yet.

EVA: Darling, I hate to remind you but ever since the ceiling of the Harrison building caved in and nearly killed the Manager, Sidney Hopcroft is about your only hope of surviving as an architect in this city.

GEOFFREY: I can do without Sidney Hopcroft, thank you very much.

[*The door opens.* RONALD *enters with two bottles of bitter lemon*]

RONALD: Here we are. Two very bitter lemons. [*He pours out two bitter lemons and a scotch*]

EVA: Thank you.

RONALD: I think I'm going to have something more than that, if you'll excuse me. Bit quieter than last Christmas, eh?

GEOFFREY: What?

RONALD: Last Christmas. Remember that? Round at your place?

GEOFFREY: Yes.

EVA: Yes.

RONALD: Good gracious me. You have to laugh now. Old Hopcroft. [*He laughs*] Always remember old Hopcroft. Doing very well. Did you know that? Doing frightfully well. Seems to have a flair for it. Wouldn't think so to look at him. Always found him a bit unprepossessing. Still—the chap to keep in with. The rate he's going.

EVA: Yes.

GEOFFREY: [*picking up* RONALD's *book*] Is this good?

RONALD: Oh, yes. Yes, quite good. Very amusing. Bit—saucy, in parts. Mrs Minns found it under one of the boys' mattresses. Nearly finished her there and then, poor old thing. Bitter lemon.

EVA: Thanks.

RONALD: Bitter lemon.

GEOFFREY: Thank you.

RONALD: [*raising his glass of scotch*] Well, Happy Christmas. Good health. God bless.

EVA: Happy Christmas.

GEOFFREY: Happy Christmas.

RONALD: [*after a pause*] Sorry to hear about your problems, Geoff.

GEOFFREY: How do you mean?

RONALD: I meant, the Harrison thing. Hear it fell through . . . Oh, I'm sorry, perhaps that's the wrong expression to use—bit unfortunate.

GEOFFREY: That's all right.

EVA: It wasn't actually Geoff's fault.

RONALD: No. no, I'm sure—knowing Geoff. Unthinkable. I mean, that local paper's as biased as hell. I refused to read that particular article. So did all my friends.

EVA: [*after a pause*] Just because Geoffrey was doing something totally new for a change . . .

GEOFFREY: How's the bank doing, then?

RONALD: Oh, well. We're not in the red, yet. No thanks to me, mind you.

[*A bell rings*]

GEOFFREY: Is that the front door?

RONALD: No. It's the – er – bedroom bell, actually. We've never bothered to have them taken out. They always come in useful. Boys with measles and so on.

EVA: Shall I go up to her?

RONALD: No, no, I'll . . .

EVA: No, it's all right. I don't mind . . .

RONALD: Well, that's very good of you. Probably nothing important. Wants the page of her magazine turning over or something.

EVA: I hope not.

RONALD: What's the harm, I say. As long as it keeps her happy.

EVA: Yes.

[EVA *goes out, closing the door*]

RONALD: I mean, who are we to argue with a woman, eh? You can never win. Hopeless. Mind you, I'm talking to the wrong chap, aren't I?

GEOFFREY: What?

RONALD: I mean you seem to do better than most of us.

GEOFFREY: Oh, yes. [*He sits in the armchair*]

RONALD: You seem to have got things pretty well organized on the home front. [*He laughs*]

GEOFFREY: Well, it's just a matter of knowing . . .

RONALD: Ah yes, that's the point. I never really have. Not really. I mean, take my first wife. Distinguished-looking woman. Very charming. Seemed pretty happy on the whole. Then one day, she suddenly ups and offs and goes. Quite amazing. I mean, I had literally no idea she was going to. I mean, we had the flat over the bank at the time, so it wasn't as if I was even very far away and on this particular day, I came up for lunch and she'd laid on her usual splendid meal. I mean, I had absolutely no complaints about that. I think my very words were something like, jolly nice that, see you this evening. And when we knocked off for tea, I came upstairs and she'd just taken off. Well, I hunted about for a bit in case she'd got knocked down or gone shopping and lost her memory or something and then she wrote, some time later, and said she'd had enough.

So I was forced to call it a day. Some time later again, I took up tennis to forget her and married Marion. Of course, that's all forgotten now. All the same, sometimes in the evening I can't help sitting here and trying to work it all out. I mean, something happened. Something must have happened. I'm just not sure what. Anyway. Under the bridge, eh? All I'm saying really, is some people seem to have the hang of it and some of us just aren't so lucky.

GEOFFREY: Hang of what?

RONALD: Well — this whole women business, really. I mean, this may sound ridiculous, but I've never to this day really known what most women think about anything. Completely closed book to me. I mean, God bless them, what would we do without them? But I've never understood them. I mean, damn it all, one minute you're having a perfectly good time and the next, you suddenly see them there like — some old sports jacket or something — literally beginning to come apart at the seams. Floods of tears, smashing your pots, banging the furniture about. God knows what. Both my wives, God bless them, they've given me a great deal of pleasure over the years but, by God, they've cost me a fortune in fixtures and fittings. All the same. Couldn't do without them, could we? I suppose. Want another one of those?

GEOFFREY: No, thanks.

[*The door opens.* EVA *enters*]

[GEOFFREY *rises and sits again*]

EVA: [*coming in swiftly and closing the door*] Brrr.

RONALD: Ah.

EVA: Forgot to put my coat on. [*She puts her coat on*]

RONALD: Anything serious?

EVA: No. [*Kneeling by the stove to warm herself*] She says she wants to come down.

RONALD: Here? Is that wise?

EVA: She says she wants a Christmas drink with us since we're all here.

RONALD: Oh well. Sort of thing she does. Calls you all the way upstairs to tell you she's coming all the way downstairs. Your drink there.

EVA: Thanks.

RONALD: And how's that mad dog of yours? Still chewing up

your guests?

GEOFFREY: Er – no . . .

EVA: No, we had to – give him away.

RONALD: No, really?

EVA: Yes – he got a bit much. He was really getting so expensive to keep. And then these people we know who've got a farm – they said they'd have him.

RONALD: Oh, dear. I didn't know that. That's a shame.

EVA: Yes, it was an awful decision to make. We just felt – well . . .

GEOFFREY: You did, you mean.

EVA: Darling, we couldn't afford to keep him.

RONALD: Well, old Dick Potter will be relieved, anyway. What did he have to have? Three stitches or something, wasn't it?

EVA: Something like that.

RONALD: Doesn't seem to have done him any harm, anyway. He should be half-way up some Swiss mountain by now. Hopefully, those two lads of ours are safely roped to him.

EVA: Oh, is that where they've gone?

RONALD: Yes. Something I always meant to take them on myself. Anyway, we'll have to do without old Dick to jolly us up this year, I suppose.

GEOFFREY: That's a pity.

[*The door opens.* MARION *sweeps in. She wears a negligée. She stands dramatically and flings out her arms*]

MARION: Geoff, darling, it's sweet of you and Eva to come round to see me.

GEOFFREY: [*rising*] Oh, that's O.K.

MARION: No, you don't know how much it means to me. It really is terribly, terribly sweet of you.

GEOFFREY: That's all right, we were . . .

MARION: And at Christmas, particularly. Bless you for remembering Christmas. [*She collapses into the armchair*]

RONALD: Look, Marion, you're going to freeze to death. For goodness' sake, put something on, woman.

MARION: I'm all right.

RONALD: Let me get you your coat. You've only just got out of bed.

MARION: Darling, I am quite all right. And I am not sitting in my kitchen in a coat. Nobody sits in a kitchen in a coat.

Except tradesmen. It's unheard of. Now, offer me a drink.

RONALD: Look, dear, you know the doctor said very plainly . . .

MARION: [*snapping fiercely*] Oh, for the love of God, Ronnie, it's Christmas. Don't be such an utter misery. [*To the others*] He's Scrooge, you know. He's Scrooge in person. Have you noticed, he's turned all the heating off.

[RONALD, *dignified, goes to the trolley and pours* MARION *a drink.* GEOFFREY *sits by the table*]

Oh, it's heavenly to be up. When you've lain in bed for any length of time, on your own, no-one to talk to, with just your thoughts, don't you find your whole world just begins to crowd in on you. Till it becomes almost unbearable. You just lie there thinking, oh God, it could've been so much better if only I'd had the sense to do so and so — you finish up lying there utterly filled with self-loathing.

EVA: I know the feeling.

RONALD: [*handing* MARION *a glass*] Here you are, dear.

MARION: Heavens! I can hardly see it. Is there anything in here? No it's all right. I'll just sit here and inhale it. [*Turning to* GEOFFREY *and* EVA] How are you, anyway?

EVA: Well, as I told you we're — pretty well —

MARION: I don't know what it is about Christmas but — I know it's supposed to be a festive thing and we're all supposed to be enjoying ourselves — I just find myself remembering all the dreadful things — the dreadful things I've said — the dreadful things I've done and all those awful hurtful things I didn't mean — oh God, I didn't mean them. Forgive me, I didn't mean them. [*She starts to cry*]

RONALD: Look, darling do try and jolly up just for a bit, for heaven's sake.

MARION: [*savagely*] Jolly up? How the hell can — I — jolly — up?

EVA: Marion, dear . . .

MARION: Do you know what I saw in the hall just now? In the mirror. My face. My God, I saw my face. It was like seeing my face for the first time.

RONALD: Oh, come on. It's not a bad face, old sausage.

MARION: How could anything be so cruel? How could anything be so unutterably cruel?

RONALD: [*to* GEOFFREY] Now, you see, this is a case in

point. What am I supposed to do? I mean, something I've said has obviously upset her, but you tell me – you tell me.

MARION: [*pulling* GEOFFREY *to her*] Geoff – Geoff – Geoff – did you know, Geoff, I used to be a very beautiful woman? I was a very, very beautiful woman. People used to stare at me in the street and say, "My God, what a beautiful, beautiful woman she is." People used to come from miles and miles just to take my picture . . .

RONALD: Marion.

MARION: I mean, who'd want my photograph now? Do you want my photograph now? No, of course you don't. Nobody wants my photograph now. Can anybody think of anyone who'd want a photograph of me now? Please, someone. Someone, please want my photograph.

RONALD: [*bellowing*] Marion! Nobody wants your damn picture, now shut up.

[*A silence.* GEOFFREY *and* EVA *are stunned.* RONALD *removes his eyeshade and adjusts his scarf*]

[*The first to recover*] Now then, what were we saying?

[*The doorbell rings*]

EVA: [*after a pause*] Doorbell.

RONALD: Bit late for a doorbell, isn't it?

[*They sit. The doorbell rings again*]

EVA: Shall I see who it is?

RONALD: Yes, do. Have a look through the little glass window. If you don't like the look of them, don't open the door.

EVA: Right.

[EVA *goes into the hall*]

RONALD: Can't think who'd be ringing doorbells at this time of night.

GEOFFREY: Carol singers?

RONALD: Not at this time. Anyway, we don't get many of them. Marion always asks them in. Insists on filling them up with hot soup and chocolate biscuits as if they were all starving. Had a great row with the chap next door. She made his children as sick as pigs.

[EVA *enters. As she does so the doorbell rings. She closes the door behind her*]

EVA: I couldn't be sure but it looks suspiciously like the Hopcrofts. Do you want them in?

RONALD: Oh, good grief, hardly.

GEOFFREY: Heaven forbid.

RONALD: If we sit quiet, they'll go away.

EVA: Well, there's the hall light.

RONALD: That doesn't mean anything. People always leave their hall lights on for burglars. I don't know why they bother. I mean, there must be very few households who actually choose to spend their evenings sitting in the hall with the rest of the house in darkness.

GEOFFREY: If I know the Hopcrofts, they won't give up easily. They'll come round the side.

MARION: Why don't you just go in the hall and shout "Go away" through the letter-box?

RONALD: Because he happens to have a very large deposit account with my bank.

[*The doorbell rings*]

EVA: They can smell us.

RONALD: I think we'll compromise and turn off the lights in here. Just to be on the safe side. [*Going to the door*] Everybody sit down and sit tight. [*By the switch*] Ready? Here we go.

[*The room plunges into darkness. Just two streams of light – one from the door and one from the window*]

Now if we all keep absolutely quiet, there's no chance of them – ow! [*He cannons into* EVA *who gives a cry*] I'm terribly sorry. I do beg your pardon. Was that your . . . ?

EVA: That's all right.

GEOFFREY: Ssh.

RONALD: I wish I knew where I was.

GEOFFREY: Well, stand still. I think someone's coming round the side.

EVA: Ssh.

[MARION *starts to giggle*]

RONALD: Marion. Quiet.

MARION: I'm sorry I've just seen the funny side . . .

GEOFFREY: Ssh.

[SIDNEY *and* JANE *appear at the back door. They wear party hats, are decked with the odd streamer, have had more drinks than they are used to and have a carrier bag full of goodies. They both press their faces against the back door, straining to see in*]

MARION: It's them.

GEOFFREY: Ssh.

[*Pause*]

RONALD: I say . . .

EVA: What?

RONALD: I've got a nasty feeling I didn't lock the back door.

MARION: Oh, no . . .

[GEOFFREY *and* EVA *hide in front of the table.* RONALD *steps up into a corner by the window. The back door opens slowly*]

SIDNEY: Hallo?

JANE: [*unwilling to enter*] Sidney . . .

SIDNEY: Come on.

JANE: But there's nobody . . .

SIDNEY: The door was open, wasn't it? Of course there's somebody. They're probably upstairs.

JANE: But, Sidney, they might . . .

SIDNEY: Look, would you kindly not argue with me any more tonight, Jane. I haven't yet forgiven you for that business at the party. How did you manage to drop a whole plate of trifle?

JANE: I didn't clean it up, Sidney, I didn't clean it up.

SIDNEY: No. You just stood there with the mess at your feet. For all the world to see.

JANE: Well, what . . .

SIDNEY: I have told you before. If you drop something like that at a stand-up party, you move away and keep moving. Now come along.

JANE: I can't see.

SIDNEY: Then wait there and I'll find the light.

[*A pause.* SIDNEY *crosses the room.* GEOFFREY *and* EVA *creep to the sideboard. The light goes on* SIDNEY *and* JANE *are by the separate doors. The other four are in various absurd frozen postures obviously caught in the act of trying to find a hiding-place.* JANE *gives a short squeak of alarm. A long pause*]

MARION: [*eventually*] Boo.

SIDNEY: Good gracious.

RONALD: [*as if seeing them for the first time*] Ah, hallo there.

It's you.

SIDNEY: Well, you had us fooled. They had us fooled there, didn't they?

JANE: Yes, they had us fooled.

SIDNEY: Playing a game on us, weren't you?

ALL: Yes.

EVA: Yes, we were playing a game.

SIDNEY: Completely fooled. Walked straight into that. Well, Happy Christmas, all.

ALL: [*lamely, variously*] Happy Christmas.

SIDNEY: [*after a pause*] Well.

JANE: Well.

   [*A pause*]

RONALD: Would you like a drink? Now you're here.

SIDNEY: Oh, thank you.

JANE: Thank you very much.

SIDNEY: Since we're here.

RONALD: Well. What'll it be? [*He goes to the trolley*]

SIDNEY: Sherry, please.

JANE: Yes, a sherry.

SIDNEY: Yes. We'd better stick to sherry.

RONALD: Sherry . . . [*He starts to pour*]

SIDNEY: Sorry if we surprised you.

MARION: Quite all right.

SIDNEY: We knew you were here.

RONALD: How?

SIDNEY: We saw the car.

JANE: Saw your car.

RONALD: Oh. Yes.

   [*A pause.* SIDNEY *blows a party "blower"*]

EVA: Been to a party?

SIDNEY: Yes.

JANE: Yes.

GEOFFREY: You look as if you have.

SIDNEY: Yes. Up at Walter's place. Walter Harrison.

RONALD: Oh – old Harrison's.

SIDNEY: Oh of course, you'll know him, won't you.

RONALD: Oh, yes.

GEOFFREY: Yes.

SIDNEY: [*to* GEOFFREY] Oh, yes, of course. Asking you if

you know old Harrison. I should think you do know old
Harrison. He certainly remembers you. In fact he was saying
this evening . . .

RONALD: Two sherries.

SIDNEY: Oh, thank you.

JANE: Thank you very much.

SIDNEY: Compliments of the season.

JANE: Of the season.

RONALD: Yes. Indeed.

[*A pause*]

SIDNEY: What a house. Beautiful.

MARION: Oh, do you like it? Thank you.

SIDNEY: No. Old Harrison's. What a place.

JANE: Lovely.

RONALD: Didn't know you knew him.

SIDNEY: Well, I won't pretend. The reason we went was half
pleasure and half − well, 'nuff said. Follow me? You scratch
my back, I'll scratch yours.

RONALD: Ah.

[*A pause*]

JANE: It's a nice kitchen . . .

MARION: At the Harrisons'?

JANE: No. Here.

MARION: Oh. Glad you approve.

[*A pause*]

JANE: [*very, very quietly*] Sidney.

SIDNEY: Eh?

JANE: [*mouthing and gesticulating towards the carrier bag*]
Their presents.

SIDNEY: What's that? [*He looks at his flies*]

JANE: [*still mouthing and miming*] Shall we give them their
presents now?

SIDNEY: Yes, yes, of course. That's why we've brought them.

JANE: We brought you a present.

SIDNEY: Just a little seasonal something.

RONALD: Oh.

MARION: Ah.

EVA: Thank you.

JANE: [*to* EVA] No, I'm afraid we didn't bring you and your
husband anything. We didn't know you'd be here, you see.

SIDNEY: Sorry about that.

EVA: Oh, never mind.

GEOFFREY: Not to worry.

JANE: We could give them the hm-mm. You know, that we got given this evening.

SIDNEY: The what?

JANE: You know, the hm-mm. That we got in the thing.

SIDNEY: What, that? They don't want that.

JANE: No, I meant for hm-mm, you know. Hm-mm.

SIDNEY: Well, if you want to. Now, come on. Give Ron and Marion their presents. They're dying to open them.

RONALD: Rather.

MARION: Thrilling.

JANE: [*delving into her carrier and consulting the labels on various parcels*] Now this is for Ron. [*Reading*] To Ron with love from Sidney and Jane.

SIDNEY: [*handing Ronald the present*] That's for you.

RONALD: Thank you. [*He unwraps it*]

JANE: Now then, what's this?

SIDNEY: Is that Marion's?

JANE: No, that's from you and me to Auntie Gloria. [*Rummaging again*] Here we are. To Marion with love from Sidney and Jane.

SIDNEY: This is for you. [*He gives* MARION *her present*]

MARION: Oh, super ... [*To Ronald*] What've you got, darling?

RONALD: [*gazing at his present mystified*] Oh, yes. This is very useful. Thank you very much.

MARION: What on earth is it?

RONALD: Well, it's—er—[*taking a stab at it*] —looks like a very nice set of pipe cleaners.

JANE: Oh, no.

SIDNEY: No, those aren't pipe cleaners.

RONALD: Oh, aren't they?

SIDNEY: Good gracious, no.

RONALD: Oh, no. Silly of me. Just looked terribly like them for a minute. From a certain angle.

SIDNEY: You should know those. It's a set of screwdrivers.

JANE: Set of screwdrivers.

SIDNEY: Electrical screwdrivers.

JANE: You should know those, shouldn't you?

[SIDNEY *and* JANE *laugh.* MARION *opens her present*]

MARION: [*with a joyous cry*] Oh, look! It's a lovely bottle of
  gin. Isn't that kind?

RONALD: Oh, my God.

SIDNEY: Bit of Christmas spirit.

MARION: Lovely. I'll think of you when I'm drinking it.

JANE: [*still rummaging*] To the boys with love from Sidney and
  Jane. [*She produces two rather ghastly woolly toys – obviously
  unsuitable*]

SIDNEY: That's just a little something.

JANE: Just for their stockings in the morning.

MARION: Oh, how nice.

RONALD: They'll love these . . .

SIDNEY: That the lot?

JANE: No, I'm just trying to find the hm-mm.

SIDNEY: Well, it'll be at the bottom somewhere, I should think.

JANE: I've got it. It's nothing very much. We just got it this evening out of a cracker actually. We were going to keep it for our
  budgie but we thought your George might like it. For his collar.
  [*She holds up a little bell on a ribbon*]

EVA: Oh.

SIDNEY: So you'll know where he is.

JANE: As if you couldn't guess.
  [SIDNEY *barks genially and hands them the bell*]

SIDNEY: Woof woof!

EVA: Thank you.

SIDNEY: [*to* GEOFFREY] Woof woof. [*No response*] Woof
  woof.

GEOFFREY: [*flatly*] Thanks a lot.

SIDNEY: That's your lot. No more.

RONALD: I'm terribly sorry. I'm afraid we haven't got you anything at all. Not really much of ones for present buying.

SIDNEY: Oh, we didn't expect it.

JANE: No, no.
  [*A pause.* SIDNEY *puts on a nose mask.* JANE *laughs. The
  others look horrified.* MARION *pours herself a gin*]

SIDNEY: Well – [*he pauses*] – you know who ought to be here?
  now?

JANE: Who?

SIDNEY: Dick Potter. He'd start it off.

JANE: With a bit of help from Lottie.

SIDNEY: True. True.

RONALD: Yes, well, for some odd reason we're all feeling a bit low this evening. Don't know why. But we were just all saying how we felt a bit down.

JANE: Oh . . .

SIDNEY: Oh dear oh dear.

RONALD: Just one of those evenings, you know. The point is you'll have to excuse us if we're not our usual cheery selves.

MARION: I'm perfectly cheery. I don't know about anybody else.

RONALD: That is apart from my wife who is perfectly cheery.

SIDNEY: Oh, that's quite understood.

JANE: I have those sometimes, don't I?

SIDNEY: You certainly do. You can say that again. Well, that's a shame.

RONALD: Yes.

EVA: [after a slight pause] My husband was saying to me just now, Sidney, that he feels terribly guilty that you keep on asking him to do jobs for you and he just hasn't been able to manage them.

SIDNEY: Yes. Well, he's a busy man.

EVA: Sometimes. But he really is dying to do something for you before long.

GEOFFREY: Eh?

EVA: He's really longing to.

SIDNEY: Oh, well in that case, we'll see.

EVA: If you could keep him in mind.

SIDNEY: Yes, I'll certainly keep him in mind. Really rather depends.

GEOFFREY: Yes, it does rather.

EVA: He'd love to.

SIDNEY: [after a pause] Well now, what shall we do? Anyone got any ideas? We can't all sit round like this, can we? Not on Christmas Eve.

JANE: No, not on Christmas Eve.

SIDNEY: Spot of carpentry, spot of plumbing, eh? I know, what about a spot of electrical work? [At the radio] Well, we can have a bit of music to start off with, anyway. [To RONALD] This work all right, does it?

RONALD: Yes, yes, but I wouldn't . . .

SIDNEY: Get the party going, bit of music . . . [*He switches on the radio and begins to dance a little*]

JANE: Bit of music'll get it going.

SIDNEY: Hey . . .

JANE: What?

SIDNEY: You know what we ought to do now?

JANE: What?

SIDNEY: We ought to move all the chairs back and clear the floor and . . .

[*The radio warms up and the room is filled with the sound of an interminable Scottish reel which plays continually. Like most Scottish reels, without a break. This effectively drowns the rest of* SIDNEY *and* JANE's *discussion. He continues to describe with graphic gestures his idea to* JANE. JANE *claps her hands with excitement. They move the table, stove and chairs out of the way.* SIDNEY *then wheels the trolley away past* MARION's *armchair. She grabs a bottle as it goes by*]

RONALD: [*yelling above the noise*] What the hell's going on?

SIDNEY: [*yelling back*] You'll see. Just a minute. [*He turns the radio down a little*] Now then. We can't have this. We can't have all these glum faces, not at Christmas time.

JANE: [*scurrying about collecting a bowl of fruit, a spoon, a tea-cosy, colander and tea towel from the dresser and draining-board*] Not at Christmas time. [*She opens the gin bottle and puts a glass near it on the trolley*]

SIDNEY: So we're going to get you all jumping about. Get you cheerful.

RONALD: No, well, I don't think we really . . .

SIDNEY: No arguments please.

RONALD: Yes, but all the same . . .

SIDNEY: Come on then, Eva, up you get.

EVA: [*uncertainly*] Well . . .

SIDNEY: Come on. Don't you let me down.

EVA: No . . . [*She rises*]

GEOFFREY: I'm afraid we both have to . . .

EVA: No, we don't. We'll play.

GEOFFREY: What do you mean, we'll . . .

EVA: If he wants to play, we'll play, darling.

[JANE *begins to roll up the carpet*]

SIDNEY: That's grand. That's marvellous. That's two — come on —

any more?

MARION: What are we all doing? Is she going to be terribly sweet and wash our floor?

JANE: No, we're playing a game.

SIDNEY: A game.

MARION: Oh, what fun . . .

RONALD: Marion, I really don't think we should . . .

MARION: Oh, don't be such a misery, Ronnie. Come on.

RONALD: Oh . . .

SIDNEY: That's telling him, that's telling him. Now then, listen very carefully, everyone. This is a version of musical chairs called Musical Dancing.

JANE: Musical Forfeits.

SIDNEY: Musical Dancing. It's called Musical Dancing.

JANE: Oh, I thought it was called Musical Forfeits.

SIDNEY: Musical Dancing. It's very simple. All you do – you start dancing round the room and when I stop the music you all have to freeze in the position you were last in . . .

[GEOFFREY *sits on the high stool*]

Don't let him sit down. [*To* GEOFFREY] Come on, get up.

EVA: [*sharply*] Get up.

[GEOFFREY *gets up*]

SIDNEY: Only to make it more difficult, the last person caught moving each time gets a forfeit. At the end, the person with the least forfeits gets the prize. [*To* JANE] What's the prize going to be?

JANE: [*producing it from the carrier*] A chocolate Father Christmas.

SIDNEY: A chocolate Father Christmas, right. Everything ready your end?

JANE: I think so.

SIDNEY: Got the list?

JANE: [*waving a scrap of paper*] Yes.

SIDNEY: Right. You take charge of the forfeits. I'll do the music. Ready, everybody? Right. Off we go.

[SIDNEY *turns up the music loud. The four stand looking faintly uneasy.* JANE *and* SIDNEY *dance about to demonstrate*]

Well, come on then. Come on. I don't call that dancing. Everybody dance. Come on, dance about. Keep dancing till the music stops.

[MARION *starts to dance, in what she imagines to be a classical ballet style. She is extremely shaky*]

That's it. She's doing it. That's it. Look at her. Everybody do what she's doing. Lovely.

[*The others begin sheepishly and reluctantly to hop about*]

And – stop! [*He cuts off the music*] Right. Who was the last?

JANE: Ron.

SIDNEY: Right. It's Ron. Ron has a forfeit. What's the first one?

JANE: [*consulting her list*] Apple under the chin.

SIDNEY: Apple under his chin, right. Put an apple under his chin.

RONALD: Eh? What are you doing?

[JANE *puts the apple under his chin*]

JANE: Here. Hold it. Go on, hold it.

RONALD: Oh, don't be so ridiculous, I can't possibly . . .

MARION: Oh, for heaven's sake, darling, do join in. We're all waiting for you. Don't be tedious.

RONALD: [*talking with difficulty*] This is absolutely absurd. I mean how am I to be . . .

SIDNEY: [*over this*] And off we go again. [*He turns up the music*]

[*They resume dancing.* MARION *is the only one who moves around: the others jig about on one spot.* SIDNEY *shouts encouragement*]

And – stop! [*He stops the music*]

JANE: Eva!

SIDNEY: Right, Eva. What's Eva got?

JANE: [*consulting list*] Orange between the knees.

SIDNEY: Orange between the knees, right. If you drop it you get another forfeit automatically.

[JANE *gives* EVA *her orange*]

And off we go again.

[*Music. From now on the forfeits come quick and fast.* JANE *reading them out,* SIDNEY *repeating them.* RONALD *gets the next* [spoon in mouth]. *The music continues.* GEOFFREY *gets the next* [tea-cosy on head]. *They dance on.* MARION *gets the next* [ironically, swallowing a gin in one]. RONALD *opens his mouth to protest at this last forfeit of* MARION's. *In doing so he drops his spoon*]

[*Gleefully*] Another one for Ron!

JANE: Another one for Ron . . .

RONALD: What?

JANE: Pear on spoon in mouth . . .

SIDNEY: Pear on spoon in mouth . . . [*He gets up on the table and conducts*]

RONALD: Now listen I . . .

[*JANE rams the spoon handle back in RONALD's mouth. She balances a pear on the other end*]

SIDNEY: And off we go . . . !

[*The permutations to this game are endless and SIDNEY's list covers them all. Under his increasingly strident commands, the dancers whirl faster and faster whilst accumulating bizarre appendages. JANE, the acolyte, darts in and out of the dancers with a dedicated frenzy. GEOFFREY throws his tea-cosy to the floor. JANE picks it up and wraps a tea towel round his leg. She then pours another gin for MARION. SIDNEY, at the finish, has abandoned the idea of stopping the music. He screams at the dancers in mounting exhortation bordering on the hysterical*]

That's it. Dance. Come on. Dance. Dance. Come on. Dance. Dance. Dance. Keep dancing. Dance . . .

*It is on this scene that –*

*the* CURTAIN *falls*

# ABSENT FRIENDS

First produced at the Library Theatre, Scarborough, on June 17th 1974 and subsequently at the Garrick Theatre, London, on July 23rd 1975 with the following cast of characters:

| | |
|---|---|
| Paul | Peter Bowles |
| Diana | Pat Heywood |
| John | Ray Brooks |
| Evelyn | Cheryl Kennedy |
| Colin | Richard Briers |
| Marge | Phyllida Law |

The play directed by Eric Thompson
Designed by Derek Cousins

# ACT ONE

*3 p.m. Saturday.*
*The open plan living room of a modern executive-style house.*
*Archways leading off to the kitchen and back doors. Another to*
*the front door and bedrooms etc. Primarily furnished with*
*English Swedish style furniture. A lot of wrought iron for gates*
*in lieu of doors and as used for room dividers. Also artistic frost-*
*ed glass. Doubtful pictures. Possibly a bar. It all cost a great deal*
*of money. Parquet floor with rugs.*
*At the start,* EVELYN, *a heavily made-up, reasonably trendily*
*dressed, expressionless girl, is sitting by a pram which she is rock-*
*ing absently with one hand whilst gazing blankly out of the*
*window. Near her, on the table, underneath suitable coverings, tea*
*is laid out in the form of sandwiches and cakes. Only the teapot*
*and hot water jug are missing.* EVELYN *chews and sings to*
*herself.*
*After a moment,* DIANA *enters. She is older, mid to later thir-*
*ties. She always gives the impression of being slightly fraught. She*
*smiles occasionally but it's painful. Her sharp darting eyes don't*
*miss much after years of suspicions both genuine and unfounded.*

DIANA: Have you got him to sleep?
EVELYN: Yes.
DIANA: [*looking into the pram*] Aaah! They look so lovely like
    that. Like little cherubims.
EVELYN: [*unenthusiastic*] Mmm.
DIANA: Just like little cherubims. [*Anxious*] Should he be
    covered up as much as that, dear?
EVELYN: Yes.
DIANA: Won't he get too hot?
EVELYN: He likes it hot.
DIANA: Oh. I was just worried he wasn't getting enough air.
EVELYN: He's all right. He doesn't need much air.
DIANA: Oh, well. . . [*She looks about her*] Well, I think we're
    all ready for them. John's on his way, you say?
EVELYN: Yes.
DIANA: How is he these days? I haven't seen John for ages.

EVELYN: He's all right.

DIANA: I haven't seen either of you.

EVELYN: We're all right.

DIANA: Not for ages. Well, I'm glad you could come this afternoon. Colin really will appreciate that, I'm sure. Seeing us all. [*Pause.*]

Paul should be home soon. I think he's playing his squash again.

EVELYN: Oh.

DIANA: Him and his squash. It used to be tennis — now he's squash mad. Squash, squash, squash. Can't see what he sees in it. All afternoon hitting a ball against a wall. It's so noisy. Bang, bang, bang. He's not even out of doors. No fresh air at all. It can't be good for him. Does John play squash?

EVELYN: No.

DIANA: Oh.

EVELYN: He doesn't play anything.

DIANA: Oh, well. He probably doesn't need it. Exercise. Some men don't. My father never took a stroke of exercise. Till he died. He seemed fit enough. He managed to do what he wanted to do. Mind you, he never did very much. He just used to sit and shout at we girls. Most of the time. He got calmer though when he got older. After my mother left him. [*Looking into the pram*] Did you knit that little jacket for him?

EVELYN: No.

DIANA: Pretty. [*Pause*] No, there are times when I think that's the principal trouble between Paul and me. I mean, I know now I'm running myself down but Paul basically, he's got much more go — well, I mean let's face it, he's much cleverer than me. Let's face it. Basically. I mean, I was the bright one in our family but I can't keep up with Paul sometimes. When he has one of his moods, I think to myself, now if I was really clever, I could probably talk him round or something but I mean the thing is, really and truly, and I know I'm running myself down when I say this, I don't think I'm really enough for him. He needs me, I can tell that; he doesn't say as much but I know he does. It's just, as I say, I don't think I'm really enough for him. [*She reflects*] But he couldn't do without me. Make no mistake about that. He's got this amazing energy. I don't know where he finds it. He goes to bed long after me, he's up at dawn, working down here — then off he goes all day. . . . I need my eight hours, it's no good. What I'm saying is really, I wouldn't blame him. Not altogether. If he did. With someone else. You know, another woman. I wouldn't blame him, I wouldn't blame her. Not as long as I was told. Providing I know, that I'm told — all right. Providing I feel able to say to people — "Yes, I am well aware that my husband is having an affair with such and such or whoever. . . it's quite all right. I know all about it. We're both grown-up people, we know what we're doing, he knows I know, she knows I know. So mind your own business." I'd feel all right about it. But I will not stand deception. I'm simply asking that I be told. Either by him or if not by her. Not necessarily now but sometime. You see.

[*A pause.* EVELYN *is expressionless* ]

I know he is, you see. He's not very clever and he's a very bad liar like most men. If he takes the trouble, like last Saturday, to tell me he's just going down the road to the football match, he might at least choose a day when they're playing at home. [*She lifts the tablecloth and inspects the sandwiches* ] I hope I've made enough tomato. No, I must be told. Otherwise it makes my life impossible. I can't talk to anybody without them. . . . I expect them, both of them, at least to have some feeling for me. [*She blows her nose* ] Well.

[*The doorbell rings* ]

Excuse me. . .

[DIANA *goes out*]

[*Offstage dialogue*]

MARGE: Only me.

DIANA: Marge!

MARGE: I've been shopping, don't laugh.

DIANA: Leave your coat?

MARGE: Oh yes!

[*Sound of shopping bags dropping and laughter* ]

DIANA: How's Gordon?

MARGE: Not too bad. . . [*Bustling in laden with bags*] . . . poor little thing — lying there — with his face as white as a sheet. . .

DIANA: [*returning*] Poor thing. . .

MARGE: He looks dreadful. . . . Hallo, Evelyn.

EVELYN: Hallo.

MARGE: Oh! Look who's here! Little baby Walter.

EVELYN: Wayne.

MARGE: What?

EVELYN: It's Wayne. His name's Wayne.

DIANA: [*laughing*] Walter. . . .

MARGE: I thought it was Walter.

DIANA: Marge, honestly. You can't have a baby called Walter.

MARGE: Well, I don't know. Somebody must have done. . . . [*She screams with laughter. Peering into the pram*] Oh look. Look at his skin. It's a lovely skin, Evelyn.

EVELYN: Thank you.

MARGE: Beautiful skin. Hallo, Baby Wayne. Hallo, Wayne. Google – google – google.

DIANA: Ssh, Marge, she's just got him to sleep.

MARGE: [*quieter*] Diggy diggy diggy. [*Whispering*] Lovely when they're asleep.

DIANA: Yes. . .

MARGE: [*whispering*] Looks like his Daddy. Looks like John.

DIANA: You don't have to whisper, Marge. Just don't shout in his ear.

MARGE: [*back to her carriers etc.*] Look at all this lot. I can't go anywhere.

DIANA: What have you got there?

MARGE: You know what I'm like. You know me. . .oh, guess what I did get?

DIANA: What?

MARGE: Are you ready?

DIANA: Yes.

MARGE: Brace yourself. I got the shoes.

DIANA: You bought them?

MARGE: Just now and I don't care. I passed the shop on the way here. I thought it's no good, I don't care, it's now or never, I'm going to have them, I must have them. So I got them.

DIANA: I must see.

MARGE: Just a minute. Gordon'll go mad. . . [*Rummaging*] Now, which one did I put them in?

DIANA: It is a shame about Gordon. Gordon's ill, Evelyn, he can't come.

EVELYN: Oh.

MARGE: No. He finally got it. It's been going round and round for months, I knew he'd get it eventually. He was perfectly all right last night, then he woke up this morning and he'd got it. . . . [*Finding her shoe bag within another bag*] Here we are. . . [*Finding something else*] Oh — nearly forgot. That's for you.

DIANA: For me?

MARGE: It's only a little thing. But I saw one while I was in there and I knew you'd seen mine and wanted one. . .

DIANA: Oh, yes. . .

MARGE: [*to* EVELYN] It's a holder. For those paper towels in the kitchen. Paper towel holder. Have you got one?

EVELYN: No.

MARGE: Remind me, I'll get you one.

DIANA: That's so thoughtful. I must pay you for it.

MARGE: You'll do no such thing.

DIANA: No, Marge, I insist. You're always buying us things.

MARGE: I enjoy it. I like buying presents.

DIANA: [*producing her purse*] How much?

MARGE: I won't take it, put it away.

DIANA: How much was it?

MARGE: Diana, will you put that purse away this minute.

DIANA: No, I'm sorry, Marge, I'm going to pay you.

MARGE: Diana, will you put that away this minute. Evelyn, tell her to put it away. . .

[EVELYN, *during this, has moved to the door and is on the point of going out* ]

DIANA: [*noticing her*] You all right, dear?

EVELYN: Fine.

DIANA: Where are you off to then?

EVELYN: To the lavatory.

DIANA: Oh. I see. Beg your pardon.

[EVELYN *goes out* ]

[*selecting coins from her purse*] Twenty p. There you are. I don't know how much it was but there you are.

MARGE: Oh, really. [*She leaves the money on the table*]

DIANA: Am I glad to see you.

MARGE: Why's that?

DIANA: She's been here for ages.

MARGE: Who do you mean — oh, yes. Miss Chatterbox.

DIANA: I know she's been up to something. I don't trust

her. I never did.

MARGE: I must show you my shoes. [*Starts to unpack them*] How do you mean?

DIANA: I know that girl's been up to something.

MARGE: Oh, you mean with. . .?

DIANA: She and Paul. I know they have.

MARGE: Well. . . [*Producing a pair of very unsuitable shoes*] There, you see. Aren't they nice?

DIANA: Lovely.

MARGE: They had them in blue which was nicer, actually. But then I had nothing else that would have gone with them.

DIANA: He didn't want them to come round here today. That's how I know they're up to something.

MARGE: Who?

DIANA: Evelyn and John. He didn't want them round.

MARGE: Who? Paul didn't?

DIANA: No.

MARGE: [*parading around in her shoes*] Look, you see. . .these tights aren't right with them but. . .

DIANA: I mean, why should he suddenly not want them round? They've been round here enough in the past and then all of a sudden he doesn't want to see them.

MARGE: Odd. There was another sort, you know, with the strap but I found they cut me across here.

DIANA: They suit you.

MARGE: Yes, I'm very pleased.

DIANA: I tried to get her to say something.

MARGE: Evelyn?

DIANA: Just now.

MARGE: Oh. Did she?

DIANA: No. She's not saying anything. Why should she? I know Paul, you see. I know he's with someone. I'm sure it's her. He came home, went straight upstairs and washed his shirt through the other night. I said, what's got into you? He said, well, what's wrong with me washing my shirt? I said, you've never washed anything in your life. He said, well, we all have to start some time. I said, lovely, but why do you want to start doing it in the middle of the night. And he had no answer to that at all. Nothing. He just stood there with it dripping all over the floor.

MARGE: Well. . .

DIANA: After twelve years, you get to know someone.

MARGE: I wonder if these will go with that other coat.

DIANA: What's she doing up there?

MARGE: Well, she's. . .

DIANA: I bet she's having a really good snoop around.

MARGE: Oh, Di. . .

DIANA: I bet that's what she's up to. I've never trusted her an inch. She's got one of those really mean little faces, hasn't she?

MARGE: Well. . .

DIANA: I bet it was her that went off with my scarf, you know.

MARGE: I shouldn't think so. Why don't you talk it over with Paul?

DIANA: Paul? We haven't talked for years. Not really. Now he's had his own way and sent the children off to school, there's even less to talk about. I don't know why he wanted them at boarding school. They're neither of them happy. I know they're not. You should see the letters they write.

MARGE: I don't know what to say. . . [*to pram*] Poogy, poogy. Hallo, Walter.

DIANA: Wayne.

MARGE: Hallo.

DIANA: Don't for God's sake wake him up. He's been bawling his head off half the afternoon. I don't think she feeds him properly.

MARGE: He looks nice and chubby.

DIANA: It doesn't look all there to me.

MARGE: Di!

DIANA: No, truthfully, you look at its eyes.

MARGE: He's asleep.

DIANA: Well, you look at them when it wakes up. Don't tell me that's normal. I mean, our Mark's were never like that. Nor were Julie's. And she's had to wear glasses.

MARGE: She looks lovely in her little glasses.

DIANA: Paul doesn't think so. He won't let her wear them when she's at home.

MARGE: Well, I think he's a lovely baby. I was on at Gordon again the other day about adopting one.

DIANA: What did he say?

MARGE: Still no. He won't hear of it. He's frightened of it, I think. He keeps saying to me, it's not like a dog, Marge. We can't get rid of it if we don't like it and I say, we will like it, we'll grow to like it and then he says, well what happens if we adopt one and then it grows up to be a murderer? Then what do we do? They'll blame us.

DIANA: It's not very likely.

MARGE: Try convincing him. No, he's just going to keep on going with his tests. . . till the cows come home. That reminds me, I must ring him up. I said I would as soon as I got here. See if he's coping. Do you mind?

DIANA: No, go ahead.

MARGE: He's got the phone by his bed.

[MARGE *starts to dial*]

[EVELYN *returns*]

DIANA: Find everything?

EVELYN: Fine. [*She checks the baby with a glance then sits and starts to read a magazine*]

DIANA: Marge is just phoning her husband.

EVELYN: Oh.

MARGE: [*as she stands waiting for an answer, indicating her shoes*] Do you like these, Evelyn?

EVELYN: Fantastic.

MARGE: [*into phone*] Hallo. . . Jumjums? It's Margie, darling. How are you feeling. . . oh. . . oh. Well listen, Jumjums, can you manage to get across to the chest of drawers, sweetie? . . . by the window, yes. . . you'll find them in the top drawer. . . that's right, darling. . . can you manage that all right on your own. . . right [*Pause. To them*] He wants the nose drops, he's all bunged up, poor love. . . [*She stands listening*]

DIANA: [*to EVELYN*] What are you chewing, dear?

EVELYN: Gum.

DIANA: Oh.

EVELYN: Want a bit?

DIANA: No thanks. We'll be having our tea soon.

MARGE: [*into phone*] Oh, darling. . . you must be careful, Jumjums. . . yes, I know it shouldn't be there. . . never mind, well rub it, rub it better. [*Covering the phone, to the others*] Banged his leg. . . [*into phone*] All right? I'll be here if you want me. You know the number. I'll be home soon. . . yes. . . yes, I will. I'll phone you later. Bye bye, Jumjums, bye bye,

darling. Bye. [*Pause*] Bye bye. [*Pause*] Bye. [*Rings off*]
Honestly, I don't know what I want children for, living with
Gordon. I get through first aid tins like loaves of bread.

DIANA: He's very unlucky, isn't he?

MARGE: Oh, he is. He's so big, you see. I think that's one of
his troubles. Being so big. Nothing's really made his size.
He bangs his head on buses. He can't sit down in the cinema
and he has trouble getting into his trousers. It's a terrible
problem. Sixteen stone eight.

DIANA: Yes, that is big.

MARGE: It is, it's very big. His face is small but then he's got
quite a small head. It's the rest of him. Somebody the other
day said he looked like a polythene bag full of water. [*She
laughs*]

[*DIANA laughs*]

Oh, dear, you have to laugh.

DIANA: Poor Gordon. It's not fair.

MARGE: He's all right. Bless him. Keeps me out of mischief.
[*They laugh*]

[*A silence. They look at* EVELYN *who chews on, reading* ]

DIANA: [*with a look at* MARGE] Enjoying that, are you?

EVELYN: It's all right. . .

MARGE: Oh. I've still got these on. [*She starts to change her
shoes*]

DIANA: Be funny seeing Colin again. Three years.

MARGE: I only knew him slightly. He was Gordon's friend
really.

DIANA: Yes. It's a pity he'll miss Colin.

MARGE: What exactly happened to this fiancée of his? Did she
just die?

DIANA: Drowned.

MARGE: Drowned, oh. . .

DIANA: In the sea.

MARGE: Oh.

[*Throughout the following* MARGE *follows* DIANA's *lips
carefully echoing the odd word in agreement* ]

DIANA: We knew him very well, you know. He and Paul were
inseparable. And then Colin's job moved him away and he
used to write to us occasionally and then he wrote and said
he'd met this Carol girl and that they were going to get married

— which was a great surprise to us because we always said he'd never let anything get that far and then the next thing we heard, she'd drowned. So I said to Paul, we'd better invite him over. I mean, we're still his friends. I doubt if he's got any where he is now because it takes him ages to get to know people and then I thought, well, it might be awkward, embarrassing knowing what to say to him, just Paul and me and since he knew Gordon and you slightly and John — he doesn't know Evelyn of course — I thought it would be nice if we just had a little tea party for him. He'll need his friends.

MARGE: Well, you know me, I'm bound to say the wrong thing so shut me up or I'll put my foot in it. Was she young?

DIANA: Who?

MARGE: His fiancée.

DIANA: Carol? About his age, I think.

MARGE: Oh. Tragic.

DIANA: Yes. [*Aware of* EVELYN *again*] What are you reading, dear?

EVELYN: Nothing.

DIANA: No, what is it?

EVELYN: [*wearily turning back a page and reading flatly*] Your happiness is keeping that man in your life happy. Twelve tips by a woman psychiatrist.

DIANA: Oh.

MARGE: We can all learn from that.

EVELYN: [*reading on remorselessly*] Tip number one: send him off in the morning with a smile. How many of us first thing just don't bother to make that little extra effort. Have you ever graced the breakfast table without a comb through your hair. Go on, admit it, of course you have. You're only human. Or not done that little extra something to take the shine off your early morning nose. No wonder he escapes behind his paper. . .

DIANA: I must read that.

EVELYN: [*unstoppable*] Go on, live a little and give him the surprise of his life.

DIANA: Yes, that's lovely, Evelyn. . .

EVELYN: Make yourself into his news of the day. You'll live with him till the evening. Tip number two: go on, pamper yourself with a full beauty treatment.

DIANA: Yes, thank you, Evelyn.

EVELYN: What?

DIANA: That's lovely. I'll read it later.

MARGE: We can all learn something from that.

EVELYN: I'm not doing that for my bloody husband. He can stuff it.

[*Pause*]

MARGE: I'd hate to drown. [*Pause*] I don't mind anything else. Poison, hanging, shooting – that's never worried me but I'd hate to drown. You look so awful afterwards.

DIANA: Now, we mustn't get morbid. We're here to cheer Colin up when he comes. I know this all happened two months ago now but he's bound to be a bit down. We mustn't let him dwell on it.

MARGE: No. You're quite right.

[*A silence. PAUL enters. He has on his track suit bottoms and a sweater. He has obviously been taking exercise* ]

PAUL: [*as he comes in*] Have you seen my shoes anywhere. . .? [*Breaking off as he sees that they have company*] Oh, hallo there.

MARGE: Hallo, Paul.

EVELYN: [*barely glancing up*] 'Llo.

PAUL: Mothers' Meeting is it? How are you, Marge?

MARGE: Very well, thank you.

PAUL: How about you, Evelyn?

EVELYN: Eh?

PAUL: Keeping fit?

EVELYN: Yes.

PAUL: [*looking into pram*] What's in here then? Tomorrow's dinner?

EVELYN: No.

PAUL: Oh. I thought it was tomorrow's dinner.

DIANA: Did you have a good game?

PAUL: All right. So so. Not really. Dick didn't turn up. Had to play with this other fellow. Useless. Finished up giving him eight start and playing left-handed. I still beat him. Then he fell over his racquet and broke his glasses so we called it a day. Trouble with that club is, you couldn't improve your game even if you wanted to. No competition. Lot of flabby old men.

EVELYN: [*without looking up*] Hark at Mr. Universe.

PAUL: Watch it. [*To* DIANE] You seen my black shoes?

DIANA: Which ones?

PAUL: The black ones.

DIANE: They're upstairs.

PAUL: Well, they weren't there this morning. How's Gordon?

MARGE: He's not too good today, I'm afraid.

PAUL: Not again.

DIANA: What do you mean, not again?

PAUL: He's always ill. Gordon.

MARGE: Not always.

PAUL: Hasn't been to work for two years, has he?

MARGE: Course he has.

DIANA: He's exaggerating.

PAUL: He's a one man casualty ward. Why don't you get him insured, Marge? You'd clean up in a couple of days.

MARGE: Get on. . .

PAUL: Right. I'll leave you ladies to it, if you don't mind. Ta ta. Look after yourselves. I've things to do upstairs.

DIANA: Don't be too long, will you, dear?

PAUL: How do you mean?

DIANA: I mean, don't stay up there for too long.

PAUL: No, I've just got a bit of work to do, that's all.

DIANA: Well, tea will be in a minute. You'll be down for that.

PAUL: No. You don't want me down here, I'll —

DIANA: You must come down for tea. Colin's coming.

PAUL: Colin who?

DIANA: Colin. You know, Col —

PAUL: Oh, that Colin. Is he?

DIANA: Oh, don't be stupid. You know he is. I told you.

PAUL: Did you?

DIANA: I arranged it a fortnight ago.

PAUL: You never told me.

DIANA: And I reminded you this morning.

PAUL: You didn't tell me.

DIANA: This morning, I told you.

PAUL: Excuse me, you did not tell me he was coming this morning. You did not tell me anything this morning. I was out before you were up.

DIANA: Well, then it must have been yesterday morning.

PAUL: That's more likely. But you still didn't tell me.

DIANA: I told you very distinctly.

MARGE: Perhaps you just forgot, Paul.

PAUL: No. I'm sorry I didn't forget. I never forget things. You're talking to the wrong man. I run a business where it's more than my life's worth to forget things. I've trained myself not to. I never forget.

MARGE: Well, I'm sorry I. . .

PAUL: Yes, all right. Just don't give me that "maybe you forgot bit" because with me it doesn't cut any ice at all . . .

DIANA: Look, Paul, will you stop taking it out on Marge for some reason. . .

PAUL: I'm not taking it out on anybody. Look, I've got a lot of work to do upstairs. . .

DIANA: Now, Paul, you can't do that. Colin is coming. He is your friend. You can't just go upstairs. . .

PAUL: Excuse me, he is not a friend of mine. He was never a friend of mine. . .

DIANA: How can you say that?

PAUL: I just happened to know him, that's all. You'll just have to say to him when he comes that you're sorry, I had no idea he was coming, nobody told me and that I had a lot of work to do upstairs.

DIANA: You cannot do that. . .

PAUL: I'm sorry. . .

DIANA: You've got no work to do.

PAUL: That's it. No more. I'm not going on with it. I'm going upstairs. I don't want to hear any more about it. I have a lot of work to do. Excuse me please.

[PAUL *goes out. A silence* ]

DIANA: I told him Colin was coming. I told him over breakfast. While he was eating his cereal. I told him. He always does this. Every time I – [*Tearful*] I spent ages getting this ready.

MARGE: It's all right, Di. . .

DIANA: It's not all right. He's always doing this. He does it all the time. I told him. Specially. . . [*She hurries out into the kitchen*]

MARGE: Oh dear.

[EVELYN *gives an amused grunt, ostensibly at her magazine* ]
[MARGE *looks at her* ]
Evelyn, could I have a word with you?

EVELYN: What?

MARGE: I want you to answer me something perfectly honestly. I want you to be absolutely straight with me. Will you do that, please?

EVELYN: What?

MARGE: It's been brought to my notice that you and Paul. . . have. . . well. . .

EVELYN: What?

MARGE: I think you know what I'm talking about.

EVELYN: No.

MARGE: That you and her husband have been. . . is this true? Yes or no?

EVELYN: Is what true?

MARGE: Will you put that magazine down a moment, please.

EVELYN: [laying the magazine aside wearily] Well?

MARGE: Is it true or isn't it? Yes or no?

EVELYN: What?

MARGE: Have you been. . . having. . . a love affair with Paul?

EVELYN: No.

MARGE: Truthfully?

EVELYN: I said no.

MARGE: Oh. Well. That's all right then.

[Pause]

EVELYN: We did it in the back of his car the other afternoon but I wouldn't call that a love affair.

MARGE: You and Paul did?

EVELYN: Yes.

MARGE: How disgusting.

EVELYN: It wasn't very nice.

MARGE: And you have the nerve to come and sit in her house. . .

EVELYN: She asked me. [Pause] She needn't worry. I'm not likely to do it again. He'd just been playing squash, he was horrible.

MARGE: Diana knows about this, you know.

EVELYN: Then he must have told her. I didn't.

MARGE: She's not a fool. She put two and two together. He didn't want you to come here at all this afternoon. That's a sure sign of a guilty conscience.

EVELYN: Most probably because he doesn't like me very much.

MARGE: He liked you enough to. . .

EVELYN: Not after what I said to him.

MARGE: What did you say?

EVELYN: I said thank you very much. That was as exciting as being made love to by a sack of clammy cement and would he kindly drive me home.

MARGE: That wasn't a very nice thing to say.

EVELYN: He's horrible.

MARGE: What a thing to say.

EVELYN: Horrible. Worse than my husband and that's saying a lot.

MARGE: Poor John. God help him being married to you.

EVELYN: Why?

MARGE: Well. Really.

EVELYN: They all think they're experts with women. None of them are usually. And by the time they are, most of them aren't up to it any more.

MARGE: You speak for yourself.

EVELYN: I am. I've tried enough of them to know. [*She reads*]

MARGE: Your husband will catch up with you one of these days.

EVELYN: He knows.

MARGE: He knows!

EVELYN: Nothing he can do.

MARGE: Does he know about you and Paul?

EVELYN: Probably. He's not going to complain.

MARGE: Why not?

EVELYN: Well — he relies on Paul for business, doesn't he? Without Paul, he's in trouble. Business before pleasure, that's John's motto.

MARGE: Sounds as if it's yours as well.

EVELYN: There's not much pleasure to be had round this place, is there?

MARGE: I'm sorry, I find your attitude quite disgusting. Heartless, cruel and disgusting.

[EVELYN *ignores her and continues her reading* ]

[*at the pram*] Poor little child. If only he knew. Poor little Walter. Googy, googy. . . You're just a heartless little tart. . . googy, googy.

EVELYN: If you're interested, those shoes of yours are a lousy buy.

MARGE: And what would you know about my shoes?

EVELYN: I bought a pair. They split at the sides after two days and the dye comes off on your feet.

MARGE: I've nothing further to say to you.

EVELYN: Anyway, they're out of fashion.

MARGE: I don't wish to listen to you any further.

[*Doorbell. They both wait* ]

One of us had better answer that, hadn't we?

EVELYN: Yes.

[*Doorbell* ]

MARGE: I suppose it had better be me.

[DIANA *enters* ]

DIANA: That was the doorbell, wasn't it?

MARGE: Oh, was it? Yes, we thought we heard it.

DIANA: What if it's Colin? I don't know what I'm going to say if it is. . .

[DIANA *goes out* ]

MARGE: You see what you've done.

EVELYN: Beg your pardon?

MARGE: To them. To Paul and her. See the atmosphere between them. All your doing.

EVELYN: Me?

MARGE: Who else?

EVELYN: You really want to know who else?

MARGE: I hope you realise that.

EVELYN: If you really want to know who else, you'd better pass me the phone book. He's halfway through the Yellow Pages by now. If it moves, he's on to it.

[JOHN *enters. A jiggling, restless figure* ]

JOHN: Hallo, hallo.

MARGE: Hallo, John.

EVELYN: You took your time.

JOHN: It's only twenty past.

EVELYN: You took your time.

JOHN: [*amiably*] Yes. [*He jigs about*]

MARGE: Where's Di gone to?

JOHN: Dunno. Upstairs, I think. [*Sticking his head into the pram*] Hallo, son. Say hallo to Daddy.

EVELYN: Don't.

JOHN: Eh?

EVELYN: He's asleep.

JOHN: He shouldn't be. He won't sleep tonight now.

EVELYN: He never does anyway.

JOHN: Keep him awake during the day, that's the secret. Shake his rattle in his ear every ten minutes.

EVELYN: Fantastic.

JOHN: Where's Paul?

MARGE: Upstairs.

JOHN: Oh. Both gone to bed, have they? [*He laughs*]

   [MARGE *glares at* EVELYN]

   No Colin yet?

MARGE: Not yet.

JOHN: Well, I hope he hurries it up. Then we can get it over with.

EVELYN: I thought he was supposed to be a friend of yours.

JOHN: He was, yes.

EVELYN: Sounds like it.

JOHN: I haven't seen him for years. Anyway – I don't know what to say to him. I didn't know this girl of his. I mean, it's difficult.

MARGE: I don't think he'll want to talk about Carol.

JOHN: No?

MARGE: I shouldn't think so. He'll want to forget.

JOHN: I hope so. I hate death. Gives me the creeps.

EVELYN: Get on.

JOHN: It does.

EVELYN: You?

JOHN: I get all. . . uggghhh. [*He shudders*] Don't talk about it.

EVELYN: [*laughs*] Death, death, death.

JOHN: Shut up.

   [EVELYN *laughs* ]

   [*Silence.* MARGE *takes out her knitting* ]

MARGE: I hope they come down before he arrives.

JOHN: Disgraceful. On a Saturday afternoon. Whatever next. [*Pause. He jigs about some more*] I got that fuel gauge.

EVELYN: Oh.

JOHN: 90p off it. [*He laughs*] It had a loose wire. I told the girl it was faulty. She didn't know any better. 90p. [*Pause*] Got a wing mirror for 30p. Had a screw missing off it. Got one of those round the corner and he let me have some interior carpet for nothing. He was throwing it away. Not a bad day's work, eh?

EVELYN: Great.

JOHN: You're the one who wanted carpet in the car.

EVELYN: Fine.

JOHN: Can't do anything right, can I?

EVELYN: I just know you. It won't fit when you get it in.

JOHN: It'll fit.

EVELYN: No, it won't because you got it cheap.

JOHN: It'll fit.

EVELYN: Nothing you ever get for us is quite right. I've got a vacuum cleaner with elastic bands holding on the attachments because you got them cheap off another model.

JOHN: Oh, come on.

EVELYN: I've got an electric mixer I can't use because it flings the food halfway up the bloody wall.

JOHN: It's only because it's got the wrong bowl that's all. Only the bowl's wrong.

EVELYN: Then why haven't we got the right bowl?

JOHN: I'm trying to get hold of one. They're scarce.

EVELYN: But it never did have the right bowl.

JOHN: I know it didn't. How do you think I got it cheap in the first place?

EVELYN: Oh, I give up. [*She reads*]

JOHN: You're just a trouble maker you are. [*He playfully shadow boxes near her face*] Bam, bam. . .

EVELYN: Go away.

[JOHN *shadow boxes round the room* ]

[DIANA *returns* ]

JOHN: Here she is. Had a good time up there?

MARGE: Is Paul coming down?

DIANA: I have no idea. I have no idea at all. I have done my best. I have now given up. Most probably it will be left to us. In which case, we'll have to cope with Colin on our own, won't we?

JOHN: Without Paul?

DIANA: Apparently he's far too busy to see his so-called best friend.

JOHN: If Paul's not going to be here, it's going to be a bit. . .

DIANA: Quite. What's that you're knitting, Marge?

MARGE: Oh, just a sweater for Gordon.

DIANA: Lovely colour.

MARGE: Yes, I rather like it. I'm hoping he'll wear it to protect his chest. Once he goes out in that wind. . .

JOHN: How is old Gordon? Is he coming?

MARGE: I'm afraid he's not very well at the moment.

JOHN: Oh, dear. He's had this a long time, hasn't he?

MARGE: Had what?

JOHN: This – er food poisoning, wasn't it?

MARGE: That was weeks ago. This is something quite different.

JOHN: Oh. [*He jigs about*]

DIANA: Would you like to take a seat, John?

JOHN: No, it's all right, thanks. I don't like sitting down very much.

EVELYN: Sit down, for heaven's sake.

JOHN: I don't like sitting down. I don't enjoy it.

EVELYN: He'll never sit down. I don't think I've ever seen him sit down. He has his meals dancing around the table.

JOHN: I prefer standing up, that's all.

[*Pause. He jiggles* ]

DIANA: [*tense and shrill*] John, will you please sit down before you drive me mad.

JOHN: [*sitting*] Sorry. Sorry. . .

DIANA: I'm sorry.

JOHN: No, it's me, I'm sorry.

DIANA: I'm sorry, John.

JOHN: No need to be sorry. That's all right.

EVELYN: You'll never get him to sit still, I'll tell you that.

[*They sit. EVELYN sings, chews and reads. JOHN tries not to fidget. DIANA sits, staring ahead of her, steeped in worry. MARGE studies her pattern* ]

MARGE: [*at length*] I think I've gone wrong with this. I've got twelve too many stitches. How the dickens did I get twelve too many stitches.

[*At length, PAUL enters* ]

JOHN: Hallo, hallo. He's arrived.

[*PAUL stands, surveying the room, making his presence felt. He sits* ]

PAUL: Well. Here I am then.

DIANA: So we see.

PAUL: That's what you wanted, wasn't it?

DIANA: I'm not so sure.

PAUL: Well, make up your mind. I'll go upstairs again.

[*Silence* ]

JOHN: Paul, could we have a quick word about Eastfield, do you think?

PAUL: Not just at the moment, if you don't mind.

JOHN: It's just if I got your okay, I could go ahead with the order.

PAUL: Look, I'm not in the mood to talk about Eastfield just at the moment, John. We're having this riotous tea party. Rude to talk business over tea. [*He discovers the paper towel holder*] What's this? Where did this come from?

DIANA: It's nothing. It's just a holder for the paper towel in the kitchen, that's all.

PAUL: Is it ours?

DIANA: Yes.

PAUL: What have you gone and bought another one for?

DIANA: I didn't.

PAUL: I just put one up the other day. How many of the things do you want?

MARGE: Oh well. . .

PAUL: [*laughing to* MARGE] Kitchen, knee deep in paper towels.

MARGE: It's useful to have a spare.

[*Pause* ]

PAUL: I don't know what we're going to talk to this fellow about, I'm sure. We haven't seen him for three years. I don't even know this girl's name.

DIANA: Carol.

PAUL: Well, that's something. I mean, I can't see what good this is going to do for him. Coming round here talking to us about it.

DIANA: He probably won't want to.

PAUL: Then what else is there to talk about? It's just embarrassing isn't it?

DIANA: What's embarrassing? Somebody you've known for a long time loses someone very dear to them. Seems natural to ask them round and comfort them a little.

PAUL: Fat lot of comfort he'll get here.

MARGE: We can try. It'll only be for an hour.

JOHN: As long as he doesn't start talking about death, I don't mind. If he starts on about death or dying, I'm off.

EVELYN: I don't know why you came.

JOHN: Well – like Di says, it's – friendly.

EVELYN: You don't like him.

JOHN: Colin? I didn't mind him.

EVELYN: You said you didn't like him.

JOHN: I didn't mind him.

PAUL: I didn't like him.

DIANA: You went round with him enough.

PAUL: I did not.

DIANA: You used to come round to our house every Friday and Saturday. You and him. We used to call you the flower pot men.

PAUL: He used to follow me.

DIANA: And Colin always went off with my sister Barbara and I was stuck with you.

PAUL: Very funny.

DIANA: It's true. We both fancied Colin really.

[JOHN and MARGE laugh again ]

PAUL: That is patently untrue. That is a lie.

DIANA: I was only joking. . .

PAUL: If you want to know what it really was. . .

DIANA: I was joking.

PAUL: If you really want to know. . .

DIANA: It was a joke.

[PAUL subsides ]

PAUL: Anyway. Come to that, why do you think we both came round?

DIANA: I don't doubt it.

PAUL: Well.

DIANA: You lost out then, didn't you?

PAUL: So did you.

DIANA: You said it, not me.

MARGE: Look, we really mustn't quarrel.

DIANA: I'm not quarrelling.

PAUL: Neither am I.

MARGE: I mean, Colin's not going to want this. He'll want to feel he's among friends, not enemies.

EVELYN: [*in her magazine*] This is a rotten story in here. This fellow's gone mad just because this girl's kissed him. Running about and singing.

MARGE: I think that's meant to be romantic, Evelyn.

EVELYN: They ought to put him away for good, if you ask me.

DIANA: If you really fancied Barbara, I'm surprised you didn't go off with her. You had the chance.

PAUL: Forget I said it.

DIANA: I mean, why didn't you?

PAUL: Would you all please witness I did not start this conversation?

DIANA: Answer me that.

PAUL: You are all witnesses, thank you.

DIANA: If you fancied her that much. . .

PAUL: Oh, God.

DIANA: Never mind. You're making up for it now, aren't you?

PAUL: What do you mean by that?

MARGE: Now, Di. . .

DIANA: I said, you're making up for it now, aren't you, dearest? With your other little. . .

MARGE: Why don't we all have a cup of tea now? Wouldn't that be a nice idea?

[*The phone starts ringing* ]

PAUL: No. I want that last remark explained if you don't mind.

MARGE: Now, Paul, Paul. . .

DIANA: Never mind.

PAUL: All my other what?

MARGE: [*standing between them, arms outstretched*] Now, Di . . . Paul. . .

DIANA: You know.

JOHN: Should I answer that?

PAUL: All my other what? I want to hear the rest of that sentence.

DIANA: You know perfectly well what I'm talking about.

MARGE: Di. . . Paul . . .

JOHN: I'll answer it, shall I?

PAUL: I have not the slightest idea what you're talking about, I'm sorry.

DIANA: [*pointing at* EVELYN] Well, I'm sure she has. Ask her then.

MARGE: Di. . . Paul. . .

EVELYN: Eh?

JOHN: [*who has answered the phone*] Hallo. Could you speak up please.

DIANA: Yes, you. Don't you sit there looking so innocent and smug. I know all about you.

PAUL: What are you dragging Evelyn into this for?

JOHN: Oh, hallo Gordon. [*to* MARGE] It's Gordon.

MARGE: Gordon. Oh, my God. [*She snatches the phone from him*]

DIANA: If anyone has dragged Evelyn into this, it's you.

MARGE: Hallo, Jumjums.

DIANA: You're the one who's dragged her in, literally.

MARGE: My darling, what is it?

PAUL: I don't know what you're talking about. Will somebody kindly tell me what she's talking about.

MARGE: He's spilt his cough mixture in his bed.

DIANA: You know bloody well what I'm talking about. I'm talking about you and her, you bastard.

MARGE: Has it sunk through to the mattress, love?

EVELYN: I'm going home.

DIANA: Yes, you go home, you little bitch.

PAUL: Oh, no you don't. You stay where you are, Evelyn. If she says things like that, she's got to prove them.

DIANA: I don't have to. I know.

EVELYN: Goodbye.

JOHN: We can't go now. Colin's coming.

EVELYN: To hell with him.

PAUL: She's just hysterical.

MARGE: Can you try and sleep on the dry side until I get back?

PAUL: The woman's hysterical. Now listen, Di. . .

DIANA: [*screaming*] Don't come near me.

MARGE: Oh no. Have you got it on your 'jamas as well? [*The baby starts crying*]

EVELYN: [*furious*] You've woken him up now.

JOHN: I didn't wake him up.

PAUL: I mean, seriously, how can a man live with a woman like that?

MARGE: Jumjums, how did you get it on your trousers. . . well, look, take them off, dear. Take the bottoms off.

JOHN: Where are you going?

EVELYN: [*starting to push the pram out*] I'm taking him home.

JOHN: Oh, Evelyn. . .

PAUL: I mean, am I unreasonable?

MARGE: There's some more in the bottom drawer. The stripy ones.

JOHN: [*calling after her*] Evelyn.

MARGE: Yes, well, you will be sticky. You'll have to wash.

[*Doorbell*]

DIANA: How you can stand there looking so damned innocent. . .

PAUL: Listen, if you could tell me what I'm being accused of, I could perhaps answer you.

[*Doorbell* ]

JOHN: I think that's the doorbell.

MARGE: No, keep warm, Jumjums, keep warm. . .

[EVELYN *re-enters with the pram, baby still crying* ]

JOHN: What are you doing?

EVELYN: I can't get out that way. There's somebody at the front door.

DIANA: Get out of my house.

EVELYN: I'm trying to.

MARGE: Bye bye, darling.

JOHN: It'll be Colin.

MARGE: Bye.

PAUL: Colin?

EVELYN: I'm taking Wayne in the garden.

MARGE: Bye. [*She hangs up*]

JOHN: Don't go home, Evelyn.

PAUL: Now listen, Di, Marge. . .

EVELYN: [*as she goes out*] I can't, can I?

[EVELYN *goes out to the kitchen with the pram* ]

MARGE: He has spilt cough mixture not only on the sheet, but on the pillow.

[*Doorbell* ]

PAUL: Would you listen a minute?

MARGE: . . . his clean pyjama bottoms. .

PAUL: Marge, please. Would you mind? Di, get a grip on yourself, Di.

DIANA: What?

PAUL: Colin is here now at the door.

DIANA: Oh no.

[DIANA *runs out to the kitchen* ]

PAUL: Di. . .

MARGE: Shall I let him in?

PAUL: Would you mind, Marge. You seem to be the calmest among us.

MARGE: I am not calm, believe me. That linctus will have gone through that undersheet straight into that mattress. [*As she goes*] I don't know how I'm going to get it out, I don't.

[JOHN *and* PAUL *are left* ]

[PAUL *pacing.* JOHN *jiggling* ]

PAUL: Did you tell her?

JOHN: Who?

PAUL: Di.

JOHN: What about?

PAUL: About Evelyn and me.

JOHN: I didn't. Why should I? I mean, as we said, it was just one of those things, wasn't it?

PAUL: Right.

JOHN: Wouldn't happen again.

PAUL: Certainly wouldn't.

JOHN: There you are. We'd settled it, hadn't we?

PAUL: Did Evelyn tell Di?

JOHN: I don't think so.

PAUL: Can't see why she would.

JOHN: No reason at all. Just one of those things, wasn't it? I'm not bitter. It was a bit of a shock when she told me. But I'm not bitter.

PAUL: Somebody told her. . .

[MARGE *ushers in* COLIN ]

MARGE: Here he is.

COLIN: Paul.

PAUL: Colin, my old mate, how are you? [*he embraces him*]

COLIN: Great to see you, John. . .

JOHN: [*shaking his hand*] Hallo, Col.

COLIN: Oh, it is good to see you both. How are you?

PAUL: Great.

JOHN: Fine.

COLIN: Where are the girls then, where are the girls?

PAUL: Oh – er – Di's just out in the kitchen there.

COLIN: Doing her stuff?

PAUL: Yes, more or less. And – er – Evelyn's with the baby.

COLIN: Hey, yes. You've got a baby.

JOHN: Right.

COLIN: Boy or girl?

JOHN: Boy. Wayne. Four months.

COLIN: Fantastic. That's what you always wanted, didn't you? I always remember that. When the four of us used to get together, you know, you, me, Gordon, Paul – what was it Gordon wanted to be, a cricketer, wasn't it? – you always used to say, I just want to get married and have a son.

JOHN: Right.

COLIN: Fantastic. Congratulations. Sorry to hear about Gordon, Marge. He's ill, you say?

MARGE: I'm afraid so.

COLIN: Poor Gordon, he has all the luck. He wasn't feeling too good when I left, was he? That's right. He was sick at the farewell party.

MARGE: Something he ate.

COLIN: [*laughing, to the others*] Out of me way, out of me way. Do you remember. We were all sitting there, quietly talking and then, out of me way, out of me way. Rushing about the room, everybody scattering for cover. He flings open the door and throws up in the broom cupboard. [*he laughs*] Nothing serious, I hope?

MARGE: No, no. He always looks worse than he is. [*With a laugh*] I don't think he's quite at death's door yet.

[*Pause*]

COLIN: Good.

MARGE: I'll – see you in a minute.

COLIN: Right.

[*MARGE goes to the kitchen*]

This is all right, this place, isn't it? Very nice indeed. How long have you had this, Paul?

PAUL: Oh, nearly two years.

COLIN: Now we know where the money's going. I'd settle for this. Wouldn't you, John? Yes, I'd settle for this.

JOHN: Yes.

PAUL: You want to sit down?

COLIN: Thanks. [*He sits*] Very nice.

PAUL: How are you feeling?

COLIN: Oh, pretty fair. Lost a bit of weight lately, that helps.

JOHN: Yes.

PAUL: Col? [*Offers a cigar*]

COLIN: No thanks.

[PAUL *takes one, as an afterthought he throws one to* JOHN *who catches it* ]

JOHN: Thanks Paul.

[*Pause* ]

COLIN: What's your wife's name again, John, I forget? Before I meet her.

JOHN: Evelyn.

[JOHN *clicks his lighter intermittently in an effort to make it work* ]

COLIN: Evelyn. That's it. Di did write and tell me. I forgot. Sorry.

JOHN: That's okay. I forget it myself sometimes.

[COLIN *laughs* ]

COLIN: She's not local though, is she?

JOHN: No. She's got relatives.

COLIN: Ah. Will I approve, do you think?

JOHN: Eh?

COLIN: Do you think I'll approve of her?

JOHN: Well, yes. Hope so.

COLIN: She all right, is she, Paul?

PAUL: Eh?

COLIN: This Evelyn of his? Has he done all right for himself would you say?

PAUL: Oh, yes he's done all right.

COLIN: John could always pick them.

PAUL: Yes.

[*Pause* ]

[MARGE *enters with mats for the teapot and hot water jug* ]

MARGE: [*whispering with embarrassment*] Excuse me. We're just brewing up. Now, Di wants her handbag a minute. Is it. . .? Oh yes. Won't be a minute.

[*She goes out* ]

COLIN: She hasn't changed.

PAUL: No.

COLIN: We used to have a name for her, didn't we? When Gordon first took her out.

PAUL: Can't remember.

COLIN: It was. . . can you, John?

JOHN: No. Something. I can't remember.

PAUL: No.

COLIN: It was a beetle or a spider or something. I'll remember, it'll come to me.

[*Pause* ]

JOHN: You're looking well, Col.

COLIN: I feel well.

JOHN: You look it.

[*Pause* ]

COLIN: I'm not early, am I?

PAUL: No, no. . .

JOHN: No.

[*Pause* ]

COLIN: Yes. You've certainly done all right for yourself, haven't you, Paul?

PAUL: Now and again.

JOHN: Everything he touches.

COLIN: I bet. You two still fairly thick, I take it?

JOHN: Oh well, you know. When our paths cross. We do each other the odd favour.

PAUL: Generally one way.

JOHN: Oh, come on.

PAUL: Usually.

JOHN: Yes, usually. Not always, but usually.

PAUL: He's still the worst bloody salesman in the country. I'm the only one who'll buy his rotten stuff. I've got about five hundred tins of his rubbish. I can't give it away.

COLIN: What is it?

PAUL: Cat food. So called. That's what they call it. I've never met a cat yet who could eat it and live. Rubbish. I wouldn't give it to a dog.

COLIN: You could try it on Gordon.

JOHN: No, seriously for a moment, Paul, that's what I wanted to talk to you about. That particular line of ours isn't selling so well. It isn't so much content, it's packaging. Now, they have just brought out this new line. . .

PAUL: Go on. They've discovered the antidote.

[COLIN *laughs* ]

JOHN: No, seriously, Paul.

PAUL: Not now.

JOHN: No, seriously, one word. . .

PAUL: Seriously, John, no.

JOHN: He'll be sorry.

[MARGE *returns* ]

MARGE: [*in the same embarrassed whisper, as before*] Excuse me a minute. Just want to fetch my comb. For Di. Now where did I. . .? Oh yes.

[*She finds her own handbag and bends and rummages in it. The men watch her* ]

COLIN: The stick insect.

MARGE: [*startled*] What?

COLIN: Nothing.

[*The men laugh* ]

MARGE: [*puzzled, waving the comb*] We won't be a minute. This is for Di. A comb. For her hair. Excuse me.

[MARGE *goes out* ]

PAUL: Still at the bank, Colin?

COLIN: Yes. Still at the bank.

PAUL: That's what I like to hear.

COLIN: Yes.

[*Pause* ]

PAUL: [*rising*] Look, I think I'll just go and see if I can sort them out out there. Give them a hand. Excuse me.

COLIN: Of course.

PAUL: Won't be a sec.

COLIN: Right.

[PAUL *goes out to kitchen* ]

[JOHN *and* COLIN *rise. They sit. They rise and meet in front of table, laugh. They sit,* COLIN *back in chair,* JOHN *on pouffe. They rise.* COLIN *looks at picture behind bar* ]

COLIN: GREAT!

JOHN: TERRIFIC!

[COLIN *looks at toy on bar, as* JOHN *leaves for kitchen.* COLIN *turns, sees he is alone, and sits back in chair* ]

[*Everyone returns.* DIANA *with handbag.* PAUL *with*

*teapot followed by* JOHN. MARGE *with hot water jug.*
EVELYN *from the garden* ]

DIANA: Hallo, Colin, I'm so sorry.

COLIN: Hallo, Di. [*They kiss*]

PAUL: Back again.

JOHN: [*following* PAUL *round and under the other dialogue*]
No, the point I'm saying is, that if I were to knock off five
percent and sell the stuff to him for that much less, we could
still net a profit of not less than what? — five twenties are a
hundred — five eights are forty — less what? — three fives are
fifteen — a hundred and twenty five percent. That's an initial
outlay — including transport, of what? — four nines are thirty
six — plus, say, twenty for handling either end — that's fifty
six. Bring it to a round figure — sixty...

[PAUL, *throughout this, nods disinterested agreement, his
mind on other things. Over this:*]

DIANA: It was so nice you could come. It really was. Now you
know Marge, of course, don't you?

COLIN: Yes, yes.

DIANA: Oh, but you don't know Evelyn. This is John's Evelyn.

COLIN: How do you do.

EVELYN: 'Llo.

COLIN: Heard a lot about you.

EVELYN: Oh yes? Who from?

COLIN: Er...

DIANA: Sit down, Colin. Let me give you some tea. Sit down,
everyone. [*To* JOHN *who is grinding on to* PAUL] John
dear, do sit down.

JOHN: Oh yes, sorry.

[*Everyone sits.* DIANA *pours tea* ]

COLIN: Do you work at all, Evelyn, or does the baby take up all
your time?

EVELYN: No.

COLIN: Ah.

JOHN: She works some days.

COLIN: Oh yes, where's that?

EVELYN: Part-time cashier at the Rollarena.

COLIN: Oh. Is that interesting?

EVELYN: No.

COLIN: Ah.

DIANA: Could you pass these round, Paul? I remembered you liked it strong, Colin.

COLIN: Oh, lovely.

[*Pause* ]

MARGE: Oh! Guess who I saw in the High Street?

DIANA: Who?

MARGE: Mrs Dyson. Grace Dyson.

DIANA: Oh, her.

MARGE: I was surprised. She looked well.

DIANA: Good.

PAUL: Who's Grace Dyson?

MARGE: Oh well, you'd know her as Grace Follett probably.

PAUL: I don't think I know her at all.

JOHN: Remember Ted Walker, Colin?

COLIN: Ted Walker? Oh, Ted Walker, yes. Of course, yes.

JOHN: He's still about.

DIANA: You like yours fairly weak, don't you, Marge?

MARGE: Yes, please. But don't drown it.

[*A silence* ]

COLIN: Do you know what my biggest regret is?

DIANA: What's that, Colin?

COLIN: That none of you ever met Carol.

MARGE: Who?

COLIN: Carol. My ex-fiancée. She was drowned, you know.

MARGE: Oh, yes, yes. I know, I know.

COLIN: I wish you'd met her.

DIANA: Yes. [*A pause*] I think I can speak for all of us, Colin, when I say how very sorry we were to hear about your loss. As I hope you'll realise, we're your friends and − well − and although we didn't know Carol − none of us had the pleasure of meeting her − we feel that in a small way, your grief is our grief. After all, in this world, we are all to some extent − we're all − what's the word. . .?

PAUL: Joined.

DIANA: No.

JOHN: Related.

MARGE: Combined.

DIANA: No. Dependent.

PAUL: That's what I said.

DIANA: No you didn't, you said joined or something.

PAUL: It's the same thing. Joined, dependent, means the same.

DIANA: We are all dependent in a way for our own – and, well
... no, I'm sorry I've forgotten what I was going to say now.
I hope you understand what I meant, anyway.

COLIN: Thank you.

DIANA: [*embarrassed and relieved*] Oh well, that's got that
over with, anyway. I mean – more tea, anyone?

MARGE: Give us a chance.

[*A silence* ]

[COLIN *suddenly slaps his knees and springs to his feet.
Everyone jolts* ]

What's the matter?

COLIN: Wait there, wait there.

[COLIN *rushes out to the front door* ]

DIANA: [*in a shocked whisper*] Where's he gone?

PAUL: I don't know.

MARGE: Is he all right?

DIANA: I didn't upset him, did I, saying that?

MARGE: No. Lovely.

JOHN: I'll have a look, shall I?

DIANA: Would you, John.

PAUL: What did you want to get on to that for?

DIANA: What?

PAUL: All that going on about grief and so on.

DIANA: I only said. . .

PAUL: We're supposed to be cheering him up. He didn't want to
listen to that.

DIANA: It had to be said.

MARGE: You have to say it.

PAUL: He obviously didn't want to be reminded of it, did he?
There was no need to, no need at all. We were all getting along
perfectly happily.

DIANA: You can't sit here and not say anything about it.

[JOHN *returns* ]

JOHN: He's gone out the front door.

DIANA: Where to?

JOHN: His car, I think. He's getting something out of the boot.

PAUL: Probably going to hang himself with his tow rope. After
what she said.

DIANA: He seemed perfectly recovered. Very cheerful. I

thought someone should say something.

PAUL: Cheerful? You can see that was only skin deep.

DIANA: I couldn't.

PAUL: I was talking to him in here. You could tell. He's living on his nerves. On a knife edge. You could tell, couldn't you, John?

JOHN: He seemed quite cheerful.

PAUL: He could snap like that. Any minute. Same with anyone in this situation. Up one minute. . .

JOHN: I've never seen him quite so cheerful.

PAUL: Exactly. All the signs are there. The last thing he wanted to do was to talk about this fiancée of his. It's a known fact, people never. . .

MARGE: Oh yes, they do. My Aunt Angela. . .

PAUL: It is a known fact. . .

[*Slight pause* ]

[*Door bangs* ]

JOHN: He's coming back.

PAUL: Now, not another word about her. Keep it cheerful. For God's sake, Evelyn, try and smile, just for once.

[COLIN *returns. He carries a photo album and an envelope of loose snapshots, all contained, at present, in a large chocolate box* ]

ALL: Ah. . .

COLIN:[*breathless*] Sorry. I forgot to bring these in. It's some photos. You can see what she looked like.

DIANA: Of her?

COLIN: Yes. I thought you'd like to.

MARGE: Oh.

COLIN: Yes. There's one or two quite good ones. Thought you might like to see some. Of course, if you'd rather. . .

PAUL: No, no. . .

COLIN: She was very photogenic. Shall I sit here next to you, Di? Then I can. . . [*He sits next to* DIANA] Now then. [*Taking snaps from the envelope*] Ah yes, these are some loose ones I haven't stuck in yet. They're the most recent. Can I give those to you, Marge? I think they're mostly on holiday, those. [*He hands loose snapshots to* MARGE]

MARGE: Thank you.

COLIN: [*with the album*] These are mostly at home in the

garden at her house.

MARGE: Oh, is this her? Oh, she is lovely, Colin. Wasn't she?

DIANA: [as COLIN *opens the first page*] Oh.

COLIN: There she is again. That's with her Mum.

DIANA: She's a fine looking woman too.

COLIN: Wonderful. She's been really wonderful. She's got this terrible leg.

DIANA: Ah.

MARGE: Oh, that's a nice one. . . Do you want to pass them round, John?

JOHN: Oh yes, sure.

[MARGE *passes them to* JOHN *who in due course passes them to* PAUL *who passes them to* EVELYN ]

DIANA: That's nice. Was that her house?

COLIN: No. That's the back of the Natural History Museum, I think.

DIANA: I was going to say. . .

COLIN: Went there at Easter.

MARGE: [*at photo*] Oh.

PAUL: [*at photo*] Ah.

DIANA: [*at album*] Oh.

MARGE: Oh look, John, with her little dog, see?

JOHN: Oh yes.

COLIN: That was her mother's.

MARGE: Oh. Sweet little dog.

EVELYN: I like that handbag.

COLIN: That's her again. Bit of a saucy one. It's not very good though, the sun's the wrong way.

DIANA: I wish I had a figure like that. It's so nice you brought them, Colin.

MARGE: Oh yes.

DIANA: It's nice, too, that you can look at them without – you know. . .

COLIN: Oh no, it doesn't upset me. Not now.

MARGE: That's wonderful.

COLIN: I was upset at the time, you know.

DIANA: Naturally.

COLIN: But – after that – well, it's a funny thing about somebody dying – you never know, till it actually happens, how it's going to affect you, I mean, we all think about death at some time, I suppose, all of us. Either our death, somebody else's death. After all, it's one of the few things we have all got in common...

[JOHN *has risen and is jiggling about* ]

DIANA: Sit down, John.

[JOHN *sits reluctantly* ]

COLIN: And I suppose when I first met Carol, it must have passed through my mind what would I feel like if I did lose her. And I just couldn't think. I couldn't imagine it. I couldn't imagine my life going on without her. And then it happened. All of a sudden. One afternoon. All over. She was caught in this under-current, there was nothing anybody could do. I wasn't even around. They came and told me. And for about three weeks after that, I couldn't do anything at all. Nothing. I just lay about thinking, remembering and then, all of a sudden, it came to me that if my life ended there and then, by God, I'd have a lot to be grateful for. I mean, first of all, I'd been lucky enough to have known her. I don't know if you've ever met a perfect person. But that's what she was. The only way to describe her. And I, me, I'd had the love of a perfect person. And that's something I can always be grateful for. Even if for nothing else. And then I thought, what the hell am I talking about, my whole life's been like that. All through my childhood, the time I was growing up, all the time I lived here, I've had what a lot of people would probably give their right arm for – friends. Real friends, like John and Paul and Gordon and Di. So, one of the things I just wanted to say, Di – Paul – Marge – John – Evelyn and to Gordon if he was here, is that I'm not bitter about what happened. Because I've been denied my own happiness, I don't envy or begrudge you yours. I just want you to know that, despite everything that happened, in a funny sort of way, I too am very happy.

[*He smiles round at them serenely. A silence. A strange whooping noise. It is* DIANA *starting to weep hysterically. Unable to contain herself, she rushes out. After a moment,* MARGE *fumbles for her handkerchief and blows her nose loudly.* JOHN, *looking sickly, gives* COLIN *a ghastly smile.* PAUL *opens his mouth as if to say something, gives up.* COLIN *stands looking slightly bemused. He looks at* EVELYN. *She looks back at him, expressionless, chewing* ]

COLIN: Did I say the wrong thing?
   [EVELYN *shrugs and resumes her reading* ]


CURTAIN

# ACT TWO

*The same. Time is continuous. 4.15 p.m. All except* DIANA.

COLIN: [*worriedly*] I didn't say anything wrong, did I?

PAUL: No, no. . .

JOHN: I think she went to get the. . . [*He can't think of anything*]

MARGE: You know Di, Colin, she. . .

COLIN: Yes. Sorry.

PAUL: No, no. . .

COLIN: I'll pack these up. I didn't realise. . .

MARGE: No, no. . .

COLIN: Yes. It can be upsetting. I didn't realise. . .

[*He starts to gather up the photos. The others help by passing them to him* ]

I bet I know what the trouble is, Paul.

PAUL: What?

COLIN: Di's been overdoing it again, hasn't she? That was always her trouble. She flings herself into whatever she does. Heart and soul. Remember her with that jumble sale? I've still got this picture of her. Standing there, in the middle of all these old clothes, crying her heart out. Remember that?

PAUL: Yes.

COLIN: I mean, look at this tea. Whoever saw a tea like that?

JOHN: Any chance of a sandwich?

MARGE: Yes, I suppose we'd better. . . [*Holding up a plate of sandwiches*] John, would you like to pass these round, dear? Here, we've got some plates.

[JOHN *rises* ]

PAUL: [*also rising*] It's all right. I'll. . .

COLIN: [*who has gathered in all his photos*] Is that the lot?

MARGE: [*handing* PAUL *sideplates with paper napkins*] Here you are. [*To* COLIN] We'd all love to have another look at them later.

JOHN: [*passing round the sandwiches, muttering*] Great.

COLIN: Yes, well, possibly. I hope Di's all right.

PAUL: Oh, yes. . .

MARGE: Oh, yes. She'll be fine. Fine. She's very sensitive.

COLIN: Oh, yes. I think that's what makes her a wonderful person, you know.

MARGE: Yes, yes. I think we could all learn from her example. She's so loyal and trusting. . .

COLIN: Yes. She's got a lot of the qualities Carol had in that respect. You're a lucky man, Paul.

PAUL: Yes.

COLIN: [*laughing suddenly*] It could have been me at one point, couldn't it? Remember? Diana and me instead of Diana and you.

PAUL: Could it?

COLIN: Oh, come on, you haven't forgotten that. [*To the others*] We were both after her – him and me – at one time.

MARGE: Were you really?

COLIN: Oh, yes. And I think it's fair to say, isn't it, Paul, fair to say, that there was one moment in time when I don't think she could honestly choose between us.

MARGE: Really, I didn't know.

COLIN: Still, it all ended happily, didn't it? Lucky old Paul, and if I'd married Di, I wouldn't have met Carol. . .

MARGE: Yes.

[*Pause* ]

COLIN: Talking of Carol, it's an odd thing you know. I'm sure this is fairly common. I mean, you read about it happening but there are times when I feel that she's still around somewhere. Some part of her. Her spirit or whatever you call it. She could be in this room at this moment. Odd, isn't it?

MARGE: It does happen to people. My Aunt Angela –

COLIN: I mean, I know for certain in my mind that she's dead. There's no doubt that she's dead. I saw her lying there dead with my own eyes. . .

[JOHN *rises and jiggles about* ]

But nevertheless, as I say, I feel that here, around here some-where, she's watching us. She can't communicate but she's watching me. Taking care of me.

JOHN: [*moving to the door*] Excuse me.

MARGE: All right, John?

JOHN: Yes, I'm just going to see if – Di's all right. . .

[JOHN *goes out to the kitchen* ]

COLIN: Good old John. He still can't sit still, can he?

MARGE: No.

COLIN: You took on a real live wire there, Evelyn.

EVELYN: Oh yes?

COLIN: How do you manage to keep up with him?

EVELYN: I don't bother.

COLIN: You'll have to get up early in the morning to catch John.

EVELYN: I do. Every morning. He doesn't wake up at all unless I wake him.

COLIN: Oh well, that's marriage.

EVELYN: How do you know?

COLIN: Well, I mean. . .

MARGE: Evelyn. . .

EVELYN: What?

MARGE: Don't be so. . .

EVELYN: What?

MARGE: Never mind.

PAUL: How long had you known Carol, Colin?

COLIN: Just over a year. Fourteen months, twenty three days.

PAUL: Ah well. Time would have told.

COLIN: Told what?

PAUL: I mean, well – I mean, to be fair you hadn't time really to get to know her. Not really.

COLIN: I think I knew Carol better than I've ever known anybody before or since, Paul.

PAUL: Oh. Well. I'm sure. . .

[DIANA *returns with a jug of cream* ]

DIANA: I'm so sorry, everyone. I just wanted to make sure I'd turned the gas off. Now this is the cream for the trifle afterwards if anybody wants any. I've left that out there in the cool till we've cleared away some of this. Oh good, you've started the sandwiches.

MARGE: Yes, I hope you didn't. . .

DIANA: No, no. They're there to be eaten.

COLIN: I'm very sorry, Di, if I upset you with – what I said. . .

DIANA: Oh no, Colin, no. Not at all. John's outside checking on the baby, Evelyn.

EVELYN: Oh.

DIANA: He thought one of you should. He's wonderful with

that baby, Colin. You should see him.

COLIN: I bet.

DIANA: Does all the things a mother should and better.

[EVELYN *clicks her tongue. She picks up the magazine and buries her nose in it rudely*]

COLIN: You all right, Evelyn?

EVELYN: Eh?

COLIN: Anything the matter? You seem a bit down.

EVELYN: No. No. No...

MARGE: It's just her manner.

DIANA: You get used to it eventually.

COLIN: Oh. Do you know something, Evelyn. Now I'm talking off the top of my head now because I've only just met you, I don't really know you – but – I think Paul will back me on this, won't you, Paul – I've always had this knack – gift if you like, I suppose you could call it – for being able to sum people up pretty quickly. Sometimes I've just got to meet them, exchange a few words with them and on occasions, not always but on occasions, I know more about that particular person than they know about themselves. Now I could be wrong, as I say this is straight off the top but I would say just from the brief time I've had to study you, I would say something's bothering you. Right or wrong?

EVELYN: Right.

COLIN: There you are. Now, I'm going to go a bit further and I warn you I'm going to stick my neck right out now and say one of your worries is John. Right?

EVELYN: Amazing.

COLIN: No, not altogether. You see, I think I know what it is – [*To the others*] excuse me, I'm just putting Evelyn straight – right. Number one. John is a very high powered individual – can't sit still, always on the move. We all know him in this room very well. Probably better than you do, Evelyn. You see, we've known him for years. He's an extrovert, good brain, clever – wonderful with his hands. The sort of fellow, if you're in trouble, it's John you go to. John is number one. Never let you down. The bee's knees. But – and there's a big but – and I think everyone here will agree with this – Marge, Di, Paul, Gordon if he was here – what we, everyone of us, have always said about John is – God help the woman he marries. Because

every day of their lives together, she is going to have to get
used to the fact that John is going to be the driver while she is
going to have to spend most of her life in the back seat.

[*He pauses for effect and gets one* ]

So. My advice is, don't let your personality — because I can see
there's a lovely personality hiding under there — don't let that
get buried away. Because he won't thank you for it in the end.
Nobody will. Get in the habit of giving yourself to people, if
you know what I mean, and you'll get a lot more back, believe
me. I'm a giver. It's natural, how I was born, nothing virtuous
about it, per se — just the way I'm made. Others have to work
at it. Carol was another giver. She'd give you everything.
Everything she had.

[*Silence* ]

MARGE: True. True. . .

COLIN: Sorry. I'm preaching. I can feel it. Sorry, Evelyn. Beg
your pardon. I just happen to be an expert on John, that's all.
I'm an expert on Paul here as well. Shall I tell you about Paul?

EVELYN: No thanks.

COLIN: No. Better not. He gets embarrassed.

DIANA: Yes. Another sandwich, everyone?

COLIN: Oh, ta.

[JOHN *returns from the garden* ]

MARGE: Is he all right?

JOHN: Yes. Fast asleep now.

COLIN: Just been talking about you.

JOHN: Who has?

EVELYN: Him, mainly.

COLIN: Me, mainly.

JOHN: Oh.

MARGE: Yes, now we know, don't we, everyone?

EVELYN: We certainly do.

[*Pause. Sandwiches are passed. Everyone settles* ]

COLIN: Memory test. Do you remember, does anyone remember, the last time we were all together like this? I mean as a
group. If you count Gordon and don't count Evelyn. Does
anyone remember?

DIANA: No. When would that have been?

PAUL: Dick's anniversary.

COLIN: No, no. Months after that.

MARGE: I give up.

COLIN: Do the words Stately Home remind you of anything.

DIANA: Stately Home? You mean that place?

JOHN: That place, yes. . .

PAUL: Oh, grief. . .

MARGE: The one day of the year we chose. . .

DIANA: And it's closed.

MARGE: That was dreadful, wasn't it?

PAUL: Proper waste of petrol.

DIANA: And then the rain.

MARGE: All that rain.

DIANA: And that was the day I lost that glove.

MARGE: Yes. That's it. And then Gordon lost the convoy. We were driving up here, down there, trying to find you.

JOHN: It was all right for you. We were sitting in that lay-by for two hours while you were seeing the countryside.

COLIN: Yes, but it was a marvellous day, wasn't it?

JOHN: Was it?

COLIN: Oh, it was a great laugh − sorry, Evelyn, this must be very boring for you, love −

EVELYN: Yes.

COLIN: Remember that fabulous picnic?

DIANA: All I remember is running from one car to the other in the rain with the thermos flask.

COLIN: And we found a great place for tea.

PAUL: Where they overcharged us.

COLIN: It was great. I'll always remember that.

JOHN: Yes.

COLIN: What a marvellous day that was.

DIANA: [*doubtfully*] Yes.

MARGE: I suppose so, yes.

COLIN: You missed something there, Evelyn.

EVELYN: Sounds like it.

[*Pause* ]

COLIN: Poor old Gordon. Lying in bed while we're scoffing ourselves.

MARGE: Yes, shame.

COLIN: Now, Gordon's the opposite to John, isn't he? He's what, shy. I'd call him shy, wouldn't you, Marge?

MARGE: Well, sometimes − yes. I suppose he has been.

COLIN: Big men are like that. They're always shy.

PAUL: I'm not shy.

DIANA: You're not very big.

PAUL: I'm fairly big.

MARGE: You're not as big as Gordon.

PAUL: Nobody's as big as Gordon.

[*Pause*]

MARGE: That's because I feed him. When his stomach's not playing him up.

COLIN: Gordon was famous for his appetite.

MARGE: He still is. I like a man with an appetite.

COLIN: There you are, you see. Two more satisfied customers.

[*Pause. COLIN laughs*]

DIANA: What;

COLIN: Sorry. No, I was just remembering something.

DIANA: What?

COLIN: It was just something me and Carol — it wouldn't interest you.

DIANA: Go on.

COLIN: No, no. . .

MARGE: Go on. We want to hear about her.

COLIN: Well, it was just one of those fantastic moments, you know.

MARGE: [*romantic*] Ah. . .

COLIN: It was — well — when we first knew each other and — I forgot where it was now — I think we were walking across the common — there was nobody about — and she suddenly turned to me and she said "Colin, I think I'm ready to let you kiss me now. I'd like that very much. Would you, please?"

MARGE: Ah. . .

COLIN: And after I'd kissed her, I remember I was over the moon, literally. You should have seen me, I was singing and dancing and leaping about all over that common. . .

MARGE: Ah. . .

DIANA: Ah. . .

EVELYN: Huh.

[*Slight pause*]

PAUL: Have you given any thought as to who's going to win the League this year, Colin?

COLIN: No, not really, no.

PAUL: I rather fancy our lot this year. They're going rather well. . .

JOHN: They are.

COLIN: Well, I still follow them. What was it? Four nil last Saturday. Did you go?

PAUL: No. Yes.

COLIN: Sounded a cracker.

PAUL: It was.

DIANA: There's nothing much can come between Paul and a football game, is there, Paul? Now come on, I want all these eaten up or I won't cut the cake.

MARGE: Well, if you've got any left I'll take it home to Gordon in a bag.

PAUL: Oh my God.

COLIN: It's a wonderful spread, Di. Really wonderful. Right up to standard.

DIANA: Thank you.

COLIN: Di's teas. Famous. I remember having a few of those over the years. Don't you Paul?

PAUL: Eh?

COLIN: Remember when we used to go round to tea? To Di and her sister Barbara's?

PAUL: Oh yes.

COLIN: Every weekend. Mind you, Paul was in such a state, he could never eat it though. He'd say to me, how the hell am I supposed to sit down opposite a fantastic looking girl like that and be expected to eat anything. That's the last thing on my mind. He really had it bad.

DIANA: For Barbara?

COLIN: Barbara? Come off it. For you.

DIANA: Oh.

PAUL: No, I didn't.

COLIN: Look he's shy. He's gone shy. Big men, I told you. Tell her about the table napkin.

PAUL: Shut up.

COLIN: All right. I'll tell them. We used to go round to tea, you see, to their house – did I ever tell you this, John?

JOHN: Don't think so.

PAUL: Look, Colin –

DIANA: Shut up, Paul, I want to hear.

MARGE: We want to hear.

COLIN: I think it was, well, practically the first time we went round to Barbara, Di and her mother's for tea and Paul was — well, he was sweating — literally sweating and all the way there he kept saying — what am I going to say to her — this was to Di. And when he got there, the girls and their mother had laid out this tea, all properly, you know. Table napkins, everything correct. . .

PAUL: Look, this was a long time ago.

COLIN: That's why I'm telling them.

DIANA: Shut up.

COLIN: Anyway, the first thing that happens, Paul and I are in the front room there, waiting — they're all out in the kitchen, giggling away, getting the tea ready — and Paul, well you know what he can be like, he gets so nervous, he's pacing up and down, sits down, gets up, sits down and then finally he leans against the wall with one hand — like this, you see — [He demonstrates] and he puts his hand right on one of those ducks. China ducks, you know, the sort people have flying up their wall. A row of them, you know. Anyway, he puts his hand on one of them and crack — bang goes one duck. So there he is, he's standing there with half a duck in each hand and we hear them coming back. No time to do anything. So he sits down to tea with his pockets full of duck.

[They laugh ]

There we are, sitting all through this tea waiting for someone to look up and say — hallo — one, two — what's happened to him. He must have migrated.

[They all laugh again ]

DIANA: We never missed it.

COLIN: No, well. He took it home, glued it together and hung it up again when we came next week.

DIANA: Typical.

COLIN: He was so worried, he could hardly keep his eyes on Di. Anyway, at the end of the meal, do you know what he did — and this shows how romantic he is underneath all that lot — he picked up that napkin that you'd been using, Di, and he put it in his pocket. Took it home to remind him of you.

MARGE: Ah.

DIANA: Is that where it went.

PAUL: I don't remember doing that.

MARGE: I think that's a lovely story. Just shows. All men are romantics at heart.

[*Pause*]

JOHN: I never did that sort of thing.

EVELYN: You nicked my Uncle's screwdriver.

JOHN: I did not.

EVELYN: He saw you taking it. He said if he comes round here again, I'll break his neck.

JOHN: You never invited me for tea.

EVELYN: You never sat down for long enough.

DIANA: Now then. More tea?

COLIN: Please.

PAUL: [*laughing suddenly*] You know something, Col?

COLIN: What?

PAUL: I've just remembered. I've still got that table napkin of hers, you know.

COLIN: Have you really?

PAUL: Yes. I use it to clean the car with.

[DIANA *picks up the cream jug and pours it slowly over* PAUL's *head.* PAUL *sits for a moment, stunned*]

[*leaping up*] Hey! What are you doing, woman?

MARGE: Di—!

COLIN: Hey, hey!

JOHN: Oy!

DIANA: Oh, I'm so sorry.

PAUL: [*outraged*] What are you doing?

DIANA: I am so sorry.

PAUL: You poured that all over me. She poured that over me.

MARGE: I'll get a cloth.

PAUL: No, I can't use a cloth. I'll have to wash it out.

MARGE: Not for you. For the chair.

[MARGE *goes out to the kitchen*]

PAUL: Bloody woman's off her head. She poured it all over me.

[PAUL *stamps off upstairs*]

DIANA: Accidents will happen.

COLIN: Well... [*He laughs awkwardly*]

DIANA: I'm sorry, Colin. You were saying?

COLIN: Was I?

DIANA: You'll have to excuse my husband, Colin, he's changed over the years. . . Now then, tea for you, John?

JOHN: Er – thank you.

DIANA: Pass your cup. Evelyn?

EVELYN: No.

DIANA: Thank you.

EVELYN: Thank you.

COLIN: Well, I daresay we've all changed in some ways.

DIANA: Possibly. Some more than most.

[MARGE *returns with a cloth, bowl of water and paper towels* ]

MARGE: Would it be all right to use this for it, Di?

[*indicates cloth*]

DIANA: Just as you like.

MARGE: Look, paper towels. Very useful. [*Examining the damage*] Oh, it's not too bad.

[MARGE *sets to work.* DIANA *hands* COLIN *his tea. Then* JOHN ]

DIANA: Is that strong enough for you, Colin?

COLIN: Oh, that's lovely, Di. That's perfect. Perfect. [*Laughing*] Just the way Carol used to make it.

DIANA: You can't say fairer than that, can you.

COLIN: Listen Di. . . .

DIANA: John. . .

[*Slight pause* ]

COLIN: Listen, Di. . . Just now, I think what Paul said just now – it may have sounded to you a bit – er – well – I think, actually, I understand what he was feeling. I know what was going through his mind. I embarrassed him with that story – I shouldn't have told it and – er – well, Paul, basically – here I go again. I told you I'm a Paul expert. . .

DIANA: So am I, Colin. So am I.

COLIN: Yes, right, point taken, surely. But. . . you see, Paul is really a very romantic man. He's soft. I've known him a long time – oh, he'll give you that old gruff bit – and the "I don't care what anyone thinks" bit – but honestly, Di, you know yourself, he's ashamed of his own nature, you see. Somewhere, he's got this idea that if he shows any sort of gentleness to people they'll think he's soft. And of course, that's what's made him the success he is today. Let's face it. Because he's managed to cover it up. And I think that in some ways you'd

be the first to say thank heavens he has. I mean. You've got
this marvellous house, full of lovely things, you've got two
fine children and − well, let's be fair, you've got just about
everything a human being could ask for. And it's a very very
sad fact of life that you don't get any of that through being
soft. That's why people like me, John, Gordon, we're never
going to get in the same bracket as Paul. Never. No, Di, I'm
afraid the only thing left for you is to love him for what he is.
Right, John?

JOHN: Right. Right.

COLIN: Marge?

MARGE: [*not quite convinced*] Yes. . .
    [*Pause*]

EVELYN: Do you happen to write for these magazines by any
chance?

COLIN: Eh?
    [*Pause.* MARGE *finishes her task*]

MARGE: I think that's done it. Shall I do over the rest while I'm
here, Di? [*She laughs*]
    [MARGE *goes out*]

JOHN: You pleased with that car of yours?

COLIN: Yes. Yes, it gets me about.

JOHN: I've always fancied the look of those. The only thing that
worries me about it is, is it slightly under-powered?

EVELYN: I bet it's got a carpet that fits.

COLIN: No, it seems to be okay. It's not a racer − but −

JOHN: No, no, quite. I think I'll consider getting one sometime.

EVELYN: A cheap one with no wheels.

JOHN: Oh, lay off, Evelyn. There's a good girl. I spend my days
slaving for her − slaving. . .
    [MARGE *returns*]

MARGE: There we are. All done. I think I've earned a spot
more tea, haven't I, Di?
    [DIANA *is in a trance of her own*]
    Di?

DIANA: It's all yours.

MARGE: Oh, righto.
    [MARGE *pours herself a cup of tea and sits in silence*]

DIANA: [*quietly at first*] When I was a little girl, you know,
my sister Barbara was very jealous of me because Mother

bought me this coat for my birthday. . .

MARGE: Oh, really?

DIANA: I'd seen it in the window of this shop when I walked to school. It was red with one of those little collars and then trimmed round the neck and the sleeves. I used to pass it every day. They'd put it on this window dummy. A little child dummy. It was a really pretty dummy. Not like some of them. A proper face. It had very very blue eyes and sort of ash coloured hair, quite short and it was standing in the middle of this sort of false grass. I wanted that coat so much. And Barbara used to say, you'll never get Mother to buy you that. But I did. And on my birthday, I put it on and I felt, oh, so happy you can't imagine. And then we were all going for a walk and we were just going out and I happened to catch sight of myself full length in the mirror in the hall. And I looked like nothing on earth in it. I looked terrible.

MARGE: Oh dear.

COLIN: What a shame.

DIANA: Yes, it was. I wanted a red one especially. Because I had this burning ambition, you see, to join the Canadian Royal Mounted Police.

MARGE: Good gracious. . .

DIANA: People used to say "You can't join the Mounted Police. You're a little girl. Little girls don't join the Mounted Police. Little girls do nice things like typing and knitting and nursing and having babies." So I married Paul instead. Because they refused to let me join the Mounted Police. I married him because he kept asking me. And because people kept saying that it would be a much nicer thing to do than. . . and so I did. And I learnt my typing and I had my babies and I looked after them for as long as they'd let me and then suddenly I realised I'd been doing all the wrong things. They'd been wrong telling me to marry Paul and have babies, if they're not even going to let you keep them, and I should have joined the Mounted Police, that's what I should have done. I know I should have joined the Mounted Police. [*Starting to sob*] I want to join the Mounted Police. Please. . . [*She starts to sob louder and louder till they become a series of short staccato screams*]

MARGE: John, for heaven's sake. Get Paul down here.

JOHN: Paul. Yes, I'll get Paul. . .

[JOHN *goes to the stairs and out.* EVELYN *has risen and is studying* DIANA *with curiosity* ]

EVELYN: What's the matter with her?

MARGE: Get out of my way. [*Shaking* DIANA] Di – Di – Di. . .

[PAUL *comes back with* JOHN *behind him.* PAUL's *hair is still wet from washing it* ]

PAUL: What's wrong? What's the matter with her?

MARGE: She's not well, Paul. You'll have to get a doctor.

PAUL: Di – Di, come on now. . .

JOHN: Shall I get her some water?

PAUL: No, we'll get her up to bed. We'll get a doctor. Give me a hand, John.

JOHN: Right.

MARGE: I'll get a cold cloth. That'll help.

[MARGE *runs out to kitchen* ]

[JOHN *and* PAUL *try to lift* DIANA *by each arm* ]

DIANA: [*fighting* PAUL *away*] Get away from me. . .

PAUL: Now, Di. . .

DIANA: Get away!

COLIN: [*who has retreated in horror to the far corner of the room, ineffectually*] Can I. . .?

EVELYN: I'll do it. Here.

[*She takes hold of* DIANA's *arm, the one that* PAUL *has relinquished.* JOHN *still has hold of the other arm* ]

DIANA: [*thrusting* EVELYN *away with some violence*] Get away from me, you bitch. . .

[MARGE *returns with a flannel* ]

JOHN: It's no good. She won't let anybody – [*Struggling with her*] – help her.

MARGE: Here, hold this. [*She thrusts the flannel into* COLIN's *hand*]

COLIN: Wah!

MARGE: Come along, out of the way.

JOHN: We could try slapping her face.

MARGE: No, we couldn't. How would you like your face slapped? Don't be silly. Come along, Di, that's it. . .

[MARGE *and* JOHN *between them start to steer* DIANA *to the door* ]

COLIN: Can I be of any. . .?

MARGE: It's all right, Colin, sit down. Easy with her, John, that's it. . . I'll phone the doctor from upstairs, Paul.

PAUL: Right.

MARGE: You're still with Harris, aren't you?

PAUL: Yes.

MARGE: Come along, John. She needs support. Support her.

JOHN: I'm trying to support her. She's bloody heavy.

[JOHN, DIANA *and* MARGE *go out. A silence. The men stand awkwardly.* EVELYN *sits and picks her nails*]

PAUL: What started that?

COLIN: I don't really know. She just started talking about the Mounted Police.

PAUL: The what?

COLIN: The Royal Canadian Mounted Police. She seemed to want to join them.

PAUL: [*shaking his head*] Well. . . [*He sits*]

COLIN: There's something very wrong there, Paul. Very wrong indeed.

[MARGE *returns busily*]

PAUL: Can you manage?

MARGE: It's all right. She's just been a little bit ill on the stairs. Nothing serious. Evelyn.

EVELYN: What?

MARGE: Paper towels. In the kitchen. Come on, this is partly your fault. You get them and clean it up.

[MARGE *goes out*]

[EVELYN *clicks her tongue and goes off into the kitchen*]

COLIN: Have you had this trouble before, Paul?

PAUL: Not quite like this.

COLIN: Worrying.

PAUL: Right.

COLIN: I think you should go up with her, you know. She probably needs you.

PAUL: Oh come on, Colin. . .

COLIN: What?

PAUL: You heard her. She doesn't want me within twenty yards of her.

COLIN: Oh yes, but that was. . . she was hysterical. I mean –

PAUL: I'm the last person.

[EVELYN *enters from the kitchen clutching a handful of paper towels*]

EVELYN: This is a right cheery afternoon this is. His lordship's bawling his head off out there as well. . .

[*She goes off to the hall*]

COLIN: I remember when Carol had flu. She wouldn't let go of my hand. Except to turn over. I sat with her for two nights in a row. But then I think the thing with Carol and me was —

PAUL: Col.

COLIN: Yes?

PAUL: Do me a favour. Just shut up for one minute about Carol, would you. I don't want to hurt your feelings but — not just at the moment. . .

COLIN: Oh, I'm sorry. I was — just thinking it — might help, you know.

PAUL: No, Colin. Really and truly, I don't honestly think it does. I mean, you and Carol were — something quite different, weren't you?

COLIN: Yes, I realise that, yes. [*He thinks for a moment*] All the same, you're wrong, you know.

PAUL: How come?

COLIN: Di didn't mean that. That she didn't want you near her.

PAUL: She convinced me.

COLIN: [*laughing*] No, no I'm sorry, Paul, you're not fooling anyone, you know. Neither's Di. Remember me? I'm the one that used to sit and talk to her for days and nights on end in the old days. Do you know what we talked about, constantly and incessantly?

PAUL: [*wearily*] Go on, amaze me. . .

COLIN: You. All you. I mean, at one time, when she used to ask me round a lot, I used to think. Hallo, I'm on to a good thing here. Can't be bad. Must mean something. And we'd sit down all evening, in her front room, drink coffee and talk about you all the time. Well, after a bit, I began to get the message. It wasn't me she was after at all. You. . . Only you were out with her sister Barbara. No, you're number one in Di's book, Paul. Always have been. I don't think you realise quite what a pedestal that woman has set you upon. She'd follow you to the ends of the earth, you know.

PAUL: She probably would at that.

COLIN: I hope you realise what you've got there?

PAUL: I do, I do.

COLIN: Stick with it, Paul, old mate.

PAUL: Thank you, Colin. Thank you very much.

COLIN: I know you will. I know you. [*Pause*] You know something? The one regret I'll always have? That Carol and I – our relationship – can never develop now into the sort of relationship you and Di must have. . .

PAUL: Oh, Colin. . .

COLIN: Never mind. Too late now. You feeling a bit brighter?

PAUL: Oh Colin, what are we going to do with you?

COLIN: Me? [*He laughs*] That's the last thing to worry about. Mind you, I'm glad I came round this afternoon. I don't know how you lot ever managed without me, eh?
[COLIN *laughs*. PAUL *laughs*. COLIN *stops laughing.* PAUL *continues. It's hysterical, almost manic, uncontrollable laughter.* COLIN *becomes concerned.* EVELYN *enters. She stares at* PAUL]

EVELYN: Oh. I'm going to fetch Wayne in. It's raining. . .
[EVELYN *goes out through the kitchen* ]
[PAUL *finally stops laughing* ]

PAUL: I'm sorry, Col. . . sorry. . .

COLIN: All right?

PAUL: Yes, yes. . .
[JOHN *enters* ]

JOHN: Right. Marge gave her one of her sleeping pills. If that doesn't get her to sleep, she says she'll phone the doctor.

PAUL: Thanks.

JOHN: Not at all, not at all. [*Looking around*] Has she gone home?

PAUL: No, she's with the baby.

JOHN: Ah. Sorry about that, Col old mate

COLIN: Oh –

JOHN: Doesn't happen every day.

COLIN: I hope not.

JOHN: You must come to our house next time. Absolute peace. Neither of us ever says a word to each other. That's the secret of a successful union. Marry a strong silent woman like Evelyn. . . [*He shadow-boxes*] Bam – bam. . . [*At the table*] Isn't anyone going to finish these?

PAUL: Help yourself.

[JOHN *munches a sandwich*]

COLIN: I must be off soon, Paul. Don't want to be in the way, you know.

[PAUL, *brooding, makes no reply*]

JOHN: [*munching*] The good thing about Evelyn — and she has her good side, although she is most careful to hide it from strangers — is that she has absolutely no sense of humour. Which is very useful since it means you never have to waste your time trying to cheer her up. Because she's permanently unhappy. Misery is her natural state. We are also fortunate in being blessed with a very miserable boy. In fact, apart from me, we are the most miserable family you are ever likely to meet and I'm working on me. Am I keeping you awake?

PAUL: Sit down.

JOHN: [*sitting*] What do you think about that deal? Worth a try.

PAUL: I don't know.

JOHN: A hundred and twenty five percent. Worth a try.

PAUL: I'll think about it.

[*The phone rings*]

Answer that will you, John.

JOHN: [*doing so*] Hallo. . . could you speak up? Gordon? . . . hallo, Gordon, matey. . . it's John, yes. . . yes, she's here . . . wait a minute. . . I'll give her a yell.

COLIN: [*moving to the door*] I'll call her.

PAUL: Tell her she can take it upstairs.

JOHN: [*still listening at phone*] Hang on, Col, she's here. . . you got it then, Marge. . . okay. . . she's got it. . . [*He goes to place the receiver and then, covering the mouthpiece, listens in. He laughs*]

PAUL: Put it down.

JOHN: [*enjoying himself*] Hang on, hang on.

COLIN: Tell her I'd like a word with him when she's —

JOHN: [*laughing*] He's burst his hot water bottle. [*listens*] He's in a shocking state.

PAUL: Put it down.

JOHN: You should hear —

PAUL: It's private, put it down.

[JOHN *does so, reluctantly*]

COLIN: I wanted a word with him.

JOHN: I don't think you would at the moment. He's a moaner, isn't he? A real moaner. Big fat moaner. Old gloom Gordon.

COLIN: He was a great left-arm bowler.

JOHN: Oh, yes. Could have played for the County.

COLIN: Easily.

JOHN: Till he wrecked his shoulder.

COLIN: Tragic, that.

JOHN: Yes. We could do with a good left-arm bowler in this County.

COLIN: He had his heart set on that as a career, didn't he?

JOHN: Yes. What is he now? Fire prevention officer, married to Marge and fat.

COLIN: I think she's very good for him, don't you?

JOHN: Yes, she's all right. I don't know how good he is for her, though. [*He lifts the phone off the hook to listen for a second*]

PAUL: [*wearily*] What are you doing?

JOHN: [*laughing*] He's shouting his head off at her still. . . [*He stays listening and pulls a face at what he hears*]

COLIN: [*moving to him*] John. . . excuse me. . . do you mind? . . . Thank you. . . [*He takes the phone from* JOHN]

JOHN: [*startled*] What are you doing?

COLIN: [*into phone*] Hallo. . . hallo. . . Marge. . . Gordon. . . Sorry if this is a private conversation. . . pardon me for butting in. . . Colin here. . . Hallo, Jumbo. . . Excuse me, Marge. . . Just wanted to say, get well soon. . . pecker up. . . I expect Marge'll be home to look after you shortly, won't you, Marge? You've got a real treasure there, Gordon, a real treasure. . . God bless. . . won't talk any longer. . . Back to nurse Marge. . . Bye-bye. . . bye-bye, Gordon. . . [*He replaces the receiver*] That's nice. Managed a quick word, anyway. . . [*He smiles*]

PAUL: Oh, my God. . .

COLIN: How was he?

COLIN: Between you and me, I don't think he's too good. Marge sounded very cut up. Very cut up indeed.

[EVELYN *pushes the baby in* ]

JOHN: You bringing him in?

EVELYN: It's raining out there.

JOHN: Rain won't hurt him. Good for him. Make him grow.

EVELYN: He's nearly off again, anyway.

COLIN: May I have a look?

EVELYN: Yes. Just don't make daft noises at him. He doesn't like it.

COLIN: [*looking into pram*] Oh, great. He's so — small, isn't he?

EVELYN: Yes. Look at him, little devil, he's really fighting to stay awake.

COLIN: He's just great. The feeling you both must have, looking at him. . . must make you so. . .

EVELYN: [*cutting him short*] He's not bad. [*She rocks the pram. To* JOHN] We're going in a minute.

JOHN: Right.

COLIN: Yes, as soon as Marge comes down, I think I must. . .

JOHN: You all right, Paul?

PAUL: Fine. I must go up in a minute. I've got a lot of work to do, upstairs.

[MARGE *comes in, blowing her nose*]

MARGE: She's nearly off to sleep. I think she'll be all right when she's rested.

COLIN: Ah, yes. Sleep. A great healer. [*Confidentially*] Hope you didn't mind me butting in on the phone call just now, Marge?

MARGE: That's all right, Colin.

COLIN: Thought as he was on, I'd have a quick word with him.

MARGE: Lovely.

COLIN: He sounded a bit. . . er. . . under the weather. . .

MARGE: He's all right.

COLIN: Not his usual cheery old self.

MARGE: He's all right.

COLIN: Sounded as if he could do with a bit of jollying up. . .

MARGE: [*more sharply*] He'll be perfectly all right the minute I get back to him, don't worry, Colin.

COLIN: Ah, well. That's good.

[PAUL *sits with his eyes closed*]

[EVELYN *rocks the pram*]

[JOHN *gazes out of the window*]

[MARGE *stands wrapped in thought*]

Well. [*Pause*] I suppose I ought to be. . . Much as I'd like to. . . Making tracks and all that.

[*Pause*]

COLIN: Yes.

   [*Pause* ]

   [*looking at his watch*] Good heavens, yes. Look at the. . . It's
a long drive. I'd better make a start. [*Pause* ] Goodbye, all. . .

MARGE: [*coming out of her reverie*] Oh, Colin, are you off?

COLIN: Yes, I think I'd. . .

MARGE: Yes. Don't forget your photographs. . .

COLIN: Oh, no. I wouldn't do that. Not likely to do that.

MARGE: I hope you — manage all right, Colin.

COLIN: Me? Oh, I'm fine. I've always fallen on my feet, you
know. . . I've still got a good job — health and strength — and
lately, I think I've found a few good friends over there as well.
Carol's parents, to name but two. I'm always round with them
these days. You know, talking over old times and things. And
if I really get a bit depressed, out come the old albums. It's a
pity you didn't meet her, Marge. You'd have got on like a
house on fire.

MARGE: Yes, I'm sure.

COLIN: Well. Goodbye, Evelyn. Been a great pleasure meeting
you.

EVELYN: Bye.

JOHN: Cheerio, old Col. See you.

COLIN: You bet. Come over and see me.

JOHN: Might just do that. When I get the new car. Have a few —
[*Drinking gesture*] . . . together.

COLIN: Any time, Paul.

PAUL: Bye, Colin. Take care.

COLIN: And you. Say goodbye to Di, will you.

PAUL: Oh, sure. She'll be sorry she missed you.

COLIN: Bye-bye, Marge. No, it's all right, I'll see myself out.
[*Hesitating*] Er — I really appreciated you all inviting me
over here, this afternoon, you know and, well. . . thanks a lot.
You've really been great. All of you.

MARGE: Goodbye, Colin. And I hope perhaps, you know — later
on — you'll. . . once you've got over. . . I mean, I know it will
be difficult for a time for you to forget about Carol. . .

COLIN: Forget her? Oh come on, Marge. You know me better
than that, don't you? [*smiling round*] Bye-bye, all.

   [COLIN *goes out. A pause*]

MARGE: He's a nice boy, isn't he?

JOHN: Good old Col. Just the same.

MARGE: Paul, I'll have to go home to Gordon in a minute.

PAUL: Yes. Fine, Marge. Fine. You do that. . .

MARGE: But if by any chance you need help – with her – you know my number. As soon as I've cleaned Gordon up, I can easily look back.

PAUL: No, we'll manage, Marge, honestly.

MARGE: She should sleep now.

[EVELYN *starts singing, still rocking the pram*]

[PAUL *sits and starts to doze*]

JOHN: [*who has sat down for once*] I'll cut that carpet up for the car tomorrow.

MARGE: [*sitting down herself for a moment*] I don't think I'd better leave Gordon on his own again when he's ill, you know. He doesn't like it. He prefers it if I'm there. [*Slight pause*] Oh, it's terrible. I haven't got the energy to move now. Once I've sat down. . . I think those shoes will go with that coat. I hope so. . . oh, look at us. Honestly. All drooping about like wet weekends. . . still, why shouldn't we, I say. There are worse ways of spending the time. Than sitting peacefully with your friends. Nice to sit with your friends now and again. Nice. . .

[EVELYN *continues her singing*]

[MARGE *daydreams*]

[PAUL *starts to snore loudly*]

[JOHN *jiggles*]

CURTAIN

# BEDROOM FARCE

## CHARACTERS

Ernest

Delia

Nick

Jan

Malcolm

Kate

Trevor

Susannah

The play was first produced at the Library Theatre, Scarborough, on June 16th 1975 and subsequently, under the direction of Peter Hall, at the National Theatre, London, on March 14th 1977.

# ACT ONE

*Saturday evening 7 p.m.*
*Three bedrooms:*
*The first, E R N E S T and D E L I A's.*
*Large Victorian bedroom in need of redecoration. The furniture including a double bed, bedside tables, dressing table etc. are all sturdy, unremarkable family pieces. A phone by the bed. Two doors, one to the landing and the rest of the house, the other to a bathroom.*
*The second bedroom is M A L C O L M and K A T E's.*
*This is smaller, probably a front bedroom in a terrace house which they are in the process of converting. It is sparsely furnished. A brand new bed, unmade, being the centrepiece. In addition an odd easy chair. One of the walls has been repapered, the rest are stripped. In one corner, a number of cardboard packages, unopened. A phone by the bed. One door leading to the landing, the bathroom and the rest of the house.*
*The third bedroom is N I C K and J A N's.*
*This is furnished in a more trendy style with a brass bedstead and some interesting antique stuff. Rugs on the floor. A phone by the bed. One door leading off to the bathroom and everywhere else. The action will alternate between these three areas.*
*At the start, N I C K is already in bed, lying looking sorry for himself.*
*M A L C O L M and K A T E's bedroom is empty.*
*D E L I A sits in her bedroom at her dressing table mirror. She is going out. She is in her slip and finishing her make-up. An elaborate operation. E R N E S T wanders in. Birdlike, bumbling, nearly sixty. He is in evening dress. He stares at D E L I A. They are obviously going to be late but E R N E S T has learnt that impatience gets him nowhere.*

E R N E S T : Have you got much further to go?
D E L I A : [*without turning*] Not long now.
E R N E S T : Good. Good show. [*he walks out humming restlessly*] No, that is definitely a damp patch, you know.
D E L I A : Mmm?

ERNEST: A damp patch. Definitely. It's getting in from somewhere. I've just been standing on the spare bed in there feeling
the ceiling. The verdict is, very very damp.

DELIA: Oh dear.

ERNEST: Yes. Which only goes to confirm my suspicion
that those chaps we had crawling about the roof for six
months didn't know their job. [*he leans out of the window
backwards*]

DELIA: What are you doing?

ERNEST: I'm trying to catch a glimpse of the re-pointing. It's
seeping in from somewhere.

DELIA: You'll fall out in a minute.

ERNEST: No. You can't see a thing. That gutterwork's obscuring
the whole. . . Good lord. That needs a spot of attention. It's
hanging off at one end. Good lord.

DELIA: Darling, you're in my light.

ERNEST: There's a whole chunk of guttering here hanging on
by a screw. [*he comes in*] Hadn't noticed that before.

DELIA: Oh, did I tell you. Susannah phoned this afternoon.

ERNEST: [*thoughtful*] Did he? Did he indeed.

DELIA: No, not he. Susannah.

ERNEST: Who?

DELIA: Susannah.

ERNEST: Oh, Susannah. Jolly good. Very worrying that guttering, you know. One light to medium monsoon, we'll have a
water-fall in the dining room.

DELIA: She sounded very agitated.

ERNEST: Oh yes.

DELIA: Things are not good between her and Trevor.

ERNEST: Ah. It's twenty past, you know.

DELIA: All right, all right.

ERNEST: We're booked for eight o'clock.

DELIA: They'll hold the table.

ERNEST: They might not.

DELIA: Of course they will.

ERNEST: You never know. Not these days.

DELIA: They'll hold the table for us. We're regulars. We go
there every year.

ERNEST: Oh, well. It's your anniversary.

DELIA: And yours.

ERNEST: True, true. I think I should have given these shoes another polish.

DELIA: Well, go and do it.

ERNEST: No, it doesn't matter. Nobody'll notice.

DELIA: It would appear that things between Susannah and Trevor are coming to a head.

ERNEST: Ah.

DELIA: He was always a difficult boy. I sometimes think if you hadn't ignored him quite as much —

ERNEST: I did?

DELIA: Of course you did. You hardly said a word to him all the time he was growing up.

ERNEST: I seem to remember chatting away to him for hours.

DELIA: Well. Chatting. I meant conversation. Conversation about important things. A father should converse with his son. About things that matter deeply.

ERNEST: Doesn't really leave them much to talk about then, does it?

DELIA: And that if I may say so is typical. No. Let's admit it. We weren't good parents. You did nothing and I tried to make up for it, and that's why he's like he is today. I mean if he'd had a stable childhood, he'd never have completely lost his sense of proportion and married Susannah. I mean, I sometimes feel on the rare occasions one does see them together that she's not really — awful thing to say but — not really resilient enough for Trevor. He wants somebody more phlegmatic. That Jan girl for instance would have been ideal. Do you remember her?

ERNEST: Jan? Jan? Jan?

DELIA: Nice little thing. Beautifully normal. She came to tea, do you remember? You got on very well with her.

ERNEST: Oh yes. She was jolly, wasn't she? She was very interested in my stamps. What happened to her?

DELIA: Oh, she married — someone else, I think. She still writes occasionally.

ERNEST: I must say I preferred her to Susannah. Never really hit it off with her, I'm afraid.

DELIA: Well, she's a very complex sort of girl, isn't she? Hasn't really made up her mind. About herself. I mean, I think a woman sooner or later has simply got to make up her mind

about herself. I mean, even if she's someone like Carolyn –
you know, Mrs Brightman's Carolyn – who looks at herself
and says, right, I'm a lump I'm going to be a lump but then
at least everyone can accept her as a lump. So much simpler.

ERNEST: I think he should have married this other one.

DELIA: Jan? I don't think she was that keen.

ERNEST: She was altogether much jollier.

DELIA: Well, we're saddled with Susannah as a daughter-in-law
– at least temporarily. We'd better make the best of it – I
think I've put these eyes on crooked – we'd better make the
best of it.

ERNEST: It's their bed. They can lie on it.

DELIA: Yes. I think that's one of the problems.

ERNEST: Eh?

DELIA: B – E – D.

ERNEST: B – E – D? Bed?

DELIA: Enough said.

ERNEST: Good lord. How do you know?

DELIA: One reads between the lines, darling. I've had a little
look around their house. You can tell a great deal from people's
bedrooms.

ERNEST: Can you? Good heavens. [*he looks about*]

DELIA: If you know what to look for. Now then. Do I wear
what I wore when I went to the Reynolds or shall I wear the
stripy thing that you loathe.

ERNEST: I'd wear the Reynolds thing.

DELIA: Or there's the little grey.

ERNEST: Oh.

DELIA: Or the blue.

ERNEST: Ah.

DELIA: No, that isn't pressed. You decide, darling. Stripy or the
other one.

ERNEST: Er...

DELIA: Or the grey.

ERNEST: Er...

DELIA: Right I've decided, it's the other one. Good. Now, in
the spare wardrobe in Trevor's old room on the top shelf,
there's a little black handbag. Could you fetch me that?...
[DELIA *goes into the bathroom*]

ERNEST: Little black handbag, right. [*looking round*] I don't think you can tell very much from this bedroom. Except the roof's leaking from somewhere.

*[As he goes out, cross fade to* NICK *and* JAN's *room.* JAN *comes in in her coat. As soon as* NICK, *lying in bed, sees her he groans ]*

JAN: Are you all right?

[NICK *moans*]

JAN: Is it painful?

NICK: Amazingly enough, yes.

JAN: Are you comfy?

NICK: Not really.

JAN: Shall I prop you up a bit?

NICK: No, no. I'll just – aaaah!

JAN: You might want to read.

NICK: How can I read? I can't do anything.

JAN: Well, your book's there.

NICK: Oh, it's maddening. A maddening thing to happen. Why this month. I mean, I'm simply bending down pulling on my socks and bang. It's totally unfair. Why me? I mean, I'm the last person in the world who should be stuck in bed.

JAN: Yes. . .

NICK: I'm a naturally active person, aren't I? Aren't I? I have to be on the go. I need to be on the go. I'm going to go mad lying here, you know. I'm going to go off my head, I know it. I've only been here since this morning and I'm dying of boredom. How long did that man say?

JAN: Well, a few days.

NICK: We know what that means. I'll be here for Christmas.

JAN: Don't be stupid.

NICK: That doctor obviously didn't know what he was talking about. Bad luck, old chap – a bottle of pills and he's off.

JAN: They're supposed to relax you.

NICK: All they've done is to give me double vision. Why me? I've got so many things I should be – aaah – should be doing. Did you get hold of the office and tell them about the meeting?

JAN: Yes, it's cancelled.

NICK: And you sent the telegram to Glasgow?

JAN: Yes and I spoke to someone at Shelgrove and told them not to expect you. And I cabled America and asked them to ring this number when convenient. O.K.?

NICK: Right

JAN: I don't know why you pay a secretary. I won't be long.

NICK: Where are you going?

JAN: I told you. Malcolm and Kate's housewarming.

NICK: Tonight?

JAN: They did invite us both. I phoned and told them what had happened. I said I'd just look in for ten minutes.

NICK: What about me?

JAN: I won't be long.

NICK: You don't want to go to Malcolm and Kate's, do you?

JAN: I said I would.

NICK: What? And sit and look at love's young dream all evening.

JAN: There'll be lots of others.

NICK: Then they won't miss you, will they?

JAN: I said I would.

NICK: Well, phone them up.

JAN: No, I want to.

NICK: Why?

JAN: Well.

NICK: What on earth for?

JAN: Well. If you must know – it's simply that – well. Simply. Susannah is going to be there.

NICK: Susannah.

JAN: Yes. I wanted to see her. It's a good opportunity and I thought I might. . .

NICK: And Trevor.

JAN: Yes. Possibly.

NICK: I should think it's highly probable. Seeing as they're married. Unless he's crippled as well.

JAN: Anyway. That's why.

NICK: And if it's a choice between Trevor and me, it's going to be Trevor.

JAN: No.

NICK: Yes.

JAN: Not at all.

NICK: Yes.

JAN: It's just I heard that – well – there's some awful trouble between them. I mean that silly bitch Susannah, she's got no idea at all. She hasn't a clue about Trevor. I know Trevor's impossible sometimes but I think I do know him probably better than anyone. . .

NICK: Oh yes, yes.

JAN: I think if I talk to them before they do something they'll regret. . .

NICK: Like her shooting him.

JAN: Don't be silly.

NICK: Look, he's a very selfish, very spoilt, self-pitying, self-obsessed. . .

JAN: I know, I know.

NICK: All right.

JAN: Just for ten minutes. I promise. Your book's there. [*she moves to the door*]

NICK: Oy!

JAN: Mm?

NICK: I take it you still prefer me?

JAN: I think so. Mostly.

[*She kisses him*]

NICK: [*wriggling*] Oh.

JAN: What is it?

NICK: Ah.

JAN: What?

NICK: This damn bed is full of crumbs.

JAN: Crumbs?

NICK: From those biscuits. I told you not to give me biscuits.

JAN: [*pulling back the side covers and attempting to brush the undersheet beneath him*] O.K., just a minute, just a minute.

NICK: Careful! Careful! CAREFUL!

JAN: All right, all right, ALL RIGHT! God, how do they do it? How do these nurses do it? They are saints. I'd go stark raving mad and strangle all the patients, I know I would.

NICK: Aaaah!

JAN: Nick, will you kindly lie still.

NICK: Ah!

JAN: There we are. Is that better?

NICK: Aah!

JAN: And stop that din. It's not that serious.

NICK: Hah!

JAN: It is not a disc. Nothing is broken. It is just a little tiny muscle.

NICK: It is not a little tiny muscle. It is the main motor

muscle that runs right up the spinal cord. . .

JAN: All right. Too bad. Sorry and all that. Won't be long. See you later.

NICK: Thanks for the sympathy.

JAN: Well, I'm afraid I have the misfortune to be born with only that much sympathy and that's your lot. You've had it all. Bye bye.

NICK: Give my love to Trevor. . . .

JAN: Oh God. [*she goes out*]

NICK: [*shouting after her, propping himself up one elbow*] Tell him with me ill in bed, the field's clear for him to — aaah! Oh blimey O'Riley. Why me? Why me?

[*Cross fade to* MALCOLM *and* KATE's ]

[MALCOLM *comes in with one of* KATE's *shoes*]

[*He looks for somewhere to hide it* ]

[*He tucks it down the bottom of the unmade bed*]

[MALCOLM *sits in the chair innocently*]

KATE: [*off, then entering*] Malcolm! Malcolm. . . I know you're up here, Malcolm. Come on, Malcolm, what have you done with it?

MALCOLM: What?

KATE: My other shoe. What have you done with it?

MALCOLM: I don't know.

KATE: Oh really. . . [*seeing the cardboard packages*] What's all this?

MALCOLM: Ah-ha.

KATE: Where did they come from?

MALCOLM: I got it today.

KATE: I didn't see you.

MALCOLM: You don't see everything.

KATE: What is it?

MALCOLM: A little surprise. Nothing much. A little house-warming present from me to you.

KATE: Whatever is it?

MALCOLM: Later, later. When they've all gone.

KATE: Whatever is it? It's an ironing board.

MALCOLM: An ironing board. . .

KATE: What have you done with my shoe?

MALCOLM: Shoe? Shoe?

KATE: [*giving up*] Oh. . .

MALCOLM: It's going to be a really good party tonight, I can feel it.

KATE: I hope so. Oooh. Something to confess.

MALCOLM: What?

KATE: You know that shelf you put up in the kitchen.

MALCOLM: Yes.

KATE: It's fallen down again.

MALCOLM: Again —

KATE: I was ever so careful.

MALCOLM: I told you it wasn't designed for great heavy weights.

KATE: I only stood the cruet on it. I deliberately didn't go near it in case it fell down. Oh, I'm terribly hot. Have I got time for a bath?

MALCOLM: Just about.

KATE: Now, the food's all going on the big table. Then I've cleared the sideboard for the drinks. And they can put their coats here on the bed — oh look, I haven't made the bed. Where is it then?

MALCOLM: What?

KATE: You know what. My blooming shoe.

[MALCOLM *whistles to himself and starts to take off his boots*.]

[*starting on the bed*] You going to wear your nice shirt?

MALCOLM: Which one?

KATE: Your nice one.

MALCOLM: All right.

KATE: You look nice in that.

MALCOLM: Yes, it's going to be a really good party. Who've we got coming then?

KATE: Oh — everyone — I asked everyone. Except Nick, he can't come.

MALCOLM: Nick?

KATE: Yes, he hurt his back, poor thing.

MALCOLM: Ah.

KATE: Jan phoned me. He hurt it this morning. She's coming though.

MALCOLM: Good. Good. [*he takes off his sweater*]

KATE: And who else is there. Ken and Margaret, of course. And John and Dorothy and Wilfrid and Gareth and Gwen and Mike

and Dave and Carole and Dick and Lottie, Gordon and Marge,
of course and — er — Susannah and Trevor. . .

MALCOLM: Trevor?

KATE: Yes.

MALCOLM: And Susannah?

KATE: Yes.

MALCOLM: Oh dear, oh dear.

KATE: Well, I had to. They've had us round twice.

MALCOLM: I see. Well, that's that, isn't it?

KATE: Well.

MALCOLM: That's that. Where is it then?

KATE: What?

MALCOLM: The shirt.

KATE: Oh, it's in the airing cupboard. I washed it.

MALCOLM: Right.

KATE: Could you turn my bath on?

MALCOLM: Right.

   [MALCOLM *goes out*]

   [KATE *finds her shoe in the bed* ]

KATE: Oh really.

   [*She eyes the present* ]

   [*She sees* MALCOLM's *boots* ]

   [*She snatches them up and stuffs them into one of the pillow
cases* ]

   [MALCOLM *returns* ]

   Very funny.

MALCOLM: Eh?

KATE: My shoe. Very funny.

MALCOLM: Ah.

KATE: And I don't want any more foreign bodies in my side of
the bed tonight, thank you very much.

MALCOLM: Foreign bodies?

KATE: You know. Hair brushes and all my bottles and jars —
you know.

MALCOLM: Wasn't me.

KATE: You and your jokes. Is my bath running?

MALCOLM: Yes. Now look, you say Jan's coming and
Susannah's coming and Trevor's coming?

KATE: Yes.

MALCOLM: That's marvellous. If Trevor and Susannah don't

have a fight, then it's ten to one Jan and Susannah will have a fight. . .

JAN: I hope not.

MALCOLM: Well, the first sign of any trouble they're all out, I'm telling you. This is going to be a good party. I'm not having any of that. [*he has put on his shirt*]

KATE: Has that shrunk?

MALCOLM: I don't know, has it?

KATE: It looks as if it's shrunk. Or else you're getting fat. [*She goes out*]

MALCOLM: Fat? You cheeky thing. [*calling*] Hey, Blodge. Blodge.

KATE: [*off*] What?

MALCOLM: What have you done with my shoes?

KATE: [*off*] Ah-ha.

MALCOLM: What have you done with them? What's she done with them?
   [*He sees her shoes*]
   [*He hides them in the bed*]

KATE: [*off*] Ooooh!

MALCOLM: What?

KATE: [*returning partially undressed*] Did you put that brush in my bath?

MALCOLM: Brush? What brush?

KATE: Well, you shouldn't do that. It's very unhygienic. Honestly. . . [*she goes*]
   [MALCOLM *laughs*]
   [*Cross fade to* ERNEST *and* DELIA]
   [DELIA *comes in dressed to go*]
   [*She looks about her*]

DELIA: [*calling*] Ernest! Ernest!

ERNEST: [*off*] Coming.

DELIA: Where have you got to?

ERNEST: [*enters dusting himself down*] All ready to go, are you?

DELIA: Where on earth have you been?

ERNEST: I was just having a quick squint into the loft. Seeing if I could see any signs. Water's getting in from somewhere.

DELIA: You're filthy dirty.

ERNEST: Oh, that's all right. No one'll notice.

DELIA: I have. Now, don't go and overtip tonight, will you.

ERNEST: Overtip?

DELIA: You did last year. These waiters don't like it.

ERNEST: I've never heard them object.

DELIA: I read somewhere it was just as bad form to overtip as it was to undertip. If not worse.

ERNEST: The bloke last year was pleased enough to take it.

DELIA: The Spanish one.

ERNEST: Was he Spanish? Smiling all over his face.

DELIA: You obviously don't know the Spanish. That expression was little short of scornful. Desperately embarrassing. Right, we're off. [*she goes*]

ERNEST: [*following*] I thought he was an Italian, anyway.

[*Cross fade to* NICK ]

[NICK *lying in bed has evidently been reading. He has laid down his book on the eiderdown to rest. He now pulls up the eiderdown round him a little and in doing so causes his book to fall off the end of the bed* ]

NICK: Oh no, oh no, oh no. . .

[*Cross fade to* MALCOLM *and* KATE]

[*The room is empty. From off a scream from* KATE. *She rushes in with just a towel round her pursued by* MALCOLM *now shirtless again and brandishing an aerosol can of shaving soap* ]

KATE: Now, Malcolm, stop it, do you hear, stop it.

MALCOLM: You started it.

KATE: I did not start it.

MALCOLM: You splashed me.

KATE: All right, I'm sorry.

MALCOLM: Are you sorry?

KATE: Yes, I said I'm sorry.

MALCOLM: Very sorry?

KATE: Yes, very sorry. Now, let me get dressed, Malcolm, please.

MALCOLM: All right. Splash me again, you're in trouble.

KATE: I'm getting dressed in the bathroom, I don't trust you.

[*She picks up some clothes and the aerosol can* ]

MALCOLM: Where have you hidden my shoes? [*he looks under the bed* ]

[KATE *sprays his back with the shaving soap. And darts away with a shriek* ]

MALCOLM: Right, Blodge, you going to get it, Blodge.

KATE: [*distant*] I've locked the door. You can't come in.

MALCOLM: I can wait, Blodge, I can wait. I'll get you. I'll get you.

[*The doorbell rings* ]

Somebody's arrived.

KATE: [*distant*] What?

MALCOLM: Somebody's here. That was the doorbell. [*he has wiped off the soap and has slipped on his shirt* ]

KATE: Oh no, it wasn't.

MALCOLM: [*slipping on some other shoes*] Want a bet? It was the doorbell.

KATE: [*distant*] Really? Well, you answer it then.

MALCOLM: I will.

KATE: I don't believe you, Malcolm Newton.

[MALCOLM *goes off downstairs* ]

[*off*] I don't believe you. [*she comes in still with the towel round her, the soap spray in her hand*] Where are you hiding? Malcolm? Malcolm? I can see you, Malcolm. Malcolm, I don't believe you. . .

[*Voices are heard coming upstairs*]

Oh, my God.

[*She runs to the door* ]

[*It is too late* ]

[*She looks round for somewhere* ]

[*As a last resort, she pulls back the covers and slides into bed* ]

KATE: Ooh!

[*She pulls out her shoes from the bed, holds them up then tucks them back under* ]

[TREVOR *enters* ]

MALCOLM: [*off*] Coats just on the bed, Trevor. I'll fix you a drink.

TREVOR: Right, thanks. [*seeing* KATE] Ah.

KATE: Hallo, Trevor.

TREVOR: Oh, hallo there.

KATE: Hallo.

TREVOR: Are you ill?

KATE: No.

TREVOR: Ah.

KATE: I'm just getting changed.

TREVOR: Ah. Er — Malcolm said it would be all right to put
    my coat on the bed. Is that O.K. with you?

KATE: Fine.

TREVOR: Won't make you too hot, will it?

KATE: Uh?

TREVOR: I mean with all the coats on top of you. Could get a
    bit hot by the middle of the evening.

KATE: Oh no. I'm not staying here. I'm just. . .resting.

TREVOR: Oh, great.

KATE: How are you?

TREVOR: Fine.

KATE: Good. Susannah?

TREVOR: She's all right. I think.

KATE: She downstairs, is she?

TREVOR: Not that I noticed.

KATE: Oh. You didn't come with her then?

TREVOR: No. We were travelling separately.

KATE: Oh. Well. . .

TREVOR: Yes. [*he laughs to himself somewhat bitterly*]
    [MALCOLM *enters*]

MALCOLM: Are you coming down for this drink, Trevor, or are
    you. . . [*seeing* KATE] Oh.

KATE: Hallo.

MALCOLM: What are you doing?

KATE: Nothing.

MALCOLM: Oh. Right. [*handing* TREVOR *his drink*] Here
    you are then.

TREVOR: Thanks.

MALCOLM: Cheers then.

TREVOR: Cheers.

MALCOLM: [*to* KATE] You all right?

KATE: Fine.

MALCOLM: Well, what do you think of our place then, Trevor?
    Our new little love-nest. What's the verdict? Not bad is it? Not
    bad. Quite nice.

TREVOR: Yes.

MALCOLM: Mind you, we've got a lot to do. Masses. This room
    for one. I mean, it's not properly furnished or anything. Still,
    we'll get it together. Give us time. Not bad though, is it?

TREVOR: No.

MALCOLM: And how are you and – er – well dare I ask – how are you and Susannah these days?

[TREVOR *laughs*]

Oh, all right. I've said enough. Said enough.

TREVOR: We're still trying to – work something – out. You know.

MALCOLM: Good.

KATE: Good.

MALCOLM: Good.

TREVOR: I don't know how successful we're being but we're trying. You know. . .

MALCOLM: Yes – well. . .

TREVOR: It's a totally draining experience though. Once you get yourself committed to a – commitment – like Susannah and I have commited ourselves to, you get a situation of a totally outgoing – non – egotistical – giving – ness. . . a total submerging, you know.

MALCOLM: Yes, yes.

KATE: Yes.

TREVOR: You feel yourself – being pushed under. . .

MALCOLM: Yes.

TREVOR: As if on top of you were a great. . . a great. . .[*he tails off*]

KATE: Yes.

MALCOLM: Yes.

KATE: Yes.

[*A long pause* ]

[MALCOLM *and* KATE *wait for* TREVOR ]

TREVOR: [*at length*] Heavy weight. God.

[*A silence*]

KATE: [*very quietly*] Malcolm, I wonder if you could possibly get my things out of the bathroom.

MALCOLM: Your what?

KATE: My things.

MALCOLM: Your –? Oh, I see. That's what you're up to. Have you got nothing on under there?

KATE: [*embarrassed*] No.

MALCOLM: [*laughing*] Do you hear that, Trevor?

TREVOR: Eh?

MALCOLM: She's got nothing on under there.

TREVOR: No, no.

MALCOLM: Hey hey! Wait there, I'll. . .

[*Doorbell rings*]

Ah, somebody else. Hang on.

[MALCOLM *darts out*]

KATE: [*calling after him vainly*] Could you fetch my clothes before you. . . Trevor, I'm going to have to ask you in a minute if you'd mind. . . Trevor.

TREVOR: Sorry, Kath. I was miles away. I'm sorry. Kath, listen.

KATE: Kate, yes.

TREVOR: I was just thinking, what is the point of it all really. You and I. Take you and me. We start out in this world with the innocence of children. We start our lives like little children.

KATE: Well, we are.

TREVOR: Have you ever studied children at close range?

KATE: Oh yes. I like children.

TREVOR: I have. You have a close look at them sometime.

KATE: I have.

TREVOR: Really closely. And then look at yourself. You'll be appalled at what's happened to you, Kath. And this − this is the test. You try and think of three − I'm only asking for three − three good reasons why you shouldn't throw yourself out of that window here and now.

KATE: I haven't got any clothes on.

TREVOR: Three good reasons, eh.

KATE: Yes.

TREVOR: See what I mean?

KATE: Yes, I follow your reasoning.

TREVOR: You do?

KATE: Yes. I don't agree with it but I think I can follow it.

TREVOR: You either don't think things out at all or you're lucky, Kath. I'll give you the benefit of the doubt.

[MALCOLM *enters with a pile of coats*]

[*He also has* KATE'*s clothes*]

MALCOLM: Whole load of people. Mike, Dave, Graham and Anna, Gareth and Gwen, Bob and Terry. . . oh, Trevor.

TREVOR: Mm?

MALCOLM: Now listen, Susannah's arrived.

TREVOR: Oh.

MALCOLM: Now, there's a house rule tonight. No arguments

with your own wife. Anybody else's wife but not your own, all right?

TREVOR: I should tell her – not me.

MALCOLM: Now, Trevor, one word you're out.

TREVOR: I'll try, Malcolm, I'll try. [*he goes out*]

MALCOLM: I must say Susannah seems in good form. I opened the door to her, she burst into tears and ran straight into the bathroom. Oh well, press on. . . Hurry up and come down. They're all arriving.

KATE: I will. Are those my clothes?

MALCOLM: Oh yes – here – [*he throws them to her*]

KATE: At last. [*she snatches them gratefully*]

[MALCOLM *opens the door to leave* ]

MALCOLM: [*calling*] John. . . Brian. . . Dave. Don't hang them there. It wasn't designed to take any sort of weight. Bring them up here. Put them on the bed.

KATE: Oh. . . [*she dives under the bedclothes and starts to dress*]

[*Cross fade to* NICK ]

NICK: [*in extreme frustration*] Aaah – aaah – aaaaah!

[*He gets up on his elbows to see if he can see his book* ]

[*in pain*] Ah!

[NICK *rolls over on to his front. He slithers sideways out of bed and finally lands on the floor on all fours with a clump. He yells again. He begins laboriously to crawl round to the end of the bed to reach his book* ]

[*getting there*] Ah-ha. Gotcha.

[*He tries to get back on to the bed. He can't make it. He brings the eiderdown slithering down on top of him* ]

Oh no. Jan. Help. Help.

[*He lies on the floor helplessly* ]

NICK: Why me? Why me?

[*Cross fade to* MALCOLM *and* KATE's. MALCOLM *enters with more coats which he throws on the bed* ]

MALCOLM: [*calling behind him*] Just along the passage there, Joan. It's the blue door.

[*As he turns to go, he passes* SUSANNAH *coming in* ]

SUSANNAH: I didn't realise there were going to be so many people.

MALCOLM: It's a party, my darling, what do you expect.

SUSANNAH: Yes.

[MALCOLM *goes*]

[*taking a deep breath*] I am confident in myself. I have confidence in myself. I am not unattractive. I am attractive. People still find me attractive. I am not afraid of people. People are not frightening. There is nothing to be frightened of.

[*During this,* KATE'S *head has popped up from under the sheets. She gapes at* SUSANNAH *in wonderment,* SUSANNAH *sees her. She jumps very nervously*]

KATE: Hallo. Sorry. I didn't mean to startle you.

SUSANNAH: I was just doing my — exercises. I do them whenever I'm alone. Or when I feel alone. They help.

KATE: Oh yes.

SUSANNAH: Trevor's here, I suppose?

KATE: Yes, yes.

SUSANNAH: He hasn't said hallo to me, I notice. No doubt he's better things to occupy him.

KATE: Well. . .

SUSANNAH: I see that woman's here.

KATE: Who's that?

SUSANNAH: Whatever her name is. Jan.

KATE: Oh, Jan. Yes. Poor old Nick's in bed. He's ill.

SUSANNAH: Oh. Is he? How lucky for her.

KATE: Excuse me. I must pop down. See things are all right.

SUSANNAH: Kate.

KATE: Yes.

SUSANNAH: Just a moment.

KATE: Yes.

SUSANNAH: Tell me something. Do you and Malcolm still have. . . how are you and Malcolm?

KATE: Oh, very well.

SUSANNAH: Truly?

KATE: Yes.

SUSANNAH: You can be honest, you know.

KATE: Yes. Well. We have a bit of a laugh. You know.

[*Doorbell rings*]

KATE: Oh, there's the. . .

SUSANNAH: I don't know if you know it but things for Trevor and me have gone totally wrong.

KATE: Yes, I heard a rumour.

SUSANNAH: I'm sure everyone's heard a rumour. We're neither of us very good at − conventional cover-ups. Is it still exciting for you?

KATE: What?

SUSANNAH: God, Trevor used to excite me. I was so excited by that man. Do you know what it feels like to be really excited?

KATE: Yes, yes, I think so.

SUSANNAH: When we weren't actually physically here in the bed. . . you know, making love − I felt empty − utterly incomplete.

KATE: Yes, it is nice sometimes, isn't it. . .

SUSANNAH: And now. Now, it's a desert. We hardly touch, you know.

KATE: Oh.

SUSANNAH: I think I actually revolt him.

KATE: Oh, surely not.

SUSANNAH: I sometimes feel that. Suddenly I've lost all my identity. Some mornings, who am I, I say. Who am I? And I don't know. I terrify myself. [*leaning towards* KATE *confidentially*] I saw this girl in the street the other day − about my age − a little bit younger. Do you know, I felt aroused by her. Attracted.

KATE: Oh.

SUSANNAH: Isn't that terrifying?

KATE: Yes.

SUSANNAH: Not that the feeling in itself is terrifying. I don't believe the feeling in itself is wrong but what it means is that all the things I used to think I knew about myself I know longer know.

KATE: [*who has been gently backing away*] Yes, yes.

SUSANNAH: I suppose you're beautifully uncomplicated, Kate.

KATE: Yes, I think so. Look, I must pop down. Do you want to. . .?

SUSANNAH: Could I just lie down for a moment?

KATE: Oh yes, yes, do. Move the coats.

SUSANNAH: Thanks. I'll pluck up courage in a minute. I'm sorry, I'm being absolutely useless.

KATE: No, no, no. Not at all. See you in a minute.

SUSANNAH: Yes.

[KATE *goes*]

180     BEDROOM FARCE

[SUSANNAH *clears a few coats from one side of the bed. Dramatically, she throws herself back on to the pillow. She strikes her head. She discovers the boots in the pillowcase. She looks puzzled. She lies back again* ]
[*Cross fade to* NICK]
NICK: [*in the same position as before*] Help...
[*Cross fade to* DELIA *and* ERNEST ]
[DELIA *and* ERNEST *return from their meal* ]
ERNEST: Well, that place has certainly gone off.
DELIA: You can say that again. Disastrous meal.
ERNEST: Three times as expensive too.
DELIA: Yes. I noticed you deliberately undertipped.
ERNEST: I didn't deliberately undertip. I just didn't bring enough money with me.
DELIA: That Spaniard looked even more miserable than last year.
ERNEST: Serve him right. Highway robbery.
DELIA: And that asparagus was out of a tin.
ERNEST: That wasn't bad.
DELIA: No, it was quite nice but it was out of a tin.
ERNEST: Oh yes, certainly out of a tin.
DELIA: I've never felt so over-dressed in my life. All those young men, none of them with a tie. And all those girls in slacks.
ERNEST: Well, they didn't bother me.
DELIA: It's all those labels sewn all over their bottoms and places I find so off-putting. I mean, nobody can seriously want to read people's bottoms. I mean, one girl had reams.
ERNEST: I think that's the thing, isn't it?
DELIA: When I was their age, I spent all my time making sure nobody could read my labels. I mean, we would rather have died than show a label.
ERNEST: We used to show the odd label, I think. On the inside of the jacket. Let the other chap see you had a tailor. Ah well, back to worrying about the roof, I suppose.
DELIA: I don't know about you but I'm still feeling distinctly peckish.
ERNEST: Are you? Yes, I am a bit.
DELIA: There's some sardines downstairs.
ERNEST: Sardines. That sounds attractive.
DELIA: On toast?
ERNEST: Rather. Let's go the whole hog if we're going to.

DELIA: Tell you what. . .

ERNEST: Um?

DELIA: Let's be really really wicked. . .

ERNEST: Eh?

DELIA: Let's eat them in bed.

ERNEST: In bed?

DELIA: Sardines on toast in bed, do you remember?

ERNEST: Good lord, yes. You've got a memory. Sardines on toast in bed, yes.

DELIA: I was expecting Trevor. . .

ERNEST: That's right. Are you sure it wasn't baked beans?

DELIA: No, not baked beans. Sardines.

ERNEST: Yes, quite right. Sardines. All right, we'll go one better. I'll go and hot them up while you get into your jim-jams.

DELIA: Oh, all right.

ERNEST: No sooner said. . .

DELIA: What fun.

ERNEST: Off you go.

[DELIA *goes into the bathroom* ]

[ERNEST *takes his pyjamas from under his pillow and goes off the other way* ]

[*Cross fade to* MALCOLM *and* KATE'*s*]

[SUSANNAH *still on the bed* ]

[KATE *ushers in* TREVOR]

KATE: She's in here, Trevor, having a lie down. Here he is, Susannah. Found him for you.

[KATE *goes out* ]

[TREVOR *wanders to the window* ]

[SUSANNAH *doesn't move*]

TREVOR: Tired?

SUSANNAH: No.

TREVOR: If you're tired, you shouldn't have come.

SUSANNAH: If I listened to you I wouldn't go anywhere at all. Mind you, you'd prefer that I'm sure. [*pause*] You don't have to stay up here with me, you know. I'm very used to being on my own. And I'm sure there's lots of people down there you'd rather be talking to.

TREVOR: I came up to see if you were all right.

SUSANNAH: You came up because Kate told you to come up. You'd never have come near me all evening if you could possibly have avoided it.

TREVOR: Look, don't get worked up. What are you getting worked up about?

SUSANNAH: Because I've every reason to be worked up.

TREVOR: Quieten down.

[*Pause* ]

SUSANNAH: You're a fine one to talk.

TREVOR: What?

SUSANNAH: If people had seen you earlier this evening. . .

TREVOR: Well —

SUSANNAH: Driving here and leaving me to walk.

TREVOR: I didn't think you were coming.

SUSANNAH: You knew I was coming.

TREVOR: I thought you wanted to stay behind.

SUSANNAH: You knew perfectly well I was coming.

TREVOR: Then why did you lock yourself in the bedroom?

SUSANNAH: Because I didn't want you in there.

TREVOR: What? In case I saw you changing? Good gracious. Husband sees his wife changing. I don't know what it is you're hiding but I bet it's fantastic.

SUSANNAH: You really are coarse, aren't you? Coarse and violent.

TREVOR: You're the one who makes me violent. I was a pacifist before I met you.

SUSANNAH: I wish I'd listened to that man.

TREVOR: What man?

SUSANNAH: That man we consulted just before we were married. The one who did the palm readings.

TREVOR: What, him?

SUSANNAH: He told me you were potentially a violent person. He was absolutely right. You've broken all my things. All my things I brought from home. All my china animals.

TREVOR: I told you, I'm sorry. I'll buy you some more.

SUSANNAH: I don't want some more. I wanted those.

TREVOR: I didn't mean to break them.

SUSANNAH: Then why did you throw a chair at them if you didn't mean to break them?

TREVOR: I don't know. I just felt like throwing a chair, that's all. No law against throwing chairs is there? It was my chair.

SUSANNAH: Potentially violent. That's what he said. That man.

TREVOR: He was an idiot.

SUSANNAH: No, he wasn't. My mother always went to him.

TREVOR: He told me I had a natural mechanical aptitude. I can't even put the plug on the Hoover. [*lying on the bed*] Well anyway, the one good thing about this party. . .

SUSANNAH: What?

TREVOR: At least we're both lying on the same bed.

SUSANNAH: [*lunging at him with a fist*] You rotten. . .

TREVOR: Ah, now who's violent.

SUSANNAH: [*hailing blows upon him*] You destroy everything, don't you? Everything. Everything.

TREVOR: [*laughing as he covers up from her blows*] What are you doing now?

SUSANNAH: [*furious*] Oh, I could so easily – oh – oh – oh.

TREVOR: Ow! Now, stop it. Stop it.

[*Eventually he pushes her off and she slips on to the floor* ]

SUSANNAH: Ow. You great bully.

TREVOR: Now, stop it. Before you're sorry.

SUSANNAH: [*getting up*] I'm not sorry. I am not sorry.

[*She snatches up the table lamp* ]

TREVOR: Now, put that down. Put it down. It's not yours.

SUSANNAH: Get away, get away, get away.

[TREVOR *approaches her* ]

[*She lunges at him with the lamp* ]

[*He grabs her wrist. He loses his balance. They both land on the bed, locked in mortal combat. Fighting for serious now, they roll on to the floor clawing and tugging at hair* ]

[MALCOLM *enters* ]

MALCOLM: Right. Who's for Cornish pasties. . . [*seeing them*] Oh no. Now, break it up. Break it up. That table lamp won't take that sort of treatment. [*putting the Cornish pasties on the floor*] Now, come on. Trevor! Susannah! Come on, break it up. [*he attempts to pull them apart*]

[KATE *appears in the doorway* ]

KATE: The plaster's coming down. What's happening?

MALCOLM: Come on, give us a hand. Give us a hand here. You pull her. I'll pull him. Pull, woman, pull.

KATE: I am pulling.

[TREVOR *and* SUSANNAH *are separated* ]

[*They stand panting, staring at each other* ]

[KATE *holding* SUSANNAH. MALCOLM *holding* TREVOR]

MALCOLM: Now, calm down. Do you hear? Calm down, both of you. Calm down. That's it.

[KATE *releases* SUSANNAH]

Now, both of you, take a deep breath.

[*With renewed energy,* SUSANNAH *suddenly clouts* TREVOR *with the table lamp*]

KATE: Stop it, stop it. Susannah...

MALCOLM: Stop that at once.

TREVOR: Ow.

[SUSANNAH *rushes out*]

TREVOR: Right — all right. [*wrenching free from* MALCOLM] Right.

[TREVOR *chases out after* SUSANNAH]

[*There are sounds of crashes downstairs*]

KATE: Malcolm, do something, please.

MALCOLM: Right. I am now personally going to drop him straight off our roof on to his head.

[MALCOLM *goes out*]

KATE: [*anxiously following him to the doorway and watching*] Oh now, Malcolm, don't you start. You must be the one to keep calm, Malcolm. Don't you start. [*picking up the Cornish pasties*] Malcolm... Malcolm... [*she hops up and down in agitation*]

[MALCOLM *returns half carrying* TREVOR]

MALCOLM: [*hurling him into the room*] Right, you get your coat. Do you hear? Get your coat. Then you're out. Straight out, mate. Come along, Kate.

[MALCOLM *goes out*]

KATE: Right. [*slipping a Cornish pasty on to the corner of the bed*] I'll leave you one of these.

[KATE *goes out*]

[TREVOR *sits on the bed recovering his breath. He feels his head*]

TREVOR: Oooh.

[JAN *comes in*]

[*She glances at him briefly*]

[*She looks for her coat, picking the others off the floor*]

JAN: I hope you're thoroughly ashamed of yourself. Both of

you. [*pause*] God, to think I nearly married you. What an escape.

TREVOR: [*muttering*] She started that one. She started that one.

JAN: I hoped that after I left you, you might have learnt to grow up. It appears that you're more retarded than ever. I mean, I realised that as long as I was there to look after you, make all your decisions you could never make, you hadn't a chance.

TREVOR: God, my head.

JAN: When are you going to grow up, Trevor?

[MALCOLM *enters* ]

MALCOLM: Excuse me, please. [*snatching up coats*] Gordon's coat. Marge's coat. Mike and Dave's coats. Gwen's coat. [*to* TREVOR] I told you, out.

[*He goes* ]

JAN: Well?

TREVOR: Just because I have an unfortunate marriage, I'm not necessarily an idiot. I try. I try all the time.

JAN: Like you did with me.

TREVOR: I particularly tried with you. I was always working flat out to make a go of it.

JAN: I don't think you noticed half the time if I was there or not.

TREVOR: I did.

JAN: Which is why I left. That didn't seem to bother you either.

TREVOR: What do you mean? I was annihilated. What are you talking about? I needed you.

JAN: Yes. I realised that from the way you came running after me.

TREVOR: I thought you'd be back.

JAN: No, thank you.

TREVOR: Never mind, eh. You're all right.

JAN: Perfectly.

TREVOR: Safe and secure with Nick.

JAN: That's right.

TREVOR: Some of us aren't so lucky.

[MALCOLM *enters* ]

MALCOLM: Excuse me. John's coat. Ken's coat. Margaret's coat. Dorothy's coat. [*to* TREVOR] This is your last warning. [*he goes out*]

JAN: You see? You can't go anywhere.

TREVOR: I'm a destroyer.

JAN: True.

TREVOR: Susannah said that. I destroy everything. She's right. I even destroyed you.

JAN: No, you didn't.

TREVOR: Destroyed you. So you go out and in desperation you marry the first man you happen to meet.

JAN: That's not very fair to Nick.

TREVOR: No, well. . .

JAN: I happen to love Nick.

TREVOR: Like you loved me.

JAN: No, not like I loved you. Like I love Nick. Quite different. Thank goodness. I can just about cope with Nick. I don't think I could ever have coped with you.

[MALCOLM *enters*]

MALCOLM: Bob's coat. Terry's coat. . . Anna's coat. Graham's coat. [*turning to* TREVOR, *livid*] You've ruined this party. You realise that, don't you?

TREVOR: Have I?

MALCOLM: You and that wife of yours. You've ruined fifty people's evening down there.

TREVOR: Well, I'm sorry.

MALCOLM: What's the point in being sorry now, mate.

JAN: Malcolm, don't.

MALCOLM: Him and his batty bloody wife. Sitting there in the middle of the front room crying her eyes out she is. If I had my way, I'd have you both locked up for good. . . They've all gone home, every one of them. . .

JAN: Malcolm.

MALCOLM: I'm sorry, Jan. Every one of them. I hope you're satisfied.

[MALCOLM *slams out*]

TREVOR: I might have improved if you'd stayed with me. I mean, with you, Jan, I. . . You see, Susannah I can't get near. She's incapable of giving. She won't give.

JAN: Perhaps you don't deserve anything.

TREVOR: Oh, what does that mean?

JAN: It means that before anyone's prepared to give anything, they want to make sure that the person they're giving it to is not going to hurl it back at your head the first time he chooses to lose his temper. You'll have to learn to treat people properly. There you are. End of lecture. Now I'm going home.

TREVOR: I treated you properly.

JAN: No, you didn't.

TREVOR: Not ever?

JAN: No.

TREVOR: Never at all?

JAN: Not really.

TREVOR: No?

JAN: No.

    *[He kisses her ]*
    *[She responds ]*
    *[KATE enters ]*

KATE: Oh. It's all right, Susannah, I'll bring it down. I'll bring it down to you.

    *[SUSANNAH enters ]*

SUSANNAH: That's all right.

    *[A swift glance at TREVOR and JAN, she picks up her coat and puts it on ]*

TREVOR: – er –

JAN: Susannah. . .

    *[SUSANNAH goes out ]*

JAN: Oh God.

KATE: Oh dear.

JAN: Look, can you go after her, Trevor, quickly. . . No, silly question. Oh well, I've really done it now. Sorry, Kate. I'll have to leave you with it. I'd better get back to Nick.

KATE: Right.

JAN: Goodnight all.

KATE: 'night. Malcolm's down there seeing them off.

JAN: OK.

    *[She goes ]*

KATE: Oh dear. *[she looks at TREVOR]* Oh dear. *[she goes to the window]* Oh dear, oh dear. Susannah's driving. I hope she gets home all right.

TREVOR: I don't know where I'm going to go.

KATE: How do you mean?

TREVOR: I can't go home.

KATE: Can't you?

TREVOR: How can I go home. . . .?

[*A pause* ]

KATE: We've got the little bedroom in the back. It isn't furnished or anything but we've got a camp bed.

TREVOR: You're a real friend, Kath.

KATE: Kate, yes.

TREVOR: Sorry about your party.

KATE: Oh well – get to bed early, won't we? I'll go and make the bed up for you. Look at this. Malcolm's surprise for me. In there. Malcolm's surprise.

TREVOR: Oh.

KATE: I don't know what it is.

[MALCOLM *enters* ]

MALCOLM: Right, that's it. End of party. All gone. [*seeing* TREVOR] Oh. You're still here, are you? All right. Now I warned you. . .

KATE: Malcolm. . .

MALCOLM: This your coat?

KATE: Malcolm. . .

MALCOLM: Eh?

KATE: I've said he could stay.

MALCOLM: Stay?

KATE: Just for the night.

MALCOLM: Who? Trevor? You're joking. Home.

KATE: He's got nowhere to go, Malcolm. He'll have to stay.

MALCOLM: He's got a home hasn't he? Let him go to it.

KATE:·He can't.

MALCOLM: All I know is he's not staying here. . .

KATE: I'm sorry, Malcolm, he'll have to stay.

MALCOLM: Not under my roof. Not after his behaviour tonight.

KATE: I'm sorry but he is.

MALCOLM: I'm sorry but he isn't.

KATE: Look, there's no point·in arguing.

MALCOLM: No. Quite. Out. . .

KATE: No, I'm sorry.

MALCOLM: Yes, I'm sorry too. I'm very sorry. He is not staying in this house and that is final.

KATE: Oh yes he is and that is also final.

[*Pause* ]

MALCOLM: All right. All right.

KATE: Where are you going?

MALCOLM: I'll tell you this much. If he is staying then I am definitely not staying.

KATE: Now, Malcolm.

MALCOLM: And that, my love, is that. I am not staying if he is staying so take your choice.

[MALCOLM *goes* ]

KATE: Oh.

[*A door slams* ]

Oh.

TREVOR: Sorry.

KATE: Oh.

TREVOR: Where's he gone?

KATE: [*snapping*] I don't know where he's gone, you damn fool.

TREVOR: Oh. Well.

KATE: He'll be back. I'll make up your bed.

TREVOR: Thanks. Er – Kath.

KATE: [*shouting*] Kate. My name is Kate.

TREVOR: Oh. Yes. Sorry.

KATE: Now. Sheets.

TREVOR: Look. I must get things cleared up before I go to bed.

KATE: How do you mean?

TREVOR: Well, with Jan and Nick, you see.

KATE: Jan and Nick?

TREVOR: Well, it was my fault and – word's bound to get back to Nick – and – he'll feel badly – and he might take it out on Jan – I wouldn't want that.

KATE: Who's going to tell Nick?

TREVOR: Well, Susannah for one.

KATE: Oh. Might she?

TREVOR: She might.

KATE: Oh. Are you going round tonight?

TREVOR: I'd better.

KATE: You could phone.

TREVOR: Oh no. Face to face stuff this. Has to be.

KATE: Don't forget your coat. [*she helps him into it*]

TREVOR: Don't wait up. I'll let myself in.

KATE: Oh yes, you'd better have a key – oh no, we haven't had another one cut yet. There's only Malcolm's.

TREVOR: Oh. Well, I won't be long.

KATE: It's all right, I'll wait up.

TREVOR: You're really great, Kate. Thanks.

KATE: That's all right. That coat's very big on you, isn't it?

TREVOR: I don't think it's mine.

KATE: Oh. Well, it's the only one left. You'd better take that one.

TREVOR: Yes. Right. See you later.

[*he goes*]

KATE: Bye. [*she sits on the bed looking worried*]

[*Cross fade to* ERNEST *and* DELIA's]

[DELIA, *in her dressing gown, sits in front of her mirror and starts to remove her make-up*]

[ERNEST *enters with two plates*]

ERNEST: Grub up.

DELIA: Just a minute.

ERNEST: It'll get cold.

DELIA: I've just got to take this off.

ERNEST: You can do that afterwards.

DELIA: I'm not getting into bed with my make-up on, darling. It may look beautiful in the films but they don't have to worry about laundry bills.

ERNEST: Oh well. Spot of bad news, anyway.

DELIA: Bad news?

ERNEST: Sardines were not in evidence. I had to settle for pilchards.

DELIA: Pilchards? Oh. . .

ERNEST: Don't you like pilchards?

DELIA: Well, not as much.

ERNEST: Similar. Both fish, anyway.

DELIA: Yes.

ERNEST: You had them in stock. I assumed you liked them.

DELIA: I don't necessarily like everything I buy. Those were just stores. For an emergency.

ERNEST: Ah, the old siege stores, eh?

DELIA: I bought a little of everything. I think there's even some tinned red cabbage and I certainly don't intend to eat that.

ERNEST: Oh well, I'll wolf the lot then, shall I?

DELIA: No, no, leave me a little.

ERNEST: Right. [*he slides into bed*] Aaah. Didn't put the blanket on, did we?

DELIA: Nor we did.

ERNEST: Ah. Woof. Down you go. [*he shoves his feet into the bed*] Ah, this is nice. What better way to end a day? Listening to the rain gushing through our roof. . .

DELIA: It's not raining surely?

ERNEST: Metaphorical. These aren't bad at all. You know, I think I could become a pilchard man in time.

DELIA: I'll phone Susannah tomorrow to see how they're getting on.

ERNEST: Good idea. I think we're in imminent need of a hot water bottle here, you know.

DELIA: Oh yes.

ERNEST: Bearing in mind the normal running temperature of your feet.

DELIA: Not my fault. Most woman have cold feet. It's circulation.

ERNEST: I wouldn't know about that. I haven't sampled that many.

DELIA: The girls at school did. Well, not the younger ones. Younger girls have very hot feet. Like little boys. But when we got to the sixth form, we all found we had cold feet. I think it's something to do with – maturing.

ERNEST: Very curious. Chaps I shared a hut with in the army all had overwhelmingly hot feet. . .

DELIA: I can imagine.

ERNEST: Yes, I pronounce these pilchards a success.

DELIA: Jolly good. Right, here I come.

ERNEST: Stand by for cold feet.

DELIA: Darling, you're getting fish on the sheet.

ERNEST: Oh, sorry.

DELIA: Now we're going to reek of fish all night. I don't think this was a terribly bright idea of someone's.

ERNEST: Oh well. You only live once. What the hell.

DELIA: Well, it's on your side. You have to put up with it. [*She eats*]
Oh yes, they're quite pleasant, aren't they? Not up to sardines but not bad.

ERNEST: They got my vote.

DELIA: At least we're in for a reasonably early night.

ERNEST: Yes.

DELIA: Sunday tomorrow, we can lie in.

ERNEST: Go for a walk later on if you like.

DELIA: That'd be nice.

ERNEST: If unwet.

DELIA: Rather.

ERNEST: Otherwise we'll both be crouching in the rafters with buckets.

DELIA: God forbid.

[*Cross fade to* NICK *and* JAN's. NICK *is still lying on the floor.* JAN *arrives back*]

JAN: Nick. Nick...

NICK: Aaaah.

JAN: [*seeing him*] Darling, what are you doing?

NICK: What do you think I'm doing? I've been lying here for hours.

JAN: Oh, darling. How did you get there?

NICK: I dropped my book.

JAN: [*trying to find a way to get him up*] Well, let me – how do I get you... shall I...?

NICK: No, no. Don't do that. Let me climb up you.

JAN: Right.

NICK: Can you take the weight?

JAN: Hang on. Right.

NICK: Hup – right – hold steady. Steady...

JAN: I'm trying. I'm trying.

NICK: Keep still.

JAN: You are very heavy.

NICK: Right. Nearly there.

JAN: Oh –

NICK: What?

JAN: You're on my foot.

NICK: All right.

JAN: Please get off my foot.

NICK: I will. Wait a minute.

JAN: Oh dear God, my foot.

NICK: Right. Hold on, hold on.

[JAN *loses her balance*]

[*They both crash on to the bed*]

[NICK *falling across* JAN *who is trapped underneath him*]

Aaaaah. Aaaaah. Aaaaah.

JAN: Aaaah.

NICK: Aaaah.

JAN: Oh, that was agony.

NICK: Aaaah.

JAN: Can you get off me, darling?

NICK: I cannot move at all. Ever again.

JAN: Well, try to move. I'm trapped.

NICK: I'm sorry. If I could move I would but I'm physically incapable of moving.

JAN: Can you get off my ribs? You're so heavy.

NICK: I am not heavy. I am the correct weight for a man of my height.

JAN: Well, that is still bloody heavy. [*easing herself slowly underneath him*] Hang on, I'll try and... oouf. [*she rests*]

NICK: Did you have a nice evening?

JAN: No.

NICK: Didn't think you would. Serve you right for going.

JAN: Thank you. Here we go again. [*she renews her efforts to slide from under him*] Huh. Huh. – hoo – hup. . . . oh dear God. This is going to take all night. Can't you even roll over?

NICK: Ha ha –

JAN: Well, can you be a gentleman and take your weight on your elbows?

NICK: No. That puts a direct strain on all the muscles all the way...

JAN: All right. Sorry. Oh dear. [*she laughs*] We're going to be like this for ever. People will find us in years to come. They'll all jump to the wrong conclusions, failing to realise what a rare occurrence this is. Us together on the bed.

NICK: There's no need to get unpleasant.

JAN: Sorry.

NICK: I've been working very hard lately.

JAN: Yes, all right, I'm sorry.

NICK: And now thanks to my back, we may have to get someone in for you. Try again.

JAN: Humphh – oh – I'm so weak.

NICK: You're telling me.

JAN: Nick.

NICK: Mmm?

JAN: While I've got your attention. . .

NICK: Mm?

JAN: I want to tell you something.

NICK: I can hardly avoid listening.

JAN: Good. I'm telling you because I want to tell you (a) and (b) I've a feeling if I don't a certain person will be phoning you up very shortly to tell you herself.

NICK: Who?

JAN: Susannah.

NICK: Susannah?

JAN: Well, very simply – or not very simply – I had a long talk to Trevor.

NICK: Ah-ha. . .

JAN: Which culminated in Trevor kissing me.

NICK: I see.

JAN: And to be perfectly honest, with me kissing Trevor.

NICK: Just kissing him?

JAN: Yes. Nothing else.

NICK: Oh, well. Hope you enjoyed it.

JAN: Yes I did, thank you.

NICK: Good. I hope you don't want me to start jumping about with rage.

JAN: No. Not at all. Not at all. [*she slides out from under him*] Right. Now let's get you into bed. [*without a lot of ceremony*] Come on.

NICK: Careful, careful.

JAN: Come on, it doesn't hurt.

NICK: Don't start taking it out on me just because. . .

JAN: I'm not taking it out on anyone.

NICK: As you say, you only kissed him. If you want me to knock you about, you'll have to wait until I'm better.

JAN: I don't want anything, thank you.

NICK: You only kissed him.

JAN: Yes, quite. I went to bed with all the other men at the party but I only kissed Trevor.

NICK: Oh well, that's all right. I had three or four women in while you were out actually. That explains the back.

JAN: [*unamused*] There you are.

NICK: Thank you. Can I have my book, please?

JAN: [*slamming it down*] There you are.

NICK: Thank you.

JAN: Happy?

NICK: Thank you.

JAN: [*pounding the bed rail in fury and frustration*] Aaarrrggh!

NICK: Did you say something?

JAN: I'm going to wash my hair.

NICK: Wash your hair?

JAN: Yes.

NICK: It's half past twelve.

JAN: So what.

NICK: [*mildly amused as she goes out*] Dear, dear, dear. . .

    [*Cross fade to* MALCOLM *and* KATE'*s* ]

    [KATE *wanders in. She sits unhappily* ]

    [MALCOLM *returns* ]

MALCOLM: Hallo.

KATE: Oh Malcolm.

MALCOLM: Got a bit churned up.

KATE: Yes, I know. I understand. [*pause*] They left mountains of food.

MALCOLM: Never mind. [*pause*] I was sitting in the car, that's all.

KATE: I'm glad you've come in.

MALCOLM: Oh yes. Well. As soon as I saw you'd turfed Trevor out, I came back.

KATE: Oh. Well. . .

MALCOLM: What?

KATE: He's coming back.

MALCOLM: Coming back? Here?

KATE: Yes, he's just gone round to see Jan and Nick.

MALCOLM: Jan and Nick?

KATE: Yes.

MALCOLM: Hasn't he done enough damage?

KATE: Well, he wanted to sort things out.

MALCOLM: And you told him he could come back here?

KATE: Yes.

MALCOLM: Well, how's he going to get in?

KATE: I said I'd wait up.

MALCOLM: You are soft in the head, you know that, don't you?

KATE: Probably.

MALCOLM: We're not going to get much sleep round here tonight then. Are we?

KATE: I don't know.

MALCOLM: [*rolling up his sleeves*] In that case. . .

KATE: What are you doing?

MALCOLM: [*hauling out cardboard boxes*] I'll make a start on this. If you don't come to bed I can't sleep, so I might as well do something useful.

KATE: What is that?

MALCOLM: Surprise. You'll see. I'll just fetch the tool kit. Only take me fifteen minutes. I'll put it together for you.

KATE: Oh lovely. . .

[*Cross fade to* ERNEST *and* DELIA's ]

DELIA: I feel as if I'm sleeping on board a herring trawler. This whole room reeks of fish.

ERNEST: We'll get used to it.

DELIA: I doubt it.

ERNEST: Want the light out?

DELIA: In a minute.

ERNEST: Shall I read to you for a bit?

DELIA: If you like. I'll go to sleep as soon as you start. You have been warned.

ERNEST: Oh well.

DELIA: You have a very soporific reading manner.

ERNEST: Probably. I'll read you a bit of this, shall I?

DELIA: What is it?

ERNEST: *Tom Brown's Schooldays.*

DELIA: I thought you'd read that.

ERNEST: Oh yes, rather. Always worth a re-read. Marvellous stuff. Now then. "Tom was detained in school a few minutes after the rest, and on coming out into the quadrangle, the first thing he saw was a small ring of boys, applauding Williams, who was holding Arthur by the collar. 'There, you young sneak,' said he, giving Arthur a cuff on the head with his other hand; 'what made you say that –' 'Hallo!' said Tom, shouldering into the crowd. . ."

DELIA: I can't follow a word of this.

ERNEST: Perfectly clear.

DELIA: Not to me. Who are all these people?

ERNEST: Well, we do have the disadvantage of starting on page 256. But I'm damned if I'm going all the way back to the beginning just so you can go to sleep. Shall I carry on?

DELIA: If you want to.

ERNEST: I'm asking you. I don't mind.

DELIA: Oh yes, carry on for goodness sake. Only not too loud.

ERNEST: " 'Hallo!' said Tom, shouldering into the crowd; 'you drop that, Williams; you shan't touch him.' 'Who'll stop me?' said the Slogger, raising his hand again. . ."

[*The doorbell rings*]

Good heavens.

DELIA: Was that the doorbell?

ERNEST: Sounded like it.

DELIA: It's twenty to one. Have a look and see who it is.

ERNEST: Yes, all right.

DELIA: Look out of the window.

ERNEST: Right.

[*He starts to get out of bed*]

[*Cross fade to include* NICK *and* JAN's]

[*As* JAN *comes back into the room, her hair in a towel, the doorbell rings*]

JAN: What was that?

NICK: Front door.

JAN: Funny.

NICK: Have a look.

JAN: [*going to window*] Right.

ERNEST: Looks suspiciously like Susannah.

DELIA: Oh lord. . .

JAN: [*in a low voice*] I think it's Trevor.

NICK: Oh no. Why me? Why me?

[*As* ERNEST *and* JAN *go out their respective exits to open their front doors, a sight of* MALCOLM *starting to unpack his assemble-it-yourself bedroom surprise. A great clattering and clanking of tools*]

[KATE *sits on the bed watching*]


CURTAIN

# ACT TWO

*Lights up on all three areas.*
MALCOLM *and* KATE's *room is now strewn with tools from* MALCOLM's *tool box and littered with wrapping paper removed from the easy-to-assemble-it-yourself dressing table which is scattered about in various pieces.*
MALCOLM *has unfurled the plan and is crouching on the floor studying it.*
KATE *sits on the bed watching.*
NICK *is in bed as usual.*
DELIA *is in bed.*

KATE: It's going to be lovely when it's all put together.
MALCOLM: As soon as I've made head or tail of this plan. [*He studies it*]
    [ERNEST *returns to* DELIA ]
ERNEST: She's – er – just gone in the bathroom downstairs.
DELIA: I suppose I'll have to come down.
ERNEST: There's no need to go downstairs – it's a bit parky. I told her to come up here when she's ready. Then you can talk.
DELIA: Does she want to talk to me?
ERNEST: Presumably. I can't think of anyone else she'd want to talk to.
DELIA: No.
ERNEST: She seems in a rather – distraught state. Could be a long session. Shall I make us some cocoa?
DELIA: Yes. I'd better try and make myself reasonably presentable.
    [DELIA *goes to the bathroom* ]
    [ERNEST *goes back downstairs* ]
    [*Lights down on them* ]
    [TREVOR *enters with* JAN, *still with a towel round her head* ]
JAN: It's Trevor, darling.
NICK: [*without much geniality*] Good lord.
TREVOR: Hi, Nick.

JAN: Nice coat. Is it new?

TREVOR: Er – yes.

JAN: Smart.

NICK: Is there just the one of you in it, or are there more?

TREVOR: What?

JAN: Let me take it.

TREVOR: Thanks.

NICK: What can we do for you?

JAN: Sit down, Trevor.

TREVOR: Thanks.

NICK: At ten to one in the morning.

TREVOR: Well – [*he looks at* JAN] Well –

JAN: Would you rather I wasn't here?

TREVOR: Well –

JAN: It's all right, I'll make some tea. Then I've got to dry my hair.

TREVOR: Right. Thanks.

[JAN *goes*]

[TREVOR *sits brooding*]

[NICK *waits*]

MALCOLM: I'm going to need the Phillips.

KATE: The who?

MALCOLM: Phillips screwdriver. It's in the car. I'll get it. Won't be a minute.

[MALCOLM *goes out*]

[*Lights down in their area*]

TREVOR: Look, Nick...

NICK: Yes?

TREVOR: Something happened tonight you've got to know about.

NICK: Yes?

TREVOR: Jan and I – we met at that party and we... and Susannah came... and we were together and etcetera etcetera and... it was nothing at all... nothing to it at all... but I wanted you to be the first to know about it.

NICK: Thank you.

TREVOR: You see, I don't know if you've heard but I've been going through this whole thing... this whole... me and Susannah and well.

NICK: That's O.K., I quite understand.

TREVOR: You do?

NICK: Yes, yes. Of course. See you again soon then.

TREVOR: Yes.

NICK: I'd see you out only I've wrecked my back, you see. I can't get up. Absolute agony.

TREVOR: Yes, yes. Fine. [*he remains seated*]
  [*Cross fade to* ERNEST *and* DELIA*'s* ]
  [DELIA *is coming out of the bathroom in her dressing gown as* ERNEST *returns* ]

DELIA: Well, where is she?

ERNEST: Still in the downstairs bathroom.

DELIA: What on earth is she up to?

ERNEST: Well, I don't really know. I passed the door just now on my way to the kitchen and I thought I heard voices.

DELIA: Voices?

ERNEST: She appears to be talking to someone. Or to herself.

DELIA: To herself, I hope. Unless she's using our downstairs bathroom for secret assignations.

ERNEST: You never know. She's a very peculiar sort of girl altogether. I hope she isn't going to be much longer. I'd rather like to go to bed.

DELIA: Well, you mount guard down there, darling. And bring her up when she's finished whatever it is she's doing.

ERNEST: Right. It's very chilly down there, you know. The Aga's gone out.

DELIA: Oh lord.
  [ERNEST *goes out* ]
  [DELIA *gets into bed and reads a magazine* ]
  [*Cross fade to* NICK *and* JAN ]
  [JAN *enters with two mugs of tea* ]

JAN: Have you finished talking?

NICK: I don't know if he has. I have.

JAN: [*giving* NICK *his tea*] Here. [*approaching* TREVOR] Trevor – Trevor. . . he's asleep.

NICK: He's what?

JAN: Ssh.

NICK: What do you mean, ssh? He can't sleep here. Wake him up. Wake up!
  [TREVOR *grunts* ]

JAN: Leave him for a minute.

NICK: He really is the limit, isn't he? Why doesn't he go home and sleep? Like anyone else.

JAN: Because Susannah's probably locked him out. Look, I'll just go and dry my hair. When I've done that, I'll wake him and pack him off.

NICK: He really is the limit.

JAN: You don't want me to wake him up now, do you? He'll only start talking to you again.

NICK: All right, all right. Leave him, leave him. . .

JAN: He looks so peaceful.

NICK: Ha ha.

[JAN *goes to the bathroom, taking* TREVOR's *mug of tea for herself*]

[*Cross fade to* KATE *and* MALCOLM's]

[MALCOLM *returns*]

MALCOLM: Here we are. Right. I'm going to take it out on the landing.

KATE: Can't you do it here?

MALCOLM: It's a surprise. Anyway there's more room out there.

KATE: Oh, all right.

MALCOLM: [*consulting the plan*] Now, where do we start? "Locate panel A which will form the inner side of the drawer unit – figure 1". Panel A? Ah – yes, right – now. . .

KATE: She's very odd isn't she, Susannah? A very odd person.

MALCOLM: You're right there. . . Support bar B. Where's that?

KATE: She said something very peculiar to me.

MALCOLM: B? B? B? Don't tell me they haven't given me a B.

KATE: She said she got attracted by other girls in the street.

MALCOLM: Who said that?

KATE: Susannah.

MALCOLM: I didn't know she was like that.

KATE: I don't think she is really.

MALCOLM: Well, fancy that. Ah-ha. Support bar B.

KATE: No, I don't think she's like that. You could tell if she was.

MALCOLM: Well, it's not normal, is it? For a woman? Fancying girls in the street.

KATE: No, but – well –

MALCOLM: You don't feel like that, do you?

KATE: No, but. . .

MALCOLM: I didn't think so.

KATE: No.

MALCOLM: Not you. Mrs Normal, that's you.

KATE: That doesn't sound very exciting, does it?

MALCOLM: Suits me. Locking bar C for the second drawer.

KATE: You don't think I'm too normal, do you?

MALCOLM: How can you be too normal?

KATE: Well. . . you see things, you know. And you think, well
  – I might be missing out on something.

MALCOLM: How do you mean?

KATE: Well. . .

MALCOLM: You're happy enough, aren't you?

KATE: Yes. I just thought that I might be – I could be a more
  exciting person. Perhaps.

MALCOLM: You're all right.

KATE: But are you excited at all by me, Malcolm?

MALCOLM: Oh yes. Mad about you. . . Where the hell is locking bar C?

KATE: No. Seriously.

MALCOLM: What are you on about?

KATE: Well, I looked at those magazines of yours.

MALCOLM: Magazines? What magazines?

KATE: The ones you hid under your socks in the drawer.

MALCOLM: Oh. You found those did you?

KATE: Well I couldn't help it. I mean, I'm in and out of your
  sock drawer all day. I mean, I didn't mind. . .

MALCOLM: Somebody gave them to me at work. I didn't even
  read them.

KATE: I did.

MALCOLM: Oh.

KATE: No, I just think perhaps I could be more exciting. For
  you. I'd hate you to get bored.

MALCOLM: I'm not bored. I'm just trying to find locking bar C.

KATE: You will tell me if you get bored with me, won't you?

MALCOLM: Yes, sure sure.

KATE: And I promise to tell you.

MALCOLM: What?

KATE: If I get bored with you.

MALCOLM: You don't get bored with me, do you?

KATE: No. No. Not often.

MALCOLM: What, you mean – when we're – in bed? Here?

KATE: Not often. . .

MALCOLM: Well, that's nice.

KATE: Only once or twice.

MALCOLM: Bored?

KATE: No, not bored. You know, it's just I have my mind on other things.

MALCOLM: You mean, other men.

KATE: No. Ordinary things like, shall we have a carpet in the hall or shall we stain the floorboards. That sort of thing. They're all to do with us. In a way.

MALCOLM: You mean to tell me while I'm — giving my all — you're lying there thinking about floorboards?

KATE: Only sometimes.

MALCOLM: Bloody hell. [*he snatches up some of the pieces*] I'm going in the hall.

KATE: Have I hurt your feelings?

MALCOLM: No. Not at all. I'm just going in the hall.

[MALCOLM *goes out angrily*]

KATE: I just don't want to get boring.

[*Cross fade to* ERNEST *and* DELIA's]

[DELIA *in bed*, SUSANNAH *comes in cautiously*]

SUSANNAH: Hallo.

DELIA: Susannah. Come in, dear, how are you? A late visit.

SUSANNAH: Yes.

DELIA: We were just — going to bed. I think Ernest is making us some cocoa.

SUSANNAH: Oh.

DELIA: We often have cocoa. Sometimes hot milk but usually cocoa.

SUSANNAH: Oh.

[*A pause*]

DELIA: Now. What's the problem?

SUSANNAH: It's —

DELIA: Mmm?

SUSANNAH: It's just. . .

DELIA: Mmm?

SUSANNAH: What am I going to do, Delia?

DELIA: You're talking about you and Trevor.

SUSANNAH: I've lost his respect.

DELIA: Oh surely not. What makes you think that?

SUSANNAH: When he's there deliberately making love to another woman. Knowing. . .

DELIA: Trevor was?

SUSANNAH: Knowing that I was bound to come in and see them.

DELIA: Another woman?

SUSANNAH: Yes.

DELIA: Who was this?

SUSANNAH: Oh, that woman. Jan. . .

DELIA: Jan? Not *the* Jan?

SUSANNAH: Do you know her?

DELIA: Oh yes, yes.

SUSANNAH: He's brought her here, has he?

DELIA: Oh yes, several times. I mean, not since he's been married to you. This was years and years and years and years ago. I mean, he's never looked at another woman. I mean, not since he's been – busy married to you. If there's one thing his father and I always instilled in him from birth it was loyalty. Loyalty to us. Loyalty to the ones he loves. And especially loyalty to the woman he marries.

SUSANNAH: He despises me.

DELIA: Oh, nonsense.

SUSANNAH: Do you know what it's like to be ignored?

DELIA: Well, yes. As a matter of fact I do. We all do. We all get ignored sooner or later. Ernest ignores me dreadfully. I have to tell him everything three times before he'll lift a finger.

SUSANNAH: Not only mentally.

DELIA: Oh. Oh, I see. [*patting the bed*] It's this old trouble is it?

SUSANNAH: Partly.

DELIA: Oh dear. Dear me. My mother used to say, Delia if S E X ever rears its ugly head, close your eyes before you see the rest of it.

[ERNEST *enters with a tray* ]

ERNEST: Cocoa is served.

DELIA: Oh, well done.

ERNEST: [*handing* SUSANNAH *a cup*] Susannah.

SUSANNAH: Thank you.

[ERNEST *gives* DELIA *a cup and sits*]

ERNEST: Well, now, what are we all chatting about?

DELIA: Nothing. Nothing that need concern you, dear.

ERNEST: Oh. On to — those things, are we? Good health.

SUSANNAH: We were talking about physical relationships.

ERNEST: Oh, were you? Jolly good.

SUSANNAH: Delia was saying it's probably the cause of all our problems.

ERNEST: Really?

DELIA: I said — something like that, yes.

ERNEST: Did we have any problems? I didn't think we had. I don't think I had any problems. Probably have a problem now but I don't remember having any then. [he laughs]

DELIA: Darling, I wonder if you'd like to slip in to the bathroom for a moment.

ERNEST: Bathroom?

DELIA: Just for a moment.

ERNEST: Oh, all right.

SUSANNAH: You don't have to go.

DELIA: Yes, I think he does have to. I'd prefer it.

ERNEST: Right. I'll — be in the bathroom then.

[ERNEST goes into the bathroom ]

DELIA: I'm sorry. I find it rather difficult to talk about this sort of thing in front of Ernest.

SUSANNAH: Isn't that — awkward for you?

DELIA: No, no. We just don't talk about it. We never have talked about it. I think there's far too much talking about it anyway. I mean, I think people would be far happier if they were just left to get on with it.

SUSANNAH: But if they have difficulties — hang-ups. . .

DELIA: Well, if you have difficulties surely you go to your doctor. Talk to him. They love talking about it. Mine does. In fact, he's got an almost macabre interest in it. For a man of his age.

SUSANNAH: I mean, mental problems. That affects how you approach everything. I mean, I am physically afraid of Trevor. He's a very violent, passionate person really and I — I don't think I can be.

DELIA: Oh dear. That is difficult. Of course, Ernest never was. I spent most of my time trying to get him to notice me at all.

SUSANNAH: Can you tell me about it?

DELIA: About what?

SUSANNAH: About — that side of it. With you and your husband.

DELIA: Don't forget your cocoa.

SUSANNAH: No thank you, I —

DELIA: Don't you want it?

SUSANNAH: No, I —

DELIA: Something else then?

SUSANNAH: No, it's —

DELIA: Tea? Have a cup of tea. I'll make you a cup of tea.

SUSANNAH: No, it's —

DELIA: Nothing like tea. [*rising*] Yes, that is a problem for you, isn't it. I don't know quite know what we do about that. Wait there, I won't be a moment.

  [*DELIA goes out* ]
  [*Cross fade to* NICK *and* JAN's ]
  [*NICK in bed.* TREVOR *still asleep* ]
  [*JAN comes in from the bathroom to fetch her comb* ]

NICK: He's starting to snore.

JAN: I'll wake him in a minute.

NICK: Please do. . .

  [*Cross fade to* MALCOLM *and* KATE's ]
  [*KATE still on the bed* ]
  [*MALCOLM enters for another section* ]

MALCOLM: Why don't you get into bed?

KATE: I'm all right.

MALCOLM: [*rummaging about in his tool box*] Well, I'll try and be less boring for you in future.

KATE: I didn't mean that.

MALCOLM: Tomorrow night I'll come to bed in a funny hat.

KATE: Oh crikey. What have I started?

MALCOLM: I don't know. And this damn plan's no use, either. [*very irritably*] One-inch sevens, where are they?

KATE: One-inch what?

MALCOLM: Never mind. Nobody ever told me before I was boring. And I've been with a few, I can tell you.

KATE: Yes, I know, you've told me.

MALCOLM: They weren't bored. None of them were bored. No woman who's been in bed with me has ever complained of boredom. That was the last thing on their mind. If I were you, I'd start worrying that there wasn't something wrong with you.

KATE: That's what I am worrying about.

MALCOLM: You'd do well to. You'd do right to. [*marching to the door and turning for a parting shot*] You ask Doreen Foster if she was bored with me. She'll tell you. . .

[*He goes out* ]

[*Cross fade to* ERNEST *and* DELIA's ]

[SUSANNAH *stands alone* ]

SUSANNAH: I am confident in myself. I have confidence in myself. I am not unattractive. I am attractive. People still find me attractive.

[*During this,* ERNEST *emerges from the bathroom. Seeing her, he attempts to tiptoe across to fetch his book from the bedside table without disturbing her* ]

SUSANNAH: I am not afraid of people. People are not frightening. There is noth – [*she sees* ERNEST]

ERNEST: [*embarrassed*] Just – fetching a book. Carry on. [*he goes to the door*] *Tom Brown's Schooldays.* Fearfully good. Read it, have you? No? Carry on.

[*He goes* ]

[SUSANNAH *wanders slowly out the other way* ]

[*Cross fade to* NICK *and* JAN's ]

[TREVOR *suddenly wakes up* ]

TREVOR: No, the point is, Nick. . .

NICK: Huh what?

TREVOR: What? Sorry, did I. . .

NICK: You just startled me.

TREVOR: Have I been asleep?

NICK: Yes.

TREVOR: Sorry.

NICK: Quite all right.

TREVOR: I don't think I was asleep, I was. . . Nick, Nick you're a friend, aren't you? I mean, I know there's Jan and all that – she was mine, now she's yours and you're the luckiest man in the world but – I think I know you. And I trust you.

NICK: Thank you.

TREVOR: And I'd like to know more about you.

NICK: Ah.

TREVOR: And frankly, I'd like you to know more about me. [*bounding up*] I know, I've got a great idea. Why don't we take a walk? Now? Why not? Come for a walk?

NICK: I can't come for a walk, Trevor. I've told you. I have a splintered spine. I'm lying here in agony.

TREVOR: Oh. Tell me about Jan, then.

NICK: Jan?

TREVOR: Jan as she is now. I mean, when you met her, when she came to you from me was she badly destroyed?

NICK: No.

TREVOR: Had I in fact destroyed her?

NICK: No, I think she'd forgotten about you completely by the time she met me.

TREVOR: But you see what I'm driving at, though?

NICK: No.

TREVOR: If I destroyed Jan, maybe I'm destroying Susannah in the same way. Maybe I'm just a destroyer of people.

NICK: Now that is possible.

TREVOR: You think that is possible.

NICK: No. Look, Trevor, I don't want to belittle your powers of destruction in any way but it does appear to me that whereas Jan is a perfectly ordinary, normal — reasonably normal — woman — fairly well-balanced — that, in my experience, nothing short of a nuclear charge is likely to destroy — Susannah from our brief acquaintance was born a wreck, is even now a wreck and will probably die one.

TREVOR: [*taking this in*] You think it's an inherent part of Susannah's character?

NICK: Yes.

TREVOR: Not me at all.

NICK: No. I don't think you've helped but. . .

TREVOR: That's an interesting theory.

NICK: Just a thought. I mean, you must have known what you were taking on when you married Susannah.

TREVOR: She seemed to understand.

NICK: Ah well, yes. Most woman look as if they understand. Then you find half of them haven't a bloody clue what you're talking about.

TREVOR: Is that what you find with Jan?

NICK: I find the best of Jan is that she's amusing occasionally, very efficient when she wants to be — pretty bright, and the worst is that she can be totally self-obsessed, erratic, bad-tempered and unreliable. But taking it all in all, I could have done worse.

TREVOR: I found her a very gentle person.

NICK: Really? Well. . .

TREVOR: Odd, isn't it? How one person to someone can be something different to someone else? [*he lies on his back on the bed beside* NICK. *Reflectively*] I remember one day. . .

NICK: What the hell are you doing?

TREVOR: I remember this one magic day when Jan and I, we went off together. . .

NICK: Look, Trevor, you've got your shoes all over the eiderdown.

TREVOR: [*casually shifting his feet*] Sorry. We went to the seaside. It was one of those perfect days. . .

NICK: Look, Trevor –

[JAN *enters brushing her hair* ]

JAN: Oh, that looks cosy. What are you up to?

NICK: Look, Jan, will you tell him to get his feet off my eiderdown?

JAN: Trevor! Shoes off, please.

NICK: Not just his shoes off. Get off altogether. What's he doing lying on my bed anyway?

JAN: He's not doing any harm.

NICK: He's doing considerable harm. This is my bed. I don't happen to want people sprawling all over it.

TREVOR: [*getting up*] Sorry. Sorry, I didn't realise.

NICK: What nobody in this house seems to realise or appreciate is that I am in considerable physical discomfort. In fact, a great deal of pain. And it is not helped when people sprawl all over the damn bed.

JAN: Come on, Trevor. Come and help me wash up.

TREVOR: Right. Sorry, Nick mate. Sorry.

JAN: We'll leave him to it.

NICK: And will somebody remember to remind me that I have to phone Arthur Hewitson tomorrow morning at home.

JAN: All right, all right.

[JAN *and* TREVOR *go out* ]

NICK: [*yelling after them*] And don't you two start anything in there. Do you hear me? Do you – aaaah. [*he lies back*]

[*Cross fade to* MALCOLM *and* KATE's ]

[KATE *lying on the bed, wincing at the sound of heavy*

*hammering in the hall* ]

[*A clatter* ]

MALCOLM: [*off*] Oh damn and blast this thing.

KATE: Malcolm.

MALCOLM: Damn and blast it.

KATE: Malcolm, why don't you come to bed? Leave it till the morning, love.

[MALCOLM *marches in clutching two pieces of splintered wood* ]

MALCOLM: Look at that. Snapped in half. It was cut half an inch too big. I tried to get it in place and what happens, it snaps in half. Useless. Useless. I'm writing a letter to this lot. I can tell you.

KATE: You're very tired. . . it's nearly three o'clock.

MALCOLM: I am not tired.

KATE: Leave it for now.

MALCOLM: Oh no, I'm going to finish it.

KATE: Well, can I help at all?

MALCOLM: No, you cannot. This is a surprise for you. Now go on, get into bed. And go to sleep.

[*He stamps out* ]

[KATE *sadly gets into bed. As if by reflex and without really noticing what she's doing, she removes a hair brush, three makeup jars and a couple of hairsprays. She lies down. The banging starts again in the hall with renewed fury* ]

[*Cross fade to* ERNEST *and* DELIA's ]

[SUSANNAH *and* DELIA *enter* ]

[SUSANNAH *with a cup of tea,* DELIA *with a slice of cake on a sideplate* ]

DELIA: [*chatting cheerfully as they come in*] . . . no, we had elastic on ours. We had terrible problems if they got too tight round here. . . oh, he's still in the bathroom. Good. Now, we're going to have to put you somewhere, aren't we? And we haven't really got an awful lot of choice. I think you're going to have to share with me if you can bear that. Ernest can go in the spare room. He won't mind at all.

SUSANNAH: Are you sure. . .

DELIA: No trouble. Now, you're positive you're not hungry?

SUSANNAH: No.

DELIA: This time of night, I get ravenous. [*she takes a bite of cake*] Now remember, three simple rules. Feed him properly. Make sure he's clean clothes in the morning. And most important of all, don't tell him anything you don't have to. A little bit of mystery never did anyone any harm. You'll have him eating out of your hand – this is delicious for a shop cake – now, we must find you a nightie. You'll have to excuse the smell of pilchards when you first get into bed. You'll find it wears off after a little. [*holding up a nightdress*] Now, how about this?

SUSANNAH: Thank you.

DELIA: It's a bit old. . . now, what else?

[ERNEST *comes out of the bathroom* ]

ERNEST: Right. That's it. I don't care what you're talking about, I'm not sitting in that bathroom a moment longer. I have now finished *Tom Brown's Schooldays*, there is nothing else in there to read and I'm going to bed.

DELIA: Yes, we've decided to give you the spare room.

ERNEST: The what?

DELIA: The spare room. Trevor's old one. You'll be sleeping in there.

ERNEST: What, the one with the damp patch, you mean? Not on your life.

DELIA: Now don't be silly, it hasn't rained for days. Susannah's staying the night and she's sleeping with me in here.

ERNEST: In here?

DELIA: Yes.

ERNEST: In my bed.

DELIA: Just for the night. I'll come and help you make up the bed in there. Oh, and you'll probably need a bottle. You deal with the bottle. The bathroom's just through there, Susannah. Use anything you find.

[SUSANNAH *goes out* ]

[DELIA *goes out* ]

ERNEST: [*following*] I don't think I've ever spent a night like this in my life.

[*As he goes, cross fade to* NICK *and* JAN's ]

[TREVOR *comes in with a teatowel to fetch* NICK's *dirty cup* ]

[JAN *appears in the doorway* ]

[TREVOR *indicates* NICK ]

JAN: [*sotto*] Is he asleep?

TREVOR: [*sotto*] Yes.

JAN: Good. He's been absolutely foul all day.

TREVOR: Has he?

JAN: He can't bear it if he's in bed. Absolutely loathes it. He's so bad-tempered you would not believe it. I've got to put up with this for days.

TREVOR: Oh.

JAN: Imagine that all day long. Count yourself lucky you've only got Susannah. She can't be worse than him at the moment.

NICK: I am not asleep. I heard that.

JAN: Good.

NICK: Is he going home now?

JAN: No, he's sleeping here.

NICK: Who said so?

JAN: I did. Want to argue? He's sleeping on the sofa. Come on, Trevor.

TREVOR: Oh. Can I ring Kate first? She's waiting up for me, you see.

JAN: Oh, they'll have gone to bed by now.

TREVOR: No, she said she'd wait up. I'll just give her a quick ring.

JAN: If you like. I'll get the number, I've got it somewhere.

NICK: Make sure he pays for the call.

JAN: Ignore him. [*heading to the door*] I'm sure they'll have gone to bed, you know.

TREVOR: [*following her out*] I'd feel better if I phoned.
    [*Cross fade to* MALCOLM *and* KATE's ]
    [*Banging from the hall* ]

MALCOLM: [*off*] Get in, you bastard, get in will you. [*more banging*] Get in. . . [*more banging and a final crash*]
    [MALCOLM *staggers in, bleary and dishevelled* ]

KATE: Have you done it?

MALCOLM: Give me a hand in with it, will you?

KATE: [*jumping out of bed and following him off*] Oh, right, I'm dying to see it.
    [MALCOLM *and* KATE *carry on the dressing table* ]
    [*It is a lop-sided mess. They set it down* ]
    [KATE *steps back* ]
    Oh. Yes. . . yes. . .

MALCOLM: Well, it's — not quite right but. . .

KATE: It's very nice. I like the drawers. [*she pulls one out. It is stuck*]

MALCOLM: Hang on, hang on, don't force it. [*he pulls at the drawer without effect. He tugs at it. He wrestles with it and finally delivers it a mighty blow with the flat of his hand. The drawer opens* ] I'll ease them a little in the morning.

KATE: It's very handsome.

MALCOLM: Not bad.

KATE: I'm just a bit worried things might roll off the end.

MALCOLM: Roll off the end?

KATE: With it being a bit on the slant.

MALCOLM: Well, it's got to be finished off. It's got to be sanded down yet.

KATE: Oh, I see. Well. Well done.

MALCOLM: Most of their stuff didn't make sense. I had to make half this up as I went along.

KATE: That's not right is it? Are you coming to bed now?

MALCOLM: [*squinting at his masterpiece*] Yes, yes. Just a sec.

KATE: It's very late.

MALCOLM: You hop in. I'll join you.

KATE: [*getting into bed*] Don't be long.

MALCOLM: No. All I need to do, you see, is to sand down the feet at this end a bit. It's only a matter of a — of a little bit. [*he lifts the thing on to its side*] Just a moment.

KATE: What are you doing now?

MALCOLM: Won't be a moment.

　　[*The phone rings* ]

　　Who the hell can that be?

　　[KATE *answers the phone* ]

　　[*Lights up on* NICK *and* JAN's *to reveal* TREVOR *at the other end* ]

KATE: Hallo?

TREVOR: Hallo. Kate?

KATE: Yes.

TREVOR: It's Trevor.

KATE: Oh hallo, Trevor. [*to* MALCOLM, *sotto, covering the receiver*] It's Trevor. [*into phone*] Where are you, Trevor?

TREVOR: Look, I hope it's all right, I'm staying over with Nick and Jan here.

KATE: Oh, I see. I have made the bed up.

TREVOR: Yes well, thanks all the same, Kate. So just to say don't wait up.

KATE: No, right, I won't. I won't. Thank you for phoning, Trevor.

TREVOR: Yes, well. Goodnight then, Kate.

KATE: Goodnight, Trevor.

[TREVOR *rings off and goes out* ]

[*replacing the receiver*] He's not coming back after all.

MALCOLM: Good. Now then, let's have a look at this.

[*He takes out a selection of sandpapers from his tool box and sifts through them* ]

[*Cross fade to* DELIA *and* ERNEST ]

[DELIA *enters followed by* ERNEST ]

[*She takes his pillow from the bed and hands it to him* ]

DELIA: Now, you'll be perfectly comfy in there. I don't know what you're complaining about.

ERNEST: I shall probably finish up with marsh fever.

DELIA: Nonsense.

ERNEST: On your head be it. That's all I can say. . .

[ERNEST *goes out* ]

[*Simultaneously* SUSANNAH *comes in from the bathroom in her nightdress*]

DELIA: Oh, that suits you.

SUSANNAH: Thank you.

DELIA: Much nicer than on me. Do you mind sleeping that side?

SUSANNAH: No, no.

DELIA: We tend to lie in a little on Sundays so don't feel you have to get up. Actually, Ernest usually makes a cup of tea for me so maybe we'll be lucky. Right, everything you want?

SUSANNAH: [*getting into bed*] Fine.

DELIA: [*doing likewise*] Now, if I do happen to dig you with my elbows − Ernest often complains I do that − just push me out of the way. Don't worry, you won't wake me.

SUSANNAH: Right.

DELIA: Lights out, then.

[*They switch off* ]

Sleep tight.

SUSANNAH: Goodnight.

DELIA: Sweet dreams.

[*Cross fade to* NICK *and* JAN's ]

[JAN *enters ready for bed*]

JAN: Well, that's Trevor settled. It makes quite a nice bed, that sofa.

NICK: Oh good. Now perhaps you can wrench your attention round to me.

JAN: Glass of water. [*she hands it to him*]

NICK: What for?

JAN: Two of these. [*she hands him two tablets*]

NICK: They are absolutely. . .

JAN: Come on. Come on, please. I want to get to bed.

NICK: Oh.

[*He takes the pills* ]

[JAN *gets into bed* ]

Are we sleeping with the light on?

JAN: Just for a second. I want to think.

NICK: Can't you think in the dark? I mean, I thought I was supposed to get rest. This place has been like a major trunk road.

JAN: In a minute.

NICK: [*after a slight pause*] It beats me what you ever saw in that man.

JAN: Trevor?

NICK: Yes. I mean, it doesn't say much for me. I mean, if he was your first choice that makes me your second choice.

JAN: I like a contrast. Shut up, I'm thinking.

NICK: Was he. . .

JAN: Mm?

NICK: Was he – you know. Good?

JAN: Good?

NICK: In bed.

JAN: Why do men always want to know that? I mean, how am I possibly expected to answer that?

NICK: Truthfully.

JAN: If I say yes, he was marvellous, you'll sulk, won't you? Whereas if I say no, awful, you'll just lie there looking smug all night.

NICK: Not at all.

JAN: [*after a pause*] Well, I'll say this. He thinks he's awfully good.

[NICK *laughs* ]

That satisfy you?

NICK: Thank you. Thank you.

JAN: Oh, look at him. Just look at him. Why didn't I keep my mouth shut.

[JAN *switches off the light* ]

[*Cross fade to* ERNEST *and* DELIA's ]

[DELIA *and* SUSANNAH *in bed asleep* ]

[SUSANNAH *is making weird moaning noises* ]

[*She starts to flail about* ]

[DELIA *wakes up. She looks alarmed* ]

[SUSANNAH's *wails increase in volume* ]

[*She begins to claw and clutch at* DELIA ]

[DELIA *fends her off* ]

DELIA: Oh lord. Oh lord. Susannah. Susannah.

[DELIA *switches on the light* ]

SUSANNAH: [*sitting bolt upright awake*] Wah – wah –. . .

DELIA: It's all right, dear. You're all right. Just a nasty dream.

[ERNEST *comes in.*]

ERNEST: Anything wrong? I heard shouting.

DELIA: Susannah had a little dream. That's all dear. Nothing serious.

ERNEST: Oh. Did she? Did she? For your information, there is steam rising off my top blanket in there. Thought you might like to know. Goodnight.

[ERNEST *goes out* ]

DELIA: Better now, dear?

SUSANNAH: [*who has lain down again half asleep already*] Mmm.

DELIA: Goodnight.

[DELIA *switches off the light again* ]

[*A slight pause.* SUSANNAH *starts again* ]

SUSANNAH: No – no – no. . . no – no – no. . . . . no – no – please – no – no. . .

DELIA: Oh heavens. . .

[*Cross fade to* MALCOLM *and* KATE's ]

[KATE *is invisible under the sheets* ]

[MALCOLM *is on the floor and has fallen asleep in the midst of sandpapering* ]

[*Cross fade to* JAN *and* NICK's ]

NICK: [*restless unable to get to sleep*] Oooh – ow. . . [*softly*] Jan? Jan? Are you asleep? Jan?. . . ooh – ow. [*loudly*] Aaah.

JAN: [*waking up*] What?

NICK: Sorry. Did I wake you? It's just agony.

JAN: Well, try and sleep, darling.

NICK: Impossible, I'm afraid.

JAN: Well, do try. . .

   [JAN *turns over* ]

   [NICK *lies, moaning to himself softly* ]

   [*Cross fade to* ERNEST *and* DELIA's ]

   [SUSANNAH *is now quiet* ]

   [DELIA *sleeps sedately* ]

   [SUSANNAH *suddenly sits bolt upright, her eyes wide open* ]

SUSANNAH: Oooooaaaah! Trevor. . .

DELIA: [*awake in a flash*] What? What?

SUSANNAH: [*fumbling her way out of bed*] I must phone Trevor.

DELIA: Not now, dear. It's only quarter to seven.

SUSANNAH: Please, please, I want to phone Trevor.

DELIA: Well, there's a phone here. Don't go out there, you'll wake Ernest. And if you wake Ernest before he's ready, he gets very tetchy. Here we are.

SUSANNAH: I'll just phone home. [*she dials*]

DELIA: It's far too early to telephone anyone. Far too early. . .

SUSANNAH: It's ringing.

DELIA: And Trevor hates being woken up early. I could never get him to school on time. He's worse than Ernest.

SUSANNAH: There's no reply.

DELIA: He'll be dead to the world. Try again later on. Now go back to sleep. . .

SUSANNAH: No, no, he would have heard. I know he would have heard. I had this terrible dream. . . I'll see if he's still at Malcolm's.

DELIA: No. Now you really mustn't. It's very naughty of you. Phoning people up at this time of the morning. I absolutely forbid it.

SUSANNAH: But I'm worried to death about him. Don't you see? Don't you care?

DELIA: [*quietening her*] Yes, yes, all right, all right.

SUSANNAH: [*scrabbling for her address book in her bag*] Malcolm and Kate. . .

DELIA: You're going to be dreadfully unpopular. . .

SUSANNAH: [*dialling*] I'll ask Kate if she knows where he

went. He may still be there.

DELIA: I hope you don't carry on like this at home. You can never hope to keep a husband if you keep bobbing up and down like this all night.

[*Lights up on* MALCOLM *and* KATE ]

[*The phone rings* ]

[MALCOLM *remains asleep* ]

[KATE's *head emerges* ]

KATE: Ooooo – aaah – oh. . . [*answering*] Ho. Hoo hiss.

SUSANNAH: Kate?

KATE: Hes.

SUSANNAH: It's Susannah.

KATE: Oh. Ho.

SUSANNAH: I hope I haven't woken you.

KATE: Ho. Ho.

SUSANNAH: Is Trevor there?

KATE: No. . . no, he's not. He went to Jan's. Night night. [*she hangs up and slumps back*]

[*Lights down on* MALCOLM *and* KATE's ]

SUSANNAH: [*thunderstruck*] He's at Jan's.

DELIA: What?

SUSANNAH: [*beginning to crumple*] I knew it. I knew he would be. He's at Jan's.

DELIA: Now, Susannah.

SUSANNAH: I dreamt he was at Jan's.

DELIA: Now come along, pull yourself together.

SUSANNAH: He's gone back to Jan. I knew he'd go back to Jan. [*she flings herself on the bed weeping hysterically*]

DELIA: Now, Susannah. Susannah. I shall smack your face. Susannah.

[ERNEST *enters angrily* ]

ERNEST: Look, what the blazes are you two playing at? Banging and thumping and wailing. It's like sleeping next door to a girls' dormitory.

DELIA: Ernest dear. . .

ERNEST: It's too bad, you know. Too bad. I just this minute got off to sleep against considerable odds.

DELIA: Ernest, we have a crisis.

ERNEST: I know we have a crisis. And if I don't get my sleep, there's going to be a bigger one.

DELIA: Ernest, please. Quietly, darling. Quietly. Please. . .

ERNEST: What?

DELIA: You're going to have to do something. Will you do something, please? Then we can all get some sleep.

ERNEST: Anything.

DELIA: Right. Will you pick up that phone, please. And ring Jan whatever-her-name-is and ask to speak to Trevor. And then you can put him on to me.

ERNEST: Why should I want to ring Jan?

DELIA: Because that apparently is where Trevor is.

ERNEST: At this time of the morning?

DELIA: Especially at this time of the morning.

ERNEST: Oh, no. You don't mean to say. . .

DELIA: Apparently.

ERNEST: Oh, no. Well, I warn you, I'm not in any mood for pleasantries. Give me the number then.

DELIA: Susannah.

SUSANNAH: Mm?

DELIA: What is Jan's number? [*holding up address book*] Will it be in here?

SUSANNAH: [*nodding mutely*] Mmm.

DELIA: Where do I find it? What's her husband's surname?

SUSANNAH: Davies.

DELIA: Davies. [*handing book to* ERNEST] Look up Davies, dear, under D.

ERNEST: [*searching*] Davies? Davies? Davies? Nick and Jan Davies. Those the ones?

DELIA: That's them.

ERNEST: 26 – um – um – 74 – [*dialling*] 2 – 6 –

DELIA: Ask to speak to Trevor.

ERNEST: I shall.

   [*Lights up on* NICK *and* JAN's ]

   [*The phone rings* ]

NICK: [*waking up and trying to sit up*] Aaah. [*he lies back*]

JAN: [*asleep*] Phone's ringing.

NICK: Well, answer it darling. Will you come round and answer it. I can't reach.

JAN: [*stumbling out of bed*] Oh no.

NICK: Oh my God, it's probably America. Lights on.

JAN: What?

NICK: Lights on.

JAN: Right. [*she does so*]

NICK: Notebook, quick. Pen and notebook. Come along, darling. Quickly please, they'll hang up.

JAN: Pen and notebook.

NICK: Jan please, get a move on.

JAN: I am getting a move on.
   [*She answers the phone* ]
   Hallo? 26...

ERNEST: Hallo. Is that Jan?

JAN: Yes, just a moment please. I'll give you my husband.

ERNEST: I don't want your husband, young lady. I want to speak to my son.

JAN: Your son?

ERNEST: I know he's there. Come along.

JAN: Oh I'm sorry. I thought you were America. Just a second...
   [*to* NICK] It's not America. It's your father.

NICK: My father? Good lord. [*taking the receiver*] Hallo there, Dad.

ERNEST: Hallo, who's that?

NICK: It's Nick, Dad. How are you? When did you get back?

ERNEST: Back?

NICK: I thought you were in Rome.

ERNEST: Rome?

NICK: Who is this?

ERNEST: That's not Trevor.

DELIA: Who are you talking to?

ERNEST: Haven't the foggiest. Some fellow who thinks I'm in Rome.

NICK: Look, did you say Trevor?

ERNEST: Yes. Trevor. I'm talking to Trevor. We seem to have a crossed line...

DELIA: Oh, give that to me.

ERNEST: Bloody G.P.O. Absolutely the last straw.

DELIA: [*ultra-charming*] Hallo, who am I speaking to?

NICK: Madam, you are speaking to a man with a bad back in considerable pain. More to the point, who are you?

DELIA: I'm so sorry to disturb you. This is Trevor's mother speaking.

NICK: You want to speak to Trevor, do you?

DELIA: If it's not too much trouble. Thank you so much.

NICK: [*handing receiver to* JAN] Trevor's mother. It runs in the family.

JAN: Delia?

DELIA: [*to* ERNEST] There, that's that sorted out.

JAN: Hallo, Delia. It's Jan. Do you want a word with Trevor?

DELIA: Yes, is he with you, Jan?

JAN: Yes, he's sleeping on the sofa. I'll get him. [JAN *goes out*]

DELIA: Thank you, Jan. She is a nice girl. Her husband sounds a very grumpy thing.

ERNEST: I'm not surprised.

DELIA: Now then. She's obviously with her husband, Susannah, so there's nothing at all for you to worry about. She's just fetching Trevor. He's sleeping on their sofa apparently.

[TREVOR *blunders in* ]

[*He has been sleeping in his shirt, pants and socks* ]

NICK: Could you not use the phone in there?

TREVOR: Sorry to disturb you.

JAN: [*entering as she speaks*] No, Trevor, I said you can take it in here, Trevor.

TREVOR: [*answering phone*] Hallo.

JAN: Trev – [*apologetically to* NICK] Sorry.

TREVOR: Hallo.

DELIA: Trevor?

TREVOR: Hallo, Mum.

DELIA: I have Susannah here, Trevor. She wants to talk to you.

TREVOR: Oh. Right.

DELIA: [*holding out phone*] Susannah.

SUSANNAH: Thank you. Hallo – Trevor?

DELIA: Ernest. [*she waves him away*]

[ERNEST *stamps back into his room* ]

TREVOR: Hallo, Suse.

SUSANNAH: I thought I'd ring you.

TREVOR: Yes.

SUSANNAH: To say. I'm sorry. About this evening. . .

TREVOR: No. It was me. I'm sorry.

SUSANNAH: Well.

TREVOR: Yes, well.

SUSANNAH: Yes. Trevor, I think we ought to try again.

DELIA: [*softly*] Aaaah.

TREVOR: Yes. Yes. O.K.

SUSANNAH: Are you alone?

TREVOR: Not really.

SUSANNAH: Is she with you?

TREVOR: Yes. Yes.

SUSANNAH: Are you still keen on her?

TREVOR: No. No.

NICK: Is this going on for long?

TREVOR: Nick's here too, Suse. He's in bed. [*to* NICK] Could you say hallo to Susannah to prove you're here?

NICK: I'm not saying hallo to anyone at this time of the morning.

TREVOR: Thanks. Did you hear that, Susannah?

SUSANNAH: Yes.

TREVOR: Well. I'm sleeping on the sofa.

SUSANNAH: Oh.

TREVOR: Where are you sleeping?

SUSANNAH: With your mother.

TREVOR: Oh.

SUSANNAH: Look, I could be home in ten minutes. I've got the car.

TREVOR: Well. O.K. So could I.

SUSANNAH: Shall we do that?

TREVOR: Sure. Fine.

SUSANNAH: O.K. See you then.

TREVOR: Yes. Sure. Bye.

SUSANNAH: Bye bye.

TREVOR: Bye.

[*They both hang up* ]

DELIA: Well, everything settled?

SUSANNAH: [*hurrying to the bathroom*] I'm going to get dressed. Excuse me.

DELIA: Dressed?

TREVOR: [*to* NICK] Thanks a lot. Thanks a lot.

NICK: Want to phone anyone else while you're here?

TREVOR: No, no. That's fine, thanks. I'll be off home then. I'll just get dressed. Thanks, Jan.

JAN: All right, Trevor.

[TREVOR *goes out* ]

NICK: I'm going to get my firm to sue that man. He's set me back about a month.

JAN: Try not to be quite so unpleasant. [*she kisses him*]

NICK: Ow.

JAN: Sorry, sorry. Back to sleep now. [*she gets into bed*]

[SUSANNAH *returns from the bathroom struggling into her clothes* ]

SUSANNAH: Trevor says he's going home. So I'm going home too. Thank you for everything.

DELIA: Quite all right. Would you like a hairbrush before you go?

SUSANNAH: Hairbrush? Oh, all right.

DELIA: You ought to do a little something with yourself. For Trevor's sake.

SUSANNAH: All right.

[*She sits and does her hair* ]

[*Back at* NICK *and* JAN's, TREVOR *comes in* ]

TREVOR: I say. I say. . .

NICK: Oh no. . .

TREVOR: I'm off.

JAN: All right, Trevor. Bye bye.

TREVOR: I say. . .

JAN: Yes.

TREVOR: I wonder if I could make a quick phone call?

JAN: Phone call?

TREVOR: Would you mind? I can't get the one in there to work.

JAN: No, you have to switch it through.

TREVOR: Switch it through?

JAN: Never mind. Use this one.

TREVOR: Are you sure?

NICK: [*screaming*] Look, take the phone! Take it!

TREVOR: Thanks. Just a quick one.

JAN: I'll put the light on.

TREVOR: No, it's all right. I can see. I can see.

[TREVOR *goes to the phone table* ]

[*He fumbles about. A clatter* ]

NICK: Aaaah! Aaaah!

TREVOR: Sorry.

JAN: What —?

[*She switches on the light* ]

[TREVOR *has knocked* NICK's *glass of water on to the bed* ]

NICK: You bloody fool.

TREVOR: Sorry, sorry, sorry.

JAN: [*getting out of bed and going out*] All right, all right. Hold on, hold on.

TREVOR: Sorry. [*he dials*] I should get up and pull the sheet over this way a bit if I were you.

NICK: [*yelling*] I can't get up! For the last time, I can't get up! You idiot.

TREVOR: Sorry.

[*The phone rings in* DELIA'*s bedroom* ]

DELIA: [*answering*] Hallo.

TREVOR: Hallo, Mum. It's Trevor again.

DELIA: Trevor. Oh – you want Susannah. She's just gone. Hold on, I'll see if I can catch her. . . [*running to the door and shouting*] Susannah! Susannah!

SUSANNAH: [*very distant*] Yes.

DELIA: Telephone. [DELIA *hurries back to the phone*] She is just coming, Trevor. You just caught her.

[JAN *enters and starts to mop up* NICK, *slipping off his pyjama jacket and pulling the sheet sideways from under him so that he no longer lies on the damp patch*]

[*Meanwhile at* DELIA'*s,* ERNEST *enters hurriedly* ]

ERNEST: All right, all right, I'm coming. Who is it?

DELIA: No, darling, not for you. For Susannah.

ERNEST: Oh my God.

[SUSANNAH *bursts past* ERNEST ]

SUSANNAH: Excuse me.

DELIA: Trevor again for you, dear.

SUSANNAH: [*taking the phone*] Hallo, Trevor. I was just leaving.

TREVOR: Look, Suse, I was just thinking. I think I'd better just clear things up first.

SUSANNAH: How do you mean?

TREVOR: Well, I was thinking – Malcolm and Kate. I mean, we ruined their party last night.

SUSANNAH: Yes, I know.

TREVOR: Well. They're good friends. I don't want them to think – well – that I'm not sorry. I think I have to go round and see them.

SUSANNAH: It's a bit early, isn't it?

TREVOR: Oh no, Malcolm's always up at the crack of dawn. He won't mind, don't worry. Anyway. So could you meet me there? Then we could drive home.

SUSANNAH: All right. Malcolm and Kate's.

TREVOR: O.K. See you then.

SUSANNAH: Right. Bye.

[*They hang up*]

Thank you. Goodbye. Goodbye, Ernest.

ERNEST: Goodbye.

[SUSANNAH *rushes out*]

[ERNEST *sits on the bed*]

TREVOR: Well. See you then.

JAN: Yes.

TREVOR: Bye, Nick. Bye.

[TREVOR *goes out*]

JAN: Right. You comfortable now?

[NICK *utters a low moan*]

[*Fade out on* NICK *and* JAN]

ERNEST: I'm sorry. I am firmly of the opinion that that girl is completely potty. Not only potty but dangerously potty.

DELIA: No, she's not really. She's quite sweet. Very, very, very dim — but quite sweet-natured.

ERNEST: Am I to be allowed back into my own bed?

DELIA: Yes, it's all yours.

ERNEST: You haven't got any more people dropping in?

DELIA: Not as far as I know.

[*They get into bed*]

ERNEST: Well, once I'm in, I'm not getting out again.

DELIA: Not if you don't want to.

ERNEST: And I'll tell you something else. If you want your morning tea. . .

DELIA: Yes?

ERNEST: You're going to have to whistle for it.

[*Cross fade to* NICK *and* JAN's]

[NICK *moans*]

JAN: What is it?

NICK: [*feverishly*] Jan — promise me. Don't let him back in here again. Please don't let him back in here again. Never let that man back in here again.

JAN: [*concerned*] All right, darling, all right. I won't. . . [*she strokes his brow*]

NICK: Please, promise me.

JAN: [*soothingly*] Yes, yes.
   [*Cross fade to* MALCOLM *and* KATE's ]
   [KATE *under the bedclothes* ]
   [MALCOLM *still asleep on the floor* ]
   [*The front door bell rings* ]
   [*It rings again* ]
KATE: Mmmmm. . . . .
MALCOLM: [*wakening*] Uh. Oooh. . .
KATE: Malcolm.
MALCOLM: Oooh.
KATE: [*emerging*] Malcolm? What are you doing?
MALCOLM: I must have fallen asleep.
KATE: Was that a bell?
MALCOLM: Was it?
   [*Doorbell rings* ]
KATE: Front door.
MALCOLM: All right, I'll go. . . [*he tries to get up*] Har. . . I've
   got cramp. Cramp – cramp – cramp.
KATE: Right. Don't worry. . . [*she slips out of bed still in her
   dressing gown*] I'll go. Walk around a bit.
MALCOLM: Walk around a bit.
   [KATE *goes downstairs* ]
   [MALCOLM *manages to stand* ]
   [*His head lists over to one side* ]
   [*He seems unable to straighten it* ]
   [*The arm on which he has slept hangs uselessly. One of his legs
   seems reluctant to support him* ]
   [KATE *returns cautiously* ]
KATE: Malcolm.
MALCOLM: Uh?
KATE: Malcolm, it's Trevor.
MALCOLM: Who?
KATE: Trevor.
MALCOLM: Trevor.
   [TREVOR *enters* ]
TREVOR: Hallo, Malcolm mate. Oh, you're dressed. I'm glad I
   didn't get you up.
MALCOLM: [*bemused*] What are you doing here?
TREVOR: Malcolm – Kate, look. Look –
MALCOLM: What is he doing here?

TREVOR: I've come to say sorry.

MALCOLM: What are you doing here?

TREVOR: I realise that last night. . . unforgivable. I. . . sorry. Sue and I, we're very, well, you know –

MALCOLM: Ah.

KATE: Thank you, Trevor.

TREVOR: So.

MALCOLM: Yes. Cheerio then.

TREVOR: Yes.

[*A pause* ]

KATE: [*moving to the door*] Well. . .

TREVOR: – er – do you think I could just hang on for a couple of seconds? I arranged to meet Susannah here, you see.

MALCOLM: Here?

TREVOR: Yes.

MALCOLM: Ah.

KATE: Malcolm, would you like a bath?

MALCOLM: Bath?

KATE: It'll loosen you up. You look very tense.

MALCOLM: All right. Yes. All right.

KATE: I'll run it for you.

MALCOLM: No. I'll do it. I'll do it. You keep an eye on him.

KATE: All right.

[MALCOLM *limps lopsidedly out* ]
Well. . .

TREVOR: We're really genuinely sorry, Kate. We're both going to try to. . .

KATE: Yes. . .

TREVOR: If we possibly can.

KATE: Yes.

[*An awkward pause* ]
Look what Malcolm made last night. [*she indicates the master-piece*]

TREVOR: Ah yes.

KATE: Out of a kit. He had a bit of trouble with it. It's got to be sanded yet.

TREVOR: Yes.

KATE: You can see it's a bit down at one end.

TREVOR: Ah yes.

KATE: And the drawers are a bit stiff. But he's going to ease those.

[*They survey it* ]

TREVOR: You could maybe just — get it more even if you did this with it. . . like this.

[*He takes the top and tries to bend it to one side. The top comes away in his hand. Unsupported, the entire thing drops to pieces* ]

Ah.

KATE: [*appalled*] Oh no. Oh no.

MALCOLM: [*off*] What's going on.

KATE: Nothing, dear, nothing. Have your bath. Oh Trevor, what have you done?

TREVOR: Sorry.

[*The doorbell rings* ]

I could maybe get it together again for you. It doesn't look as if. . .

KATE: No, don't touch it, Trevor. Don't touch it at all. I'll just tell him it — suddenly collapsed. Wait there.

[*She goes* ]

[TREVOR *examines the wreckage* ]

[KATE *returns with* SUSANNAH ]

Here she is.

SUSANNAH: [*shyly*] Hallo.

TREVOR: Hallo.

KATE: [*aware of being in the way*] I'll just see if Malcolm's managing.

[KATE *goes* ]

TREVOR: Look, Suse. . . this may not work but. . . I'm going to try, you know. I'm really going to try.

SUSANNAH: Well. I'm going to try. That's all we can do really.

TREVOR: You see, I think if we could just —

SUSANNAH: Communicate —

TREVOR: Yes —

SUSANNAH: Yes. [*she sits on the bed*]

TREVOR: [*sitting next to her*] Well, we're on the bed again.

SUSANNAH: [*embarrassed*] Yes. It's a start.

TREVOR: Yes. I'll try not to rush you, Suse. I think I really rushed you.

SUSANNAH: Well. Maybe a bit.

TREVOR: My fault.

SUSANNAH: No, my fault.

[*He strokes her hair awkwardly* ]

[*She clings to him* ]

TREVOR: You cold? You're shivering.

SUSANNAH: A little bit. Tired, I think. . .

TREVOR: [*drawing the blanket round her*] Well, I think we both are. Been a busy night.

SUSANNAH: Yes. [*she kicks off her shoes and tucks up by him*] We shouldn't do this.

TREVOR: Just for a second. He's having a bath.

SUSANNAH: [*content*] Mmm. This is nice. [*she slides her feet down under the covers*] Ow.

TREVOR: What?

SUSANNAH: Something in the bed. [*she produces a saucepan*] What's this doing in here?

TREVOR: I don't know.

SUSANNAH: They have all sorts of things in their bed. I found boots in the pillowcase.

TREVOR: [*knowingly*] Ah well. People get up to strange things, you know. Some people. . .

SUSANNAH: Yes.

[TREVOR *cuddles up to her* ]

[*She holds his head in her arms* ]

SUSANNAH: I've been thinking. We must do something about our house. I think that's important. I want to start trying to make it more of a home. I — haven't been very good at that. I mean, somewhere nice. . . then you'll want to come home all the more, won't you? And I'll try and cook. I mean, really cook. . . and make sure you have some clean clothes in the morning and. . . well. You know what I mean, don't you? Trevor? Trevor. . .?

[TREVOR *is asleep* ]

[*alone*] Oh. . . I am confident in myself. I have confidence in myself. I am not unattractive. I am attractive. People still find me attractive. . .

[*Lights fade slowly during this*]


CURTAIN